MONTGOMERY COLLEGE LIBRARY
GERMANTOWN CAMPUS

T4-AEC-874

Lord
Tiana

Guide
to Language and Study Skills for College Students of English as a Second Language

Anne V. Martin
University of Southern California

Beverley McChesney
Stanford University

Elizabeth Whalley
University of Wisconsin

Edward Devlin
Monterey Peninsula College

PRENTICE-HALL, INC., ENGLEWOOD CLIFFS, NEW JERSEY 07632

Library of Congress Cataloging in Publication Data

Main entry under title:

Guide to language and study skills for college
   students of English as a second language.

  Bibliography: p.
  1. English language—Text-books for foreigners.
I. Martin, Anne V. (date)
PE1128.G8   428'.2'4   76-47494
ISBN 0-13-370452-1

© 1977 by Prentice-Hall, Inc., Englewood Cliffs, N.J. 07632

All rights reserved. No part of this book
may be reproduced in any form or by any means
without permission in writing from the publisher.

Printed in the United States of America

10 9 8 7 6 5 4 3 2

PRENTICE-HALL INTERNATIONAL, INC., *London*
PRENTICE-HALL OF AUSTRALIA PTY. LIMITED, *Sydney*
PRENTICE-HALL OF CANADA, LTD., *Toronto*
PRENTICE-HALL OF INDIA PRIVATE LIMITED, *New Delhi*
PRENTICE-HALL OF JAPAN, INC., *Tokyo*
PRENTICE-HALL OF SOUTHEAST ASIA PTE. LTD., *Singapore*

To Clara N. Bush

Contents

FOREWORD ix

PREFACE xi

1
STRUCTURAL AIDS TO WRITING 1

    Introduction, 1
    Agreement of Subject and Verb, 1
    Articles, 7
    Parts of a Group, 20
    Position of Adverbs, 26
    Word Order of Question Word Clauses (wh-Clauses), 32
    The Present Perfect Tense, 37
    Comparing Verb + Verb-*ing* (Gerund)
       with Verb + *to* + Verb (Infinitive), 43
    The Passive Voice, 58
    Spelling, 67
    Punctuation, 73

2

VOCABULARY DEVELOPMENT 87

        Introduction, 87
        Expanding Your Vocabulary, 87
        Negative Prefixes, 94
        Noun Agent Suffixes, 108
        Verb-Forming Suffixes, 111

3

FREQUENTLY USED WORD GROUPS 117

        Introduction, 117
        Do and *Make*, 118
        Adjectives, 124
        Health, 143
        Insurance, 151
        Newspaper Language, 155
        Useful Abbreviations and Acronyms, 161
        Politics and Government, 162
        Glossary of Political Terms, 167
        Legal Vocabulary, 170
        Verbs Expressing Attitudes, 177
        Evaluative Vocabulary, 183

4

STUDY TECHNIQUES 191

        Introduction, 191
        Examinations, 192
        Research Vocabulary, 196
        Taking Lecture Notes, 205
        Outlines, 213
        Summary and Paraphrase, 223
        Writing an Abstract, 229

5

ACADEMIC PAPER PREPARATION 231

        Introduction, 231
        Criteria for Evaluation, 232
        Selecting and Limiting the Topic, 233

Library Research and Note-Taking, 234
Preparing a Rough Draft, 242
Documentation, 243
Revising the Rough Draft, 250
Typing and Proofreading, 251

APPENDIX 257

Student Papers, 257
"Physical Effects of Marijuana Use," 258
"Adsorption: Granular Activated Carbon," 265

INDEX 273

Foreword

**ADVICE OFFERED BY FOREIGN STUDENTS
STUDYING IN THE UNITED STATES**

If you really plan to come to the United States to study, I've got some advice for you. You've got to start studying from the first day of classes, in an ever-increasing effort to keep track of all the courses you are enrolled in and to hand in all the assignments the professors have given you on time. But when the thing gets really hard is in the middle of the term, when you reach midterm examinations. First of all, you have to get ready for the exams while at the same time the teachers are going on with their subjects and assigning homework. At this time you will bless having studied from the beginning, since you will hardly have time to look over the topics already studied. On the other hand, teachers begin to realize that they are behind schedule (this always happens regardless of the course) and start increasing the rate at which they teach.

If a new foreign student is coming, he must be prepared in two different areas: first, he should be prepared physically and mentally, which means that he must be willing to work hard. Second, he should learn how to express his ideas in English well, and be able to read all kinds of different readings; this means that he should read a newspaper as well as a theoretical paper.

The most important advice I would give you is about study methods. I think the best way is to follow the lecturer's notes because generally the professor doesn't follow the text that he recommends, and a great part of the material that he covers doesn't appear in one book, but in several books or papers, and sometimes nowhere else.

It's hard to get accustomed to the daily routine here, people's reactions, and the speed and loneliness of this life.

Students are encouraged, at least for some courses, to work together in order to get a better understanding of the subject. There are several courses where this is very valuable, and I would say take advantage of this possibility, for it will certainly help you.

Preface

Guide to Language and Study Skills provides a bridge between the study of English as a second language and effective, creative use of English in university studies. It is designed for undergraduate and graduate students who have reached an intermediate to advanced level of English proficiency, but who need to develop and refine skills necessary for studying at a university in the United States.

Language and study skills are covered in five chapters: structural aids to writing, vocabulary development, vocabulary used frequently in everyday life, study techniques, and academic paper preparation. Each chapter consists of a number of sections. Within each section, the exercises progress from basic to more complex activities and move from structured to less structured practice, with the student gradually assuming more responsibility for his own language progress. Care has been taken throughout the book to include both spoken and written English in useful contexts, and to help the student learn appropriate, correct use of English.

The structural aids chapter provides practice in eight grammatical structures essential in academic writing, followed by a review of a number of spelling and punctuation conventions.

The vocabulary chapters present techniques for vocabulary building, introduce and practice a number of affixes, and guide the student to useful vocabulary areas encountered in student life, such as descriptive adjectives, newspaper language, and evaluative vocabulary. Throughout the vocabulary lessons, the emphasis is on student responsibility for determining which active and passive vocabulary will be useful.

Basic tools of study are presented in the study techniques chapter. Sections unique to this text include summary and paraphrase, research vocabulary, and abstracts.

The final chapter guides the student step by step in writing a documented paper, from topic selection through library research and note-taking, preparation and revision of a rough draft, to proofreading the final paper. Two papers, one written by an undergraduate and the other by a graduate, are included as examples of academic papers.

A major feature of the *Guide* is that it is both a textbook for systematic study and a handbook which the student can consult after his English courses are completed. Chapters and sections may be used sequentially or may be selected and reordered by the instructor, according to both the students' needs and the nature and length of the course. In addition, the teacher can individualize instruction by assigning sections for independent work. The material is used most effectively with a combination of class discussion and homework assignments, providing opportunity for interrelating the spoken and written language and study skills.

Because the chapters and sections of the *Guide* may be used nonsequentially, the *Guide* is appropriate for a variety of courses. It can be covered fully in 150 to 200 hours within the components of an intensive English program. It may be used in an integrated skills course at the intermediate to advanced levels, or in separate writing, vocabulary, academic orientation, or study skills classes. The objectives of the course will determine which sections of the *Guide* should be emphasized.

During the five-year evolution of the *Guide,* many people have played a part in its development. We are grateful to Marjorie Cook and Jean Petersen for their contributions, and to the following students who allowed us to use material which they wrote: Jorge Canedo, Salar Niku, Luis Nouel, Mitsuo Shimizu, and Jose Verger. We wish to thank Clara Bush, Donald Dodson, Christine Dowling, Armand Gelpi, Dorothy Riedel, and Lee Zeigler for their assistance; Alan McCornick, Frieda Politzer, and Bill Rutherford for their reactions to part of the material; and our reviewers for their helpful criticism and suggestions. In addition, we owe thanks to our colleagues and students at Stanford University and at the University of Southern California, who used experimental material and gave us valuable feedback. Finally, we express our gratitude to Tom Martin, David McChesney, and G. Whalley, without whose encouragement and support the *Guide* could not have been completed.

Structural Aids to Writing

1

1.1 INTRODUCTION

The following explanations and exercises are designed to help you eliminate from your papers the structural errors most frequently found on foreign students' papers. After studying them, use this as a basic checklist when you check over your papers. By doing so, you can make certain that your papers are free of errors in these common problem areas.

Basic Checklist

Agreement of Subject and Verb
Articles
Parts of a Group
Position of Adverbs
Word Order of Question-Word Clauses (Wh- clauses)
The Present Perfect Tense
Comparing Verb + Verb-*ing* (Gerund) with Verb + *to* + Verb (Infinitive)
The Passive Voice
Spelling
Punctuation

1.2 AGREEMENT OF SUBJECT AND VERB

Remember that a verb has to agree with its subject. An *-s* or *-es* verb ending must be used when the subject is third person singular:

Ron Wilson *rides* his bicycle from class to class.
Many students *ride* their bikes on campus.
More and more American adults *ride* bikes now.
My roommate *fixes* bikes.

When the verb occurs immediately after the subject, it is not difficult to write the correct form of the verb. When the subject and verb are separated in more complex structures, however, special attention is required to be certain that the subject and the verb agree. For example,

He chose a topic which, for the most part, *deals* with telecommunication.

The budget director presented a proposal concerning next year's plans that *was* very controversial.

A complex subject makes the choice of verb more difficult:

Some of the most significant work in this field *has* been done within the last two years.

First, three types of research *have* to be defined.

It is clear that these kinds of problems *interest* them.

The electric-powered car is a means of transportation which *seems* promising.

The research associates and graduate students, as well as the director, *recognize* that more funds will be necessary for the completion of the project.

Agreement of subject and verb requires knowledge of nouns which are not counted—that is, those which are considered mass or collective nouns. Consider the following examples and study the following lists.

Daily homework *is* a characteristic of American higher education.

Many American scientists no longer *seem* interested in natural observation because of the lack of replication which research of this type *implies.*

A major concern in the technological sciences is the difficulty of keeping up with new information which *comes* out every day.

A biotechnology research group *is* made up of people who *want* to integrate the knowledge of many fields to improve the design of man-machine systems.

Pay particular attention to *people*. In English, *people* is always used with the plural verb form: *people are, people have.* The following list includes nouns you will need to use often. For others consult a dictionary.

Non-Count Nouns. The following nouns do not occur in plural form. For example,

A little *knowledge is* a dangerous thing.
More complete *information leads* to more responsible action.

advertising	merchandise	academic subject
advice	news	areas:[1]
attendance	pollution	economics
electricity	propaganda	engineering
equipment	recreation	materials science
furniture	research	philosophy
homework	scenery	physics
information	staff	statistics
insurance	traffic	business
knowledge	transportation	mathematics
machinery		

Count or Non-Count Nouns, Abstract. These nouns occur in singular form when they are used as abstract, general concepts. They occur in the plural when they are used as concrete, countable units.

(as a general concept)	*Noise* is becoming a controversial issue.
(as individual occurrences)	*Noises* are more noticeable when you have a headache.
(as a general concept)	Life is short.
(as countable units)	Many *lives* have been lost because of carelessness.

ability	glass	race
business	group	science
capital	life	space
class	love	time
control	material	trouble
difficulty	noise	work
experience	policy	youth

Count or Non-Count Nouns, Technical. The following nouns generally occur in singular or in the form, "several kinds of (rice)...." They may occur in plural form for *technical uses only.* Contrast the following:

[1] Note: the names of several subject areas end in *s*, but they are not plural.

Cane *sugar* is produced in Hawaii.
Fruits contain various *sugars*.

He manages his *money* well.
A treasurer is in charge of collection and distribution of *monies*.

coffee/coffees   meat/meats
food/foods   plastic/plastics
fruit/fruits   salt/salts
oil/oils   sugar/sugars
money/monies   water/waters
metal/metals   wheat/wheats

Practice 1

Supply the correct form of the verb; add -*s* or -*es* if the subject is singular; leave the space blank if the subject is plural.

Examples

An insurance salesman know<u>s</u> injury statistics quite well.

Engineering materials and equipment cost___ a staggering amount of money.

1. A country's position in the world depend___ on its economic growth.
2. Modern technology comprises a body of knowledge whose application make___ it possible to introduce new models of some products every year.
3. This transformation that is likely to take place in our approach to problems enable___ us to cope with circumstances in different environments.
4. Totaling one month's expenses, which is necessary for estimating the next month's expenses, require___ gathering a lot of figures, each one of which change___ somewhat from month to month.
5. Each of these methods, by its own nature, emphasize___ different aspects of the problem which lead___ to different decisions.
6. Despite the growing realization that the internal combustion engine is largely responsible for smog in California, one out of every two Californians own___ a car.

7. The examples he use~s~ require___ more support; they are insufficient by themselves.
8. Excessive use of air conditioners cause~s~ power shortages in New York City in the summer.
9. People who live___ in glass houses shouldn't throw stones.
10. An answer to these three ideas involve~s~ consideration of four basic points.
11. Traveling by car become~s~ more expensive than traveling by plane when all of the costs are considered.
12. I don't know if this computer program is complete, but here go~es~ anyway.
13. Swimming for a half hour before going home usually give~s~ him a big appetite.
14. Good news from home always make~s~ him happy.
15. Not many of the opinions he presents in his lectures surprise___ his students.

Practice 2

Supply the correct form of *be*, *do*, or *have* in the present tense.

Examples

(be) Many people *are* allergic to dust.

(have) The downtown area *has* a complex traffic pattern.

1. (be) Communication technology __is__ a consequence of economic development.
2. (have) The change I refer to __has__ to do with our most deeply rooted values.
3. (be) There __are__ quite a few reasons why that procedure is considered obsolete.
4. (do) __Does__ the group want to stop now or keep walking?
5. (have) Does anyone you know __have__ a slide projector?

5

6. (have) As far as I know, neither one of the offices next door __are__ a photocopy machine.
7. (be) There __is__ a couple we know—Marian and Fred.
8. (do) Not only __does__ it cost a lot, it also has a reputation for breaking down.
9. (be) Mathematics __is__ necessary for an engineering student.
10. (have) No matter how long we put it off, sooner or later someone __has__ to finish the project.
11. (be) Even those students whose tuition __is__ paid by fellowship have a lot of expenses.
12. (do) Whether he __does__ homework all weekend or not, he won't take time to talk to people in the dorm.
13. (be) The science which studies the function of the brain and other organs __is__ called physiology.
14. (have) Does Mr. Petersen, the president of the company, __have__ much in common with the other company executives?
15. (be) No matter how much homework there __is__ to do, each assignment still takes a lot of time.
16. (have) General Motors __has__ a new emission control device.

Practice 3

The following paragraphs describe Amtrak, the government's program to improve train service. Add the correct form of the verb in parentheses in order to complete the verb in present or present perfect tense.

U.S. trains (have) __have__ not kept pace with trains in several other industrialized countries. In terms of passengers, there (be) __are__ four times as many rail passengers in West Germany as in the United States. In terms of speed, the USSR's "Russian Troika" (average) __averages__ 100 miles per hour and Japan's "Bullet" (make) __makes__ its runs at speeds averaging 102 miles per hour, while America's Metroliner (travel) __is traveling__ 75 miles per hour on the average.

STRUCTURAL AIDS TO WRITING

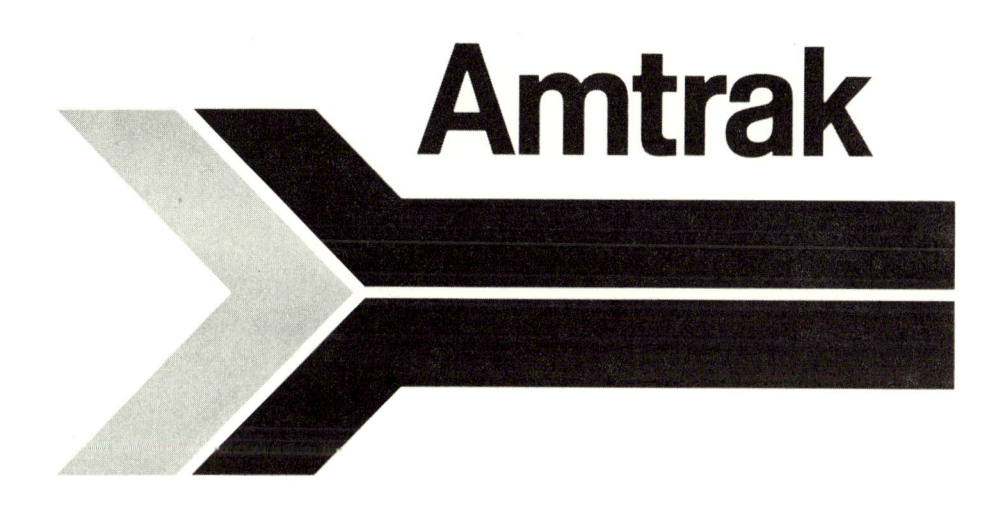

Poor rail service (pose) __poses__ problems that (extend) __extend__ far beyond the field of transportation. Environmental protection, land-use planning, and energy policy (be) __'s__ all directly affected. The search for a solution (raise) __raises__ fundamental questions concerning the respective roles of government and private enterprise.

Rather than totally nationalizing the system, Congress (plan) __plans__ to revitalize the rails gradually under the management of Amtrak, a quasi-public corporation which taxpayers heavily (subsidize) __subsidizes__. Amtrak (have) __has__ purchased efficient and attractive rail cars; frequency of service on a great number of lines (be) __is__ being changed to match public needs.

Officials (hope) __hope__ that by 1990 passenger trains will not only travel at 150 miles per hour, but will also be part of a financially self-supporting rail system. Amtrak (face) __faces__ a tough challenge.

1.3 ARTICLES

The use of articles presents some difficulty for students of English. One must know which article to use in certain situations, and when to use no article at all. While there are many exceptions, a majority of cases are covered by the explanation below. Later in this lesson, you will study some of the most common exceptions to the general patterns of *the, a, an, some.* ɸ means that *no* article is used—(ɸ John is *the* boy in my class).

Uses of *the*. The definite article *the* is used before a singular count noun when the noun is identified or its identity is understood. The use of *the* excludes all other members of that noun class.

Before Singular Count Nouns

The boy is here.	(subject)
I saw *the* boy.	(object)
The boy's bicycle is red.	(possessive)
We walked in *the* park.	(object of preposition)

Singular and Plural Count Nouns

The report arrived yesterday.
The reports arrived yesterday.

Before Other Modifiers Used with Singular Count Nouns

Another price increase has been announced by *the* steel industry.
The energy situation seems to be getting a little better.
Required courses constitute about two-thirds of *the* total number of units in his degree program.
The professor that he wants to see is out of town.

When Not to Use *the*. *The* is not used when a noun is modified by a possessive.

His course is extremely difficult.	(possessive pronouns)
John's roommate is from Florida.	(proper nouns with possessive)

The is not used when a noun is not specific or not identified by the speaker.

Specific:	*The instructions* for this exam are easy to understand.
General:	*Instructions* should always be read carefully.
Specific:	*The boys* who live next door are here to see you.
General:	*Boys* make a lot of noise.

There is a test for determining if *the* is required. Ask yourself the question "Which?" If there is a definite answer, *the* is usually required.

The instructions on my last exam were quite clear.
Which?   (the ones on my last exam—definite)

Instructions are sometimes difficult to understand.
Which?   (not specified—no definite answer)

The boys in the park make a lot of noise.
Which?   (the ones in the park—definite)

Boys make a lot of noise.
Which?   (all boys—no definite answer)

I went to *the* store.
Which?   (the one I usually go to—understood)

I went to several stores.
Which?   (not identified—no definite answer)

Practice 1

The following twelve sentences are grouped in pairs. Write *the* in the blank if it is needed; if *the* is not needed, write φ.

Examples

The history of Rome is fascinating.
φ History is my favorite subject.

φ Dogs are sometimes called "man's best friend."
The dogs of Alaska are strong.

1. I am interested in research on __×__ teaching.
2. I am interested in research on __the__ teaching of foreign languages.
3. Have you studied __the__ history of Africa?
4. __×__ history tells us that the Arab influence in Spain has been very great.
5. __The__ techniques presented in this book cannot be used to solve educational problems in my country.
6. I still hope to learn __×__ techniques which can be applied to those problems.
7. Do you know very much about __the__ War of 1812?
8. Throughout history people have never liked __×__ war.
9. The most important activity of the rebel group was to import __×__ military instructors and __×__ ammunition.
10. Were the soldiers able to get __the__ ammunition that they wanted?

11. We went to an exhibit of __×__ art from Peru and Bolivia.

12. __The__ art that I am most interested in now is Asian art.

Practice 2

Write *the* or *ϕ* in each blank.

Example

__ϕ__ interaction among students from different countries is desirable.

1. __×__ experience is a major criterion for that position.
2. One of the fields he is interested in is __ϕ__ marine biology.
3. __The__ trouble with George is that he does not know how to budget his time.
4. __×__ transportation is a major problem for some students.
5. The lawyer is gathering __a__ new evidence in the case.
6. Reports of the forest fire were on __the__ news today.
7. __×__ jogging is a popular form of exercise.
8. __The__ stores in __×__ downtown area generally open at 10 A.M.

Practice 3

Put *the* or *ϕ* in the blanks where it is required.

__The__ boy who lives in __the__ apartment next to mine is named Sandy. His __×__ hair is brown, and __×__ his eyes are too. He is nine __×__ years old and he has a lot of __×__ energy. __The__ day before yesterday, Sandy came to visit me in my __×__ apartment. __The__ problem was that he opened __the__ door of my bedroom at six o'clock in __the__ morning. While I was sleeping, he came into __the__ room and shouted, "Wake up! Wake up! __The__ sun is already shining. It's a beautiful day to go to __the__ park and play on __the__ slides and __the__ swings."

Now, you must understand that I like this boy. I even like to play __ϕ__ games with him. But I am studying engineering, and I have to do a lot of

10 STRUCTURAL AIDS TO WRITING

___ homework. Since I study best very early in ___the___ morning, I have arranged for my classes to be in ___the___ afternoon. I usually study until 3:00 A.M. and then sleep until ___ 11:00 A.M. Then I get up, read ___the___ newspaper, have ___ coffee, and go to ___ University at ___ one o'clock. When Sandy woke me up, ___The___ clock told me that I had had only a few hours of ___ sleep.

I sent Sandy ___ home, and went back to ___ sleep. ___The___ fifteen minutes later, ___The___ telephone rang. It was ___ Sandy's mother, who hoped her son had not disturbed me.

Use of *a*, *an*, and *some*. For singular nouns that can be counted but have not been identified, the indefinite articles *a* or *an* are used as weak forms of *one*.

Specific:	*The technical paper* on Dr. Johnson's research was read at the conference. Which? (the one on Dr. Johnson's research)
General:	*A technical paper* was prepared. Which? (I don't know)
Specific:	*The boy* you mentioned yesterday came to see you. Which? (the one you mentioned yesterday)
General:	*A boy* came here. Which? (not identified)
Specific:	I'd like you to meet *the old friend* I have often mentioned. Which? (the one I have mentioned)
General:	I'd like you to meet *an old friend* of mine. Which? (a friend)
Specific:	*The uncle* that Jim often mentions is going to visit him next week. Which? (the one he often mentions)
General:	*An uncle* of Jim's is going to visit him next weekend. Which? (I don't know)

Note: For plural or non-count nouns, *some* is often used to indicate an indefinite number or amount.

Specific:	*The students* in the field geography course are planning a cross-country trip.

General: *Some students* are planning a cross-country trip.
Specific: I had *carburetor trouble* last week.
General: I had *some trouble* with my car last week.

General Summary

Determine whether the noun is identified or unidentified.

1. If identified, use *the*.
2. If unidentified, determine whether the noun is singular or non-count. If singular and non-count, use *a* or *an*.

	indefinite, unidentified, general	definite, identified, specific
Singular	a boy, an apple	the boy, the apple
Plural, Non-count	φ boys, rice, freedom	the boys, the rice, the freedom

Practice 4

Fill in the blanks with *a, an, some, the,* or *φ*. There may be more than one possibility.

____The____ professor in my ____φ____ American Studies class scheduled ____a____ quiz tomorrow. It covers ____the____ problems which ____the (?)____ people of ____the____ United States encountered during ____the____ Depression in ____the____ 1930s. ____The____ quiz like this usually consists of ____φ____ one or two brief essay ____φ____ questions and about ____φ____ three simple identification questions. ____The____ Professor Jackson, or ____the____ assistant of his, grades ____the____ quizzes, records ____the____ grades, and returns ____the____ papers. ____The____ quizzes count for about 25 percent of ____the____ grade, so ____some____ student must do ____the____ good job of preparation if he wants ____a____ good grade for ____the____ course. Naturally ____A____ professor expects ____✓____ students to do ____×____ better job than others.

12 STRUCTURAL AIDS TO WRITING

Practice 5

Read this fictitious tale about a man who set up a very unusual business. Fill in the blanks with *a, an, the,* or *ϕ*.

John Peterson started _____ business about _____ six years ago. His _____ company makes _____ capes for kings. It has been _____ long time since _____ company sold _____ cape, because this _____ century has been _____ bad one for _____ kings. But John is not discouraged. He discussed _____ his business problems with his psychiatrist. _____ psychiatrist was worried about John, but John explained that although _____ business was bad in _____ cape industry, he had _____ job to rely on if his company went bankrupt.

_____ psychiatrist asked John what he would do in that _____ case. John answered, "I will get _____ job as _____ teapot."

Special Situations

This section gives examples of the use of *the* in several semantic areas. You will notice one overall pattern throughout: *the* is not used for names when they are proper names, traditional names, or titles, but it is used for descriptions.

Names and Titles. *The* is not used with names of people.

Ann Johansen is here.
She is Ann Johansen.

Exceptions:

Miss Smith, please bring *the* Ann Johansen *file.* (modifier of another noun)

Is she *the* Ann Johansen we went to school with? (when there may be more than one person with the same name)

The is used with descriptive titles *only* when a person's name is not used:

The prime minister met with the president for an hour this morning. This afternoon they were joined by the secretary of state and the foreign minister.

Queen Elizabeth has traveled throughout the Commonwealth.

Foreign Minister Jenkins left for Malaysia yesterday.

President Lincoln is one of the most famous American presidents.

The professor who is going to speak this afternoon will have lunch with the dean.

Professor Olsen will have lunch with Dean Miller.

Have you made an appointment with the doctor yet?

Dr. Hendricks will be away for two weeks.

Practice 6

Fill in the blanks with *the* or ϕ.

1. __The__ chairman of the department told _____ Dr. Johnson to see _____ Bill Peary.

STRUCTURAL AIDS TO WRITING

2. __×__ Professor Cantwin got a taxi for __×__ Senator Halflap from the state of Virginia.

3. __×__ Horace Jones you want to talk to isn't my brother. My brother is __×__ Horace Jones who lives in Topeka, Kansas.

4. Today _____ president had lunch with _____ President Omon, who is __the__ president of Bulimia.

Numbers in Reference Work. Cardinal numbers (one, two, three, [1, 2, 3,] . . .) usually follow the nouns they refer to in titles or names: *the* is not used.

Have you finished *chapter 1*?

For additional information, I refer you to *page 10*.

You will notice in *figure 7* that there was a significant increase during the ten-year period.

Will it be possible for me to borrow *Volume 2* through inter-library loan?

World War I was fought between 1914 and 1918.

Ordinal numbers (first, second, third, . . .) usually come before the nouns they refer to. *The* is used.

Have you finished *the first chapter?*

There is some more information on *the tenth page* of the report.

The seventh figure differs from the preceding ones because it covers a ten-year period.

Will it be possible for me to borrow *the second volume* through inter-library loan?

The First World War was fought between 1914 and 1918.

Practice 7

Complete these sentences. In items 1–6, use cardinal numbers after ordinal, or ordinal numbers after cardinal. In items 7–8 add any reasonable phrase with cardinal or ordinal numbers.

Example

Part one is *the first part*.

What impressed me was the increase shown in *figure 3*.

1. Section three is _____.
2. The fourth exercise is called _____.
3. The twenty-seventh paragraph is _____
   _____.
4. Problem 2 is _____.
5. The Second World War can also be called _____
   _____.
6. The chapter after the third one is _____
   _____.
7. I think you've given me the wrong volume; I need _____
   _____.
8. As I remember, the photograph is on _____
   in the seventh chapter.

Countries, Cities, and Streets. *The* is *not* used with the traditional names of countries, but it is used with the official government names of some countries when those differ from the traditional names.

ϕ Russia has one of the largest land masses of any country in the world.
The Soviet Union is made up of many republics.

ϕ Holland is very densely populated.
The Netherlands is a member of the European Economic Community.

ϕ America was inhabited long before Columbus landed on the continent.
The United States is made up of fifty states.

ϕ Panama lies between Costa Rica and Colombia.
The Republic of Panama has an advantageous position in the Western Hemisphere.

The is *not* used with the names of cities and streets.

The home of country music is ϕ Nashville, Tennessee.
ϕ New York is the largest city in the United States.
One of my friends lives on ϕ State Street.
ϕ Michigan Avenue is one of the principal streets in Chicago.

There is an important difference between First Street, which is the name of a street, and the first street, which may have any name but is the street you are coming to next. Therefore, if you are standing on Second Street, the third street over is Fifth Street.

Rivers, Oceans, Seas, Mountains, and Islands. *The* is used with the names of rivers, oceans, seas, and groups of mountains and islands, even when these are expressed in short forms.

The Pacific Ocean is larger than *the* Atlantic.

The Nile River is essential to the people who live around it.

The Caribbean Sea is a relaxing place for vacations, and so is *the* Mediterranean.

The Sierra Nevada Mountains are younger than *the* Appalachians.

The Hawaiian Islands are becoming very developed. I would prefer to spend a couple of weeks in *the* Azores.

Locations and Activities. Sometimes the noun for a place is used to refer to the activity that takes place there. In this case, *the* is not used.

I am going to ϕ school this year. (I am taking classes, referring to any level of education.)

I have to go back to ϕ school later this evening. (I plan to work in the building this evening.)

I am going to *the* school this evening. (I am going to visit the building where my children are enrolled.)

After I get my degree I plan to teach at *the* school I attended as an undergraduate. (I plan to teach at the same school I attended.)

We went to ϕ church. (We attended religious services.)

We went to *the* church around the corner for a meeting. (We went to the building.)

Time Expressions. *The* is not used with specific times.

He came at ϕ 2:00 P M
They applied to the University in ϕ June.
The plane from Mexico arrived on ϕ Monday evening.
ϕ last week was the deadline for applications.
ϕ last Friday's announcement caused a lot of confusion.

The is used with nonspecific or descriptive time phrases

He came in *the* morning.
The university was founded in *the* nineteenth century.
The plane will arrive in *the* next few minutes.

Next week is *the* last week for payment of fees.
Many community colleges were established in *the* 1960s.

Practice 8

Write *the* or φ in the blanks.

1. Who(m) have you talked to in ___the___ last couple of hours?
2. Where have you lived during ___the___ past year?
3. What have you been doing for ___the___ past ten minutes?
4. What are you planning to do today at _____ 4:00?
5. What movies did you see _____ last month?
6. How many times did you use the lab _____ last week?
7. Where were you on _____ 3rd of June?
8. What did you do on ___×___ June 25th?
9. How many tapes did you listen to ___the___ day before yesterday?
10. How many tapes did you listen to _____ yesterday?
11. What was your country like in _____ 1890s?
12. What was your country like in _____ twenties?
13. What major change has taken place in your country since the beginning of ___the___ twentieth century?
14. What books have you read about ___the___ ancient times?
15. What was the topic of _____ last week's lecture?

Practice 9

Write *a, an, the,* or φ in the blanks in the following paragraph.

An Art Exhibition

___An___ important exhibition of French art opened recently at the California Palace of the Legion of Honor. ___The___ exhibition is from ___the___ collection of industrialist Norton Simon, whose comments appear with ___×___ paintings. Simon wrote in his foreword to _____ collection catalog: " ___The___ art is ___a___ communication channel that can take ___×___ people and open them up in ___the___ unique ways. ___The___ art can start getting people to look at themselves, which is important, since one of

STRUCTURAL AIDS TO WRITING

the prime problems in _×_ society is _a_ need for _____ introspection. _The_ art can help us look not only at ourselves, but also makes it possible to see _the_ others with _a_ greater insight and sensitivity."

Practice 10

This practice reviews the entire lesson. Choose *the, a, an, some,* or *ϕ* for each blank.

_____ Ahmed arrived in _____ U.S. in _____ 1976 to work on _____ B.S. in _____ economics. He has constantly tried to make every minute count, both academically and culturally. In _____ past year he has audited _____ four classes in _____ evening besides taking _____ required courses. In addition, twice _____ week at _____ four o'clock he tutors _____ American friend who is studying _____ Arabic. He has also kept busy during _____ weekend. For example, _____ week before last he went camping with _____ friends, and _____ last weekend's excursion was _____ day at _____ typical county fair.

_____ next week Ahmed will receive his B.S. On _____ 12 th of _____ June he will leave for _____ home. We wish him well and hope sometime in _____ coming years he will return for _____ visit.

Practice 11

Choose a paragraph from a textbook or journal in your field and:

1. underline all of the articles;
2. underline all of the noun phrases and be able to explain why an article is or is not used in each phrase.

Practice 12

In ten to twelve sentences, describe an imaginary vacation trip taken by a man named John Duffy. Have him visit as many places and do as many things as possible.

Practice 13

Write a paragraph describing one of the following which has surprised you in the United States:

1. Physical conditions—the environment, climate, housing, transportation;
2. Parties, interpersonal relationships, social customs, and traditions;
3. The academic environment at universities and colleges;
4. Culture shock and adjustment.

1.4 PARTS OF A GROUP

It is common to identify one or more things in terms of larger groups to which they belong. For example,

Item	Group	Sentence
Oregon	states in the U.S.	Oregon is *one of the states.*
Bangkok	capitals	Bangkok is *one of the capitals* of Asia.
stainless steel	useful materials	Stainless steel is *one of the most useful materials* man has.
oceanography	occupations which are growing in importance	Oceanography is *one of the occupations* which are growing in importance.
Mary Race	talented women	Mary Race is *one of the most talented women* I have ever met.

Notice that the group is a count noun and is therefore plural. Compare these statements:

Mary is *the most talented woman* I have ever met.

Mary is *one of the most talented women* I have ever met.

In the first, Mary has received a higher rating than any other woman the speaker has met; in the second, Mary shares the highest rating level with a few other women.

The is used with the part when it is specifically identified.

The Nile is *one of the most important rivers* of Africa.

This is *the second of the three papers* I have to write.

The same structure is used with other quantities from *none* to *all*.

None of the buildings around here is higher than eight stories.

Any of the people I mentioned could handle that work.

The manager plans to hire *a few of the applicants* on a temporary basis.

Judy, Paul, and Sandra are *three of the most politically active students* on campus.

Several of the leading candidates appeared at a fund-raising banquet last month.

In this famous saying by Abraham Lincoln, notice that there are several examples of *some* and *all* phrases. One of the nouns, time, is a non-count noun.

You can fool *some of the people all of the time* and *all of the people some of the time,* but you can't fool *all of the people all of the time.*

Practice 1

Fill in the blank with an appropriate plural noun.

Examples

Yosemite is one of the most beautiful <u>*places*</u> I have seen.

Apples, peaches, and watermelons are some of the <u>*things*</u> I like to eat.

1. She is one of the _____ in this class.
2. Several of the _____ are going to start a car pool.
3. Music is one of the most interesting _____ I have studied.
4. Washington, D.C. and the Grand Canyon are two of the _____ everyone should see in the United States.
5. None of the _____ will be available until next week.
6. Most of the _____ I know are helpful.
7. A few of the _____ I know live off campus.
8. All of the _____ I've met so far have been interested in my reason for coming here.
9. Which two of the _____ did you learn the most from?
10. How many of the _____ have already been rented?

Practice 2

Complete these sentences with count noun groups.

Examples

The Atlantic Ocean is one of *the largest bodies of water on earth.*

Amy spent two hours looking through some of *the journals in the undergraduate library.*

1. This exercise is one of _____.
2. Last year was one of _____.
3. This week and last week have been two of _____.
4. Tokyo is one of _____.
5. The atomic bomb and bacteriological warfare have become two of _____.
6. That girl, her mother, and her sister are three of _____.
7. As far as I know, none of _____.
8. Since I have been here, many of _____.
9. Is it possible that all of _____?
10. If you are interested in learning more about apartments in the area, contact any of _____.
11. A large number of _____.
12. Some of _____.
13. To complete the registration procedure, fill out one of _____.
14. Yellowstone, the Grand Tetons, and the Grand Canyon are only a few of _____.
15. So far, none of _____.

STRUCTURAL AIDS TO WRITING

Practice 3

Use the names of the cities here to form sentences using the groups below. Notice that several groups fit more than one of the cities, so that you may sometimes use "two of the . . . ," or "some of the . . . ."

Shanghai   Berlin
Tehran   Hong Kong
Paris   Tokyo
New York   Caracas
Rio de Janeiro   Rome
Amsterdam   San Francisco

Example

Paris is one of the most famous cities in the world.

1. the most beautiful cities in the United States
2. the most historical cities in Europe
3. the most densely populated cities in the world
4. the most rapidly changing cities in the world
5. the most controversial places in Europe
6. the oldest cities in the world
7. the national capitals of Asia
8. the large cities in Brazil
9. the largest cities (in area) in the world
10. the places I want to visit when I have a lot of money and time

Practice 4

Refer to figure 1, "World Automobile Registrations." Interpret the information in the sentences below by filling in phrases using parts of a group. The group you should use is given in parentheses before the sentence.

Example

The graph covers the years 1955 and 1971. (year) These are *two of the years* covered on the graph.

1. The areas in the group called "All Others" are not specified. (world area)

    One can assume that Latin America, Africa, and the Middle East are

    _____ included in that group.

2. Auto registration in the U.S. rose by almost 10 million between 1970 and 1972. European registration increased by 10 million in just one year, 1971. (dramatic change) These are _____

    _____ shown in figure 1.

3. The number of automobiles registered in Europe in 1970 stayed relatively constant. (group) Registration in only _____ _____ was stable in 1970.
4. Registration in Asia increased nearly 15 million between 1965 and 1970. (significant five-year increase) This is _____ _____ shown in figure 1.
5. Many people might assume that auto registration has continued to increase in all four groups. (major trend) This is _____ _____ to be inferred from the graph.

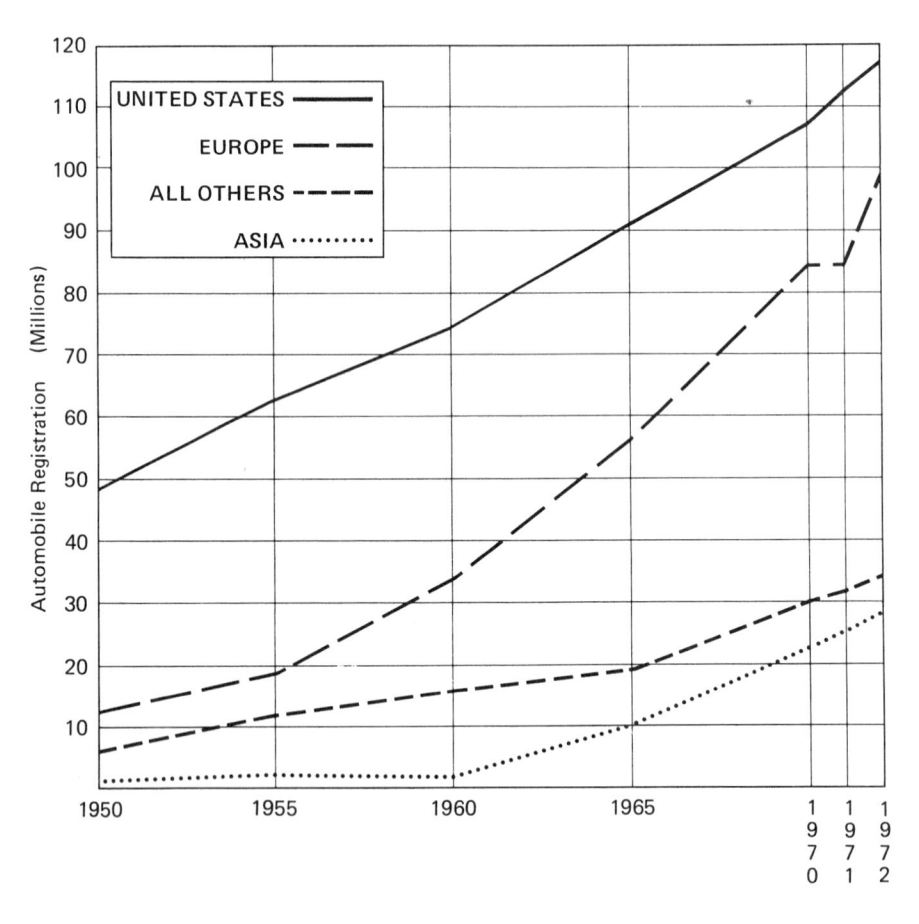

Fig. 1. World automobile registration.

STRUCTURAL AIDS TO WRITING

6. The U.S. registers more cars than any other area of the world. (obvious conclusion) That is _____ to be drawn from figure 1.

Practice 5

Study figure 2, a graph representing foreign student enrollment in United States universities between 1955–74. In class, answer the following questions.

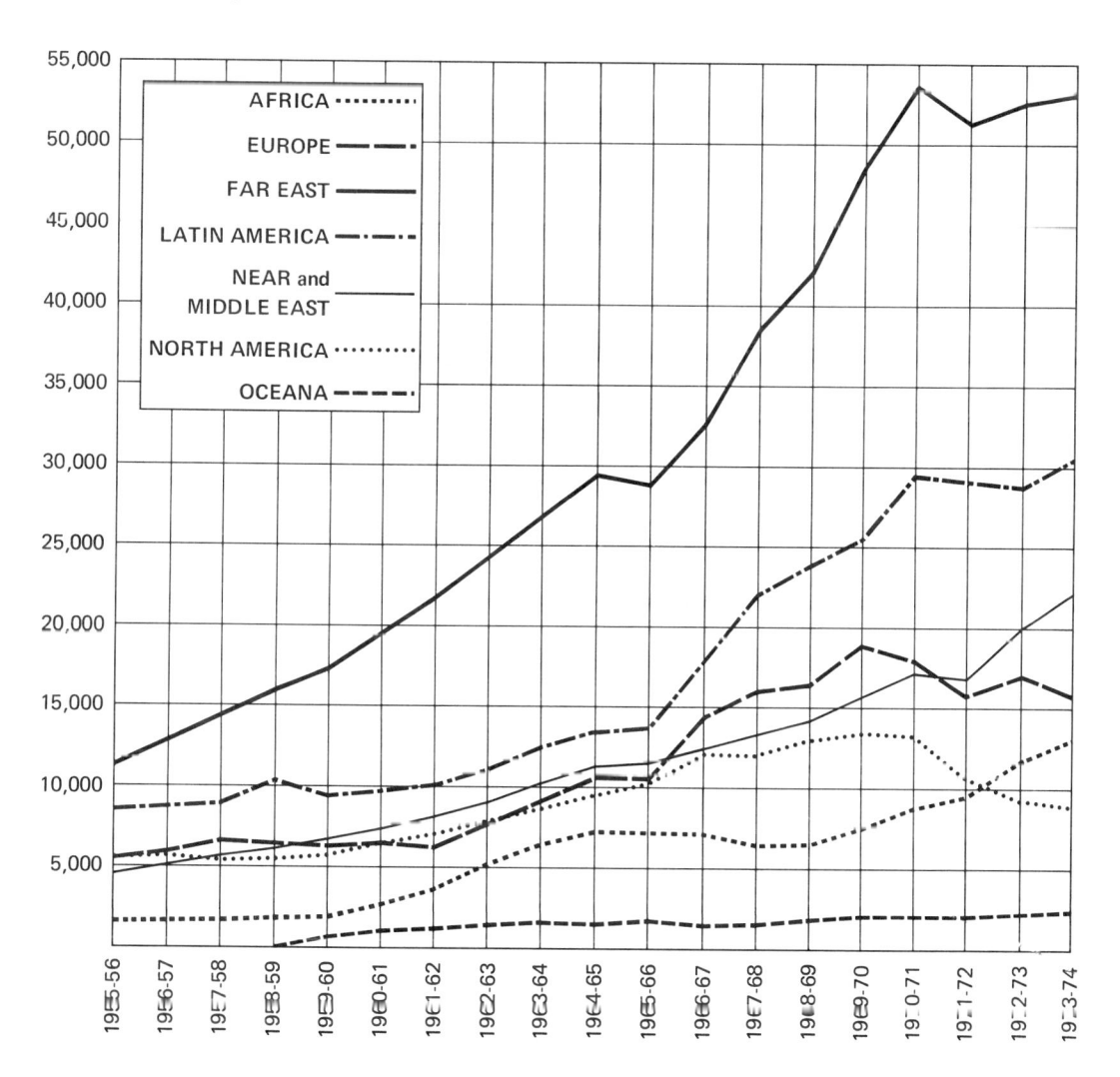

Fig. 2. Foreign students in the United States, 1955–74. From *Open Door: Report on International Educational Exchange* (New York: Institute of International Education), 1974, p. 8; and 1975, pp. 11–18.

25

1. Which region increased its enrollment most from 1966–70?
2. What are two of the most significant increases on the graph?
3. What is one of the most striking decreases in enrollment?
4. What are some of the trends in the mid-1970s?
5. What are two of the most stable enrollment patterns?

1.5 POSITION OF ADVERBS

The position of adverbs is complicated because of the many types of adverbial modifiers in English. However, most adverbs are of the following types:

Type	Examples
place	here, outside, at home, in the office
manner	quietly, fast, well, carefully, easily, unfortunately
frequency	never, rarely, still, frequently, every day
time	at 10:00 P.M., last week, soon, recently, at present, at last, finally
purpose or reason	to get a book, in order to see him
degree	hardly, barely, moderately, highly, actually, really, very much, only, just
means	by bus, by hand, on foot, via the tunnel, through the tunnel
likelihood	probably, no doubt, obviously, certainly, definitely

The basic word order of English statements is

Subject	+	Verb	+	Object
Ari		is studying		physics.
He		likes to take		evening classes.

Adverbial modifiers, including adverbs and prepositional phrases that modify verbs, are generally used in the positions shown below. Notice that adverbial modifiers are generally *not* used between the verb and the object.

Adverbial Modifier	Subject	Adverbial Modifier	Verb	Object	Adverbial Modifier
On Mondays	his professor	sometimes	ends	class	late.

Practice 1

Read the following passage about a foreign student in the U.S. Underline

STRUCTURAL AIDS TO WRITING

every adverbial modifier that you find. Notice the variety of positions in which they occur.

My Roommate Ari

My roommate Ari speaks English very well. He studied it at school for many years in order to get a scholarship. At present, he is eager to learn idioms, and he often practices new ones several times so that he will be able to use them correctly.

He is usually quite cheerful, but recently he became a little homesick. In fact, he hardly ate anything for several days. He frequently mentioned his family and said that he wanted to find out what was happening at home.

Fortunately his sister Rita, whom he likes very much, arrived here in Cleveland last week. He is definitely happier now that she is here; at last he has a chance to talk to someone from home.

Rita will probably stay at our apartment for a while. No doubt he will introduce her to some of his friends in the next few weeks. This weekend Ari plans to take her on a tour of the city.

Position Rules

There are a number of general rules to help you decide where an adverb modifier should be placed. Read the following rules and example sentences:

Place. Adverbs of place occur after the object. If there is no object, they occur immediately after the verb.

He had studied it *at school*.
His sister arrived *in Boston*.

Manner. Adverbs of manner such as *carefully, quickly, well* generally follow the object.

My roommate Ari speaks English *well*.
He wants to be able to use idioms *correctly*.

Frequency. Adverbs of frequency such as *usually, hardly ever, always* generally occur immediately before the verb.

Ari *often* practices new idioms several times.

When the main verb has several parts, the frequency adverb follows the auxiliary verb.

He has *frequently* mentioned his family.

When the verb is a form of *be*, the frequency adverb goes after the verb.

He is *usually* quite cheerful.

Adverbs of frequency which express amounts of time, such as *every day, several times, twice,* occur after the object;

He practices new ones *several times.*
He has studied it *for many years.*

or after expressions of place.

He goes to the office *every day.*
He goes to the library *once a week.*

Time. Some adverbs of time usually occur before the subject: *at present, recently, by Thursday.*

At present he is eager to learn new idioms.
Recently he has been getting a little homesick.
At last he has a chance to talk to someone from home.

Other time adverbs such as *last week* and *this weekend* may go before the subject to emphasize the time element, or may go after the object.

His sister arrived here *last week.*
This weekend Ari is taking her on a tour of the city.

Purpose or Reason. Adverbs of purpose occur after the object, or after the verb if there is no object.

He studied it *in order to get a scholarship.*

Degree. Adverbs of degree which modify verbs, such as *hardly, very, only,* usually occur before the verb. When the main verb has several parts, the adverb of degree follows the auxiliary verb.

He *hardly* ate anything for several days.

An exception to this is *very much,* which usually follows the object.

He likes his sister *very much.*

Adverbs of degree which modify adjectives go before the adjective.

He is *very* eager to learn idioms.

Means. Adverb phrases such as *on foot, by hand,* which express the means by which something happened, follow the predicate or object.

She flew to New York and then traveled to Boston *by train.*
She contacted him *by phone* when she arrived.

Likelihood. Adverbs such as *no doubt, undoubtedly, obviously* go before the subject.

No doubt he will introduce her to some of his friends.

Adverbs such as *probably, definitely, certainly* go after forms of *be,* and before other verbs.

He is *definitely* happier now that she is here.

It is important to notice that when adverbs of place and adverbs of time modify the same verb, the adverb of place comes *before* the adverb of time.

I saw Ginny *here yesterday*.
I saw Ginny *at the market at three o'clock.*

Practice 2

Rewrite these sentences, adding the word or phrase in parentheses. There may be more than one possible position for some of the modifiers.

Examples

(quite well)   After living in Paris for two years, Rita speaks French.

After living in Paris for two years, Rita speaks French quite well.

(temporarily)   She is going to stay with Ari until she finds an apartment.

She is going to stay with Ari temporarily until she finds an apartment.

1. (again)   When I first met Rita, I thought she looked just like another friend of mine, but when I saw her, I realized that there was not much resemblance.
2. (very much)   So far, she likes living in the United States.
3. (sometimes)   She wishes she were back in Paris.
4. (probably)   By now, Rita is a gourmet cook.
5. (only)   She plans to stay in the United States for a year.
6. (never)   Rita has visited her brother here before.

7. (to do research) She has a fellowship at the university medical center for eight months.
8. (fortunately) Ari lives near the city bus line so Rita can take the bus while she learns how to drive.
9. (certainly) She and Ari have enjoyed talking to each other.
10. (until 3:00 A.M.) Last night they talked with friends at Ari's apartment.

Practice 3

For each sentence a type of adverb is indicated. Add an appropriate adverb modifier of that type to each sentence. Use a different modifier in each blank.

Examples

(frequency) *I generally* try to read each assignment twice.
(manner) She wrapped the package *securely*.

1. (time) The university will announce the finals schedule —————— .

2. (purpose) They are going downtown —————————————— .

3. (likelihood) ————————————————————— he would prefer to rewrite his answer, but there isn't time to do so.

4. (degree) She had ————————————————— hung up when the phone rang again.

5. (means) As a rule, he goes to campus ————————————— .

6. (place) He likes to study ——————————————————— .

7. (frequency) Customers ————————————————— want quick service, especially during the Christmas holidays.

8. (time) He has told me how to get to his house ——————————
—————— , but I can't remember the directions.

9. (manner) If he would explain the problem ——————————
——————, I could probably solve it for him.

10. (frequency) They ————————————————— seem able to finish everything they intended to do.

STRUCTURAL AIDS TO WRITING

Practice 4

Rewrite the sentences, adding an adverb from the list below to each sentence. Add two adverbs where indicated. There may be more than one appropriate answer.

Example

Ari goes out with his friends.

Ari often goes out with his friends.

afterward	later	right away
at last	luckily	seldom
at leisure	often	sometimes
by surprise	on occasion	somewhere
eagerly	on weekends	there
generally	patiently	thoroughly
hesitantly	really	usually
instead	recently	very much
last week	regularly	even more

1. Ari enjoys going to the movies.
2. He goes with Julio.
3. They like to go to movies. (add 2)
4. They saw *One Flew Over the Cuckoo's Nest*.
5. Ari liked it, but Julio disliked it. (add 2)
6. They went to a nearby coffee shop to discuss the movie. (add 2)
7. They met Christina and Larry, who had tried to see the movie but couldn't get in.
8. They had gone to play miniature golf.
9. The four of them talked while they waited for a menu.
10. "Did you see *King Kong*?" asked Christina. "I enjoyed it."
11. "It was O.K.," said Julio, "but I liked *Black Orpheus*."
12. Someone came to take their order, and the conversation shifted to a discussion of items on the menu.

Independent Clauses

While most types of adverbs are single words or phrases, for example, He arrived *early in order to get a seat,* verb modifiers which indicate reason or time are often dependent clauses which normally follow the main clause.

Purpose or Reason: Ari decided not to go to a movie *because he had to study for a quiz the next day.*

Time: The quiz began *as soon as the professor arrived.*

Practice 5

Underline the verb modifier and explain what type each one is.

Example

They ate lunch after they had registered. (time)

1. As Frank was leaving the house, Stanley drove up.
2. He jumped up to answer the phone when it rang.
3. The class was canceled since only three students signed up for it.
4. While Earl was studying for a chemistry test, Susan brought over a surprise birthday cake.
5. He won't be able to plan his schedule until the new catalog comes out, because there have been some changes in the degree requirements.

Practice 6

Write fifteen sentences using adverbial modifiers. Choose five from the list of single-word adverbs, five from the list of phrases, and five of your own. Include one or two dependent clauses (as in Practice 5).

apparently	at some length
clearly	at your earliest convenience
immediately	by hand
indefinitely	for the time being
never	in a hurry
occasionally	in particular
perfectly	in the past two months
recently	on a large scale
temporarily	on time
tentatively	under stress
very much	with considerable effort
	with ease

1.6 WORD ORDER OF QUESTION-WORD CLAUSES (WH- CLAUSES)

You already know that the word order for statements and for yes/no questions is different.

Subject + BE

Be Statement: *Room 92E is* around the corner.

	BE + S
Be Question:	*Is* Room 92E around the corner?

	S + DO VERB
Do Statement:	Most college students *want* to travel.

	AUXILIARY + S + VERB
Do Question:	*Do* most college students want to travel?

Notice the same pattern in question word questions.

	S + BE
Be Statement:	Room 92E *is* around the corner.

	BE + S
Wh- Question:	Where *is* Room 92E? (Answer: around the corner)

	S + V
Do Statement:	That student *wants* to find Professor Green's office.

	AUX + S + V
Wh- Question:	What *does* that student *want* to find? (Answer: Professor Greene's office)

Look at this conversation among three people in an office.

Visitor:	Can you give me some information?
Receptionist:	Certainly.
Visitor:	Can you tell me *where Room 92E is?*
Receptionist:	I think it's around the corner.

Secretary:	What does he want to find?
Receptionist:	He's looking for Room 92E.

When a dependent clause begins with a question word (*where, when, how, what,* or *why*) the word order is the same as in a statement: subject + verb.

Wh- + *Subject* + *be*

I want to know where Room 92E is.

Practice 1

Transform these independent questions into dependent wh- clauses with statement word order, adding them to the following sentences.

Examples

Where is he from?   I'm not sure . . .   I'm not sure *where he is from.*

Where does he live? I think I know . . . I think I know *where he lives.*

1. What does that mean?   Please explain. . . .
2. What have you done?   I hope you realize. . . .
3. How is he feeling today?   I will ask his sister. . . .
4. How much will it cost?   First I have to ask. . . .
5. Why is he sad?   I wonder. . . .
6. When did she get here?   Do you remember . . . ?
7. What were the results?   When can you tell me . . . ?
8. What did they say?   I couldn't understand. . . .
9. How long does it take?   Maybe he knows. . . .
10. Why don't you live on campus? I'd like to know. . . .
11. When are you going to   Would you mind telling me . . . ?
    New York?
12. Which classes did your adviser You haven't notified your
    think you should take?   sponsor. . . .

These statements and questions are different from the earlier pattern.

Subject + *BE*

Something *is* wrong.

S + *BE*

What is wrong?

S + *DO VERB*

Someone *lives* next door.

S + *V*

Who lives next door?

STRUCTURAL AIDS TO WRITING

In the following sentences the word order of the dependent clause is subject + verb. Therefore, it remains the same when it is used as a dependent question word clause. In these wh- sentences the word order is subject + verb. Notice that *what* and *who* are the subjects.

wh-S + BE

Maybe he knows *what is wrong.*

wh-S + V

How would I know *who lives next door?*

Practice 2

Transform these independent questions into wh- clauses, adding them to the following sentences.

Examples

Who approved the request?	It is essential to find out *who approved the request.*
What's unusual about that?	I have no idea *what is unusual about that.*
1. Which one is correct?	Can you figure out....
2. What's so interesting?	I wish you'd tell me....
3. Who spoke at the convention?	Do you remember...?
4. Which was the most significant?	I wish I knew....
5. Who can tell me about Miles Davis?	I'm looking for someone....
6. What's bothering you?	Please tell me....
7. Which one has more potential?	What we need to determine is....
8. Who claimed that memorization was a useless activity?	I'm looking in my notes to see....
9. Which one is considered the finest?	He can show us....
10. Who suggested that we attend that lecture instead of going to the beach?	He's the one....

Practice 3

Complete this letter to a director of admissions. Use wh-clauses.

```
                                (your street)    _____
                                (city, state, country) _____
                                (today's date)   _____
```

Director of Admissions
_____ University
_____
_____

Dear Sir:

Please send me an application for admission for the coming academic year. In addition, I would like to have some information about the university. Would you please tell me the following:

       1. what . . .

       2. when . . .

       3. how much . . .

       4. how long . . .

       5. where . . .

Thank you very much for your help.

                      Sincerely,

                      (Your signature)
                      (Your printed name)

Practice 4

Complete these advertising statements with a *wh-* clause.

Examples

(to advertise toothpaste)
Think of Flash-Brite when *you think of toothpaste*.

(to emphasize quality and economy)
When you buy from us, you get what *you pay for*.

1. (to emphasize the popularity of a magazine)
   Pick up this week's issue and see why. . . .

2. (to advertise the sunny weather at a Florida resort)
   Come to Florida where. . . .
3. (to advertise a new housing development)
   Golden Hills is just what. . . .
4. (to advertise the value of the age of cheese)
   Compare our cheese to others and you'll taste what a difference. . . .
5. (to advertise the quality and comfort of a new car)
   You'll have to drive it to see how. . . .

Practice 5

Complete these sentences, adding any wh- clauses that fit in the context.

Examples

The first step is to find out which *factor he considers most significant*.

How would I know what *is happening*?

1. Above all a student has to decide what. . . .
2. A country's world position depends on how. . . .
3. What each student must do is to develop an awareness of cultural differences and to figure out how. . . .
4. Not only do we have to list all the possible alternatives, but we also have to decide which. . . .
5. It doesn't really matter who. . . .
6. Examining course catalogs from a number of universities should make it easier to choose which. . . .
7. A student must figure out when. . . .
8. Americans have a reputation for moving every few years, but there are many people in rural areas who. . . .
9. What we should do is to correct the problem first and then determine who. . . .
10. I didn't buy theatre tickets after all—I couldn't believe how. . . .

1.7 THE PRESENT PERFECT TENSE

The present perfect tense is one of the most useful means of summarizing past experience. It is therefore very important for you to understand its use in writing. This lesson reviews the formation of the tense, distinguishes between it and the past tense, and practices the use of both tenses.

Formation of the Present Perfect. The general form of the present perfect is formed by *has/have* + *past participle*:

has/have	*past participle*
Catherine has	studied astronomy for six years.
She has	taught an introductory course for two terms.
Many women have	decided to enter science professions.

In the continuous form, *been* is the past participle, followed by verb-*ing* (present participle):

has/have +	*been* + *verb*-ing
Catherine has	been studying the planet Jupiter.
She has	been teaching an introductory course.
Interest in science has	been growing for more than two decades.
People have	been showing increased interest in astronomy recently.

Present Perfect Passive. Passive constructions in the present perfect are formed by *has been/have been* + *participle of main verb*.

has been/have been +	*participle of main verb*
Catherine has been	advised to get more exercise.
The observatory employees have been	encouraged to exercise regularly.
Several tournaments have been	sponsored by the city recreation department.
Catherine has been	chosen to compete in a city-wide tennis tournament.

For a more complete review of passives, see the lesson on passives on pages 58–67.

Past vs. Present Perfect. The key to using the present perfect tense lies in an understanding of the basic difference between the time concepts of the past and the present perfect. Read these explanations and examine the contrasting examples below.

Past

The past refers to a completed experience. When you use the past tense, you emphasize completion of an event or incident at a specific time.

Present Perfect

The present perfect is a summary of past experience which continues in the present, which may recur, or which is relevant to the present. It may be continuous or occasional.

Contrasting examples:

Past	*Present Perfect*
Martin Luther King went to London several times.	My roommate has gone to London twice.
My parents went to London last year.	My parents have gone to London for the past two years.
The rainfall was heavy last year.	The rainfall has been average this year.
I read that book three years ago during my vacation.	I have read his first book, and I plan to read his second.
The present chairman began his three-year term two years ago.	He has been serving as chairman for two years.
Tennis was a minor sport until a few years ago.	Tennis has become a major American sport within the last few years.
The Davis Cup was first won by Australia in 1939.	The Davis Cup has been won by Australians many times since World War II.

Time Expressions. Another guide to the use of the past and present perfect tenses is recognition of the time expressions that are associated with them. Study these examples:

Past

ago	Michael played tennis three days *ago*.
when	He didn't learn how to play tennis *when he was a child*.
from ___ to ___	He took tennis lessons *from February to November*.

Present Perfect

since	Sharon has been playing tennis *since she was eight years old*.
so far	Sharon and Mike have played four sets *so far* this week.

Past or Present Perfect

today	He went to the tennis courts *today*, but they were crowded.
	She has been thinking about playing tennis all day *today*.
for	He played tennis every morning *for two years*, but then he quit.
	She has played tennis every morning *for two years*.
already	She *already* gave away her copy of *How to Improve Your Tennis*; he can have my copy.
	Stan has *already* bought a copy.
just	He *just* completed a four-week course at the tennis clinic.
	She has *just* begun playing a set before dinner every day.
recently	He entered a tennis tournament *recently*.
	Recently she has thought about competing in tournaments, but she doesn't think she has enough time.
yet	He didn't buy a new racket *yet*, but he plans to.
	She hasn't entered any tournaments *yet*.
	(Both tenses are used with *yet*, but present perfect is preferred by most writers.)

Practice 1

Read the following sentences carefully and determine which are correct English and which are incorrect. Rewrite the incorrect sentences. Discuss those cases in which either past or present perfect is acceptable.

1. There have been a number of traffic accidents involving bicycles this month.
2. I didn't see any movies while I worked there; I didn't see any here, so far, either.
3. I sent it in two months ago, and although I have been waiting for it to arrive, I didn't get it back yet.
4. This is the first time that Paolo and Octavio have taken a written English course.
5. The quality of audio equipment was steadily improved since 1945.
6. It is a number of years since Armstrong and Aldrin walked on the moon.

7. Chuck is looking for a used car; so far he saw three that he decided not to buy.
8. During the month that they have been there, they have traveled at least two thousand miles.
9. The time that the group spent on that project before Christmas was time well spent.
10. He has run into two old friends on this campus since he was here.

Practice 2

Use the present perfect whenever possible in these paragraphs. When it is not possible, use the past tense.

Golden Gate Park

One of my favorite places in San Francisco is Golden Gate Park. I (be) _____ there more times than I can remember. Several years ago I (live) _____ only two blocks from the south side of that beautiful park. During that time, I (spend) _____ some time in the park every week. I particularly (enjoy) _____ walking along the many paths and trails. I also (go) _____ to the Aquarium, the Japanese Tea Garden, and the de Young Museum frequently.

Since moving to Berkeley, I (continue) _____ to visit Golden Gate Park, although my visits are now much less frequent. In fact, you can count the number of times I (go) _____ there during the past three years on one hand! About a year and a half ago I (go) _____ there to see an exhibit of some of Van Gogh's most famous paintings. Last winter I (attend) _____ a harpsichord concert in the park's planetarium. And only last week I (go) _____ there and just (walk) _____ around for awhile. So, as you can see, I (go) _____ there only three times during the past two years.

Practice 3

Use the present perfect whenever possible. When it is not possible, use the past tense.

Whitman Hall

Whitman Hall (be) _____ a student-initiated project from the start. Last February, a group of eight students (petition) _____ the Housing Office to establish a house oriented to the arts. It (take) _____ several months to work out the details and to decide what to call the house. Last month the group finally (settle on) _____ the name Whitman Hall, honoring Walt Whitman, the nineteenth-century poet.

The students then (find) _____ twelve professors to support their proposal, which the Housing Office (accept) _____ the next day. Soon after that, a professor and her husband (volunteer) _____ to be faculty residents in Whitman. Since accepting that position, the couple (help) _____ the original committee define its goals. The students hope to create a relaxed, artistically oriented environment in Whitman Hall. They (make) _____ a few plans already. They (set aside) _____ two guest rooms for local artists and community leaders. In addition, they (schedule) _____ a blues concert for the beginning of Fall Quarter. Future plans will depend on the interests of the new residents.

Practice 4

Write sentences using the following time expressions. Use the present perfect wherever possible. When it is not possible, use the past tense.

1. since 1970
2. for a long time
3. a couple of days ago
4. today
5. before I came to the United States
6. from seven o'clock to eight o'clock this morning
7. since last summer
8. so far this year
9. a minute ago
10. this week
11. just now
12. already

Practice 5

For each verb, write a pair of sentences, using past in one and present perfect in the other.

Examples

The council abandoned its plan for an inter-city freeway.
The mayor has abandoned his effort to reverse the decision.

ban	formulate
design	order
develop	promise
differentiate	put
extend	request

Practice 6

Make sure that you use some present perfect structures in completing this writing assignment.

1. Summarize your experiences in the United States in a few paragraphs.
2. What have you seen and done in (a place) _____ ?
3. What are some nontechnical books that you have read during the past two years?
4. Describe an event in your childhood that has influenced your thinking.

1.8 COMPARING VERB + VERB-ING (GERUND) WITH VERB + TO + VERB (INFINITIVE)

Basic Distinction

Structures that have two verb forms (I want to go; I considered going) are quite common in English. The first verb form is the main verb (I *want* to go), which always shows tense:

I *considered* going.
I *am considering* going.
I *will consider* going.

The second verb form is *not* the main verb: it is an "object" that does not show tense:

I am considering *going.*   I want *to go.*
I was considering *going.*   I wanted *to go.*
I considered *going.*   I have wanted *to go.*
I had considered *going.*

A number of common verbs can be followed by either form, the gerund or infinitive, with no difference in meaning, such as *begin, continue, start, like, love, prefer.*

He *likes going.* (*Verb₁ + Verb₂ + -ing*)
They *started studying* in September.

He likes *to go.* (*Verb₁ + to + Verb₂*)
They *started to study* in September.

However, certain frequently used verbs can be followed by *only* one of the two forms. Study these examples and the lists at the right.

Verb₁ + Verb₂ + -ing
(gerund)

Ahmed appreciated staying with his roommate's family.

He enjoyed talking about his country with them.

He considered asking them for advice.

Verb₁ + Verb₂ + -ing

admit	find	recall
appreciate	finish	recommend
avoid	imagine	report
consider	keep	resent
delay	mind	resist
deny	miss	risk
dislike	postpone	suggest
enjoy	practice	understand
favor	quit	

Verb + to + Verb
(infinitive)

David planned to find out about a food cooperative.

He wanted to save money on food.

He persuaded his roommate to cook every other day.

Verb₁ + to + Verb₂

agree	hope	plan
arrange	intend	pretend
consent	learn	proceed
decide	mean	promise
expect	need	refuse
fail	offer	seem
happen	persuade	want
hesitate		

Some of the main verbs in the preceding lists can be followed by a dependent clause which begins with *that*. (*That* is sometimes deleted.) When the subject of the dependent clause is a verbal form, verb-*ing* is generally used. Main verbs which frequently occur in this pattern include: *recall, report, suggest, understand, agree, decide, hope, learn, promise,* and *seem.* Compare the structure and meaning of the following pairs of sentences:

Kay recalls getting up at 6:00 A.M. every day to catch the bus.
Kay recalls that getting up at 6:00 A.M. was very difficult.

STRUCTURAL AIDS TO WRITING

Abe agreed to ride to school with his roommate.
Abe agreed that riding to school with his roommate saved time.

He hoped to learn French in one summer.
He hoped (that) learning French would not take longer than one summer.

Practice 1

These are questions you may be asked often while you are in the United States. Fill in the blanks in the questions and then write out full sentence answers to them.

Examples

Do you miss (read) _____ the newspaper from your country?
No, I don't miss reading it.

Do you want (read) _____ the newspaper from your country?
Yes, I want to read it.

1. What made you decide (come) _____ here?
   _____.

2. What do you intend (study) _____ ?
   _____.

3. Do you miss (see) _____ your family?
   _____.

4. When do you expect (receive) _____ your degree?
   _____.

5. If you postpone (work) _____ full time when you return to your country, what else would you like to do?
   _____.

6. What would you appreciate (have) _____ someone send you from home? _____.

7. Are you considering (travel) _____ around the U.S. before you go home? _____.

8. Do you mind (eat) _____ the food here?
   _____.

9. What do you hope (gain) _____ by studying in the U.S.?
   _____.

10. How do you plan (use) _____ what you have learned in the U.S. when you go home? _____ .

Practice 2

Complete each sentence in this story which a research assistant told about a professor's preparations to attend a conference; add the correct form of the second verb.

Doing an Errand for a Professor

When the Institute of Electrical and Electronic Engineers (IEEE) invited Professor Michael Davis to read a paper on current injection theory at its annual spring conference, he decided (accept) _____ . While he was there, in addition to reading the paper he hoped (interview) _____ three or four applicants for an appointment in his department. He easily persuaded the university (pay) _____ for the trip since it was a professional meeting, although he had considered (pay) _____ for it himself if that were necessary. While he was there he intended (find out) _____ about some recent unpublished research which he was interested in. He also needed (catch up on) _____ other recent developments in the field; speaking to the people doing the research seemed to be a good way. Since the conference was being held in Chicago and he had been an undergraduate at the University of Chicago, he particularly wanted (go) _____ . He always enjoyed (see) _____ his old professors, many of whom were his friends.

When Professor Davis asked me if I would mind (do) _____ him a few favors before he left, I said I certainly wouldn't mind. I recalled (have) _____ to leave town in a hurry once and I remembered that he didn't hesitate (help) _____ me. He said he disliked (ask) _____ , but he knew he wouldn't enjoy (be) _____ at the conference if he left so many things undone.

"What can I do?" I asked.

"Well, I've postponed (take) _____ my car in to be fixed for a

STRUCTURAL AIDS TO WRITING

month. I can't delay (do) _____ that any longer. If you could arrange (do) _____ that for me, I'd appreciate it. I also have avoided (go) _____ to the bank, but I can't risk not (pay) _____ my income tax on time, so would you mind (deposit) _____ this check for me?"

I promised (do) _____ it as soon as the bank opened, or at least to get it to the night deposit box in the evening. Of course I understood that (get) _____ the taxes paid before April 15th was absolutely necessary. I didn't resent his (ask) _____ for help, because he had helped me many times. In fact, I wanted (do) _____ it.

Practice 3

Write ten questions beginning with question words and then answer them, using ten of the following verbs as the first verb forms and choosing your own second verb forms.

Example

Question: Why did the speaker keep his talk nontechnical?
Answer: He didn't want to risk boring the audience with a lot of statistics.

Question: What did the conference chairman do next?
Answer: He proceeded to introduce the next report.

delay	finish	refuse
decide	intend	recommend
agree	mind	suggest
keep	quit	risk
imagine	proceed	seem
consent	report	want

Practice 4

Make up a ten-item quiz which tests the use of verb-*ing* and *to* + verb. Let one of your classmates take the quiz and return it to you for correction.

Examples

He planned (live) _____ in a dormitory.
She considered (take) _____ mathematics, but she finally decided (take) _____ economics.

Two Special Verbs: stop, remember. The following two verbs can be followed by either the *-ing* form or the *to* form of the second verb, but notice the change in meaning:

stop	He stopped eating.	(stopped the activity of eating)
	He stopped to eat.	(stopped some other activity in order to eat)
remember	He remembered writing to me.	(remembered that at some time in the past he had written)
	He remembered to write to me.	(did not forget to write)

Practice 5

To practice the use of *stop* and *remember* with second verbs, read through this passage describing a student's favorite professor; after you have read it once, go back and fill in the blanks with the correct form of each verb in parentheses.

All the students immediately stopped (talk) _____ when Professor Saunders walked in the room. He was that kind of man—highly respected for his research breakthroughs, his social-political activism, and his personal interest in students. Because he often didn't remember (bring) _____ his notes or (write) _____ his ideas down before class, his excellent lectures were sometimes given off the top of his head. Years after I left the university, his lectures were the ones I remembered best.

One day (ten years after I graduated) when I was visiting the campus for an afternoon, I happened to run into Professor Saunders and he stopped (talk) _____ with me. Imagine how excited and pleased I was to see him. I had asked him to write me a recommendation ten years earlier and he still remembered (write) _____ it for me.

Practice 6

Use either the verb-*ing* or *to* + verb form of the second verbs in parentheses to complete these observations about Koyo's stay in the United States.

1. A full scholarship persuaded Koyo (come) _____ to the United States to study.

STRUCTURAL AIDS TO WRITING

2. He believed that (learn) _____ English would be useful to him in his work.
3. He appreciated (have) _____ the opportunity to travel, although he expected that (learn) _____ English would be difficult.
4. He expected (stay) _____ in the United States for about two years.
5. He considered (go) _____ to Wisconsin but finally decided (go) _____ to Duke.
6. He told his family that he would like (hear) _____ from them as often as possible.
7. He enjoyed (travel) _____ by plane.
8. I certainly recommend (look) _____ for an apartment soon.
9. He remembered (hear) _____ about the new student union on the campus.
10. He forced himself to avoid (speak) _____ his native language.

Practice 7

In this paragraph about two roommates and their cooking habits, fill in the blanks with either verb-*ing* or *to* + verb.

George MacDouglass likes to cook. He enjoys (plan) _____ meals, (try) _____ new dishes, and (prepare) _____ foods. He first learned (cook) _____ when he lived off campus at M.I.T. (Massachusetts Institute of Technology). His roommate, Paul Steward, wanted (learn) _____ , intended (learn) _____ , and promised (try) _____ (learn) _____ how to cook too, but he kept (put) _____ it off. At first they agreed (take) _____ turns cooking and washing the dishes. Paul postponed (cook) _____ so often that George finally suggested (make) _____ a different arrangement.

"We need (eat) _____ ," he told Paul, "so I'll cook and you do the dishes. How about that?"

Paul decided (accept) _____ because he knew that George would then quit (bother) _____ him. It's fortunate that George practiced (cook) _____ in college because two years later he married someone who insisted that he cook half the time.

Prepositions and Verb-*ing*

The verb-*ing* form must be used after prepositions. For example:

Many Americans are interested *in learning* about house plants.

He got some information on house plants *by writing* to the U.S. Department of Agriculture.

Notice how the verb-*ing* form is used after the prepositions *with, by, of, on,* and *about* in the following passage.

Gardening in the House

Along with increasing their interest in the environment, Americans have become interested in health foods, nonpolluting detergents, organic gardening, and house plants. House plants and indoor gardening have become as popular a topic of conversation as travel or sports. *By gardening* indoors, people who live in apartments or condominiums, and people who live in harsh climates can enjoy plants all year long. Even people in mild climates who live in single-family dwellings with space for outdoor gardens have shown great interest in having plants indoors. Clearly, Americans are getting a lot of pleasure *out of caring for* their plants and *watching* them grow.

For the novice who is doubtful *about starting* in on this hobby, there are more and more indoor garden manuals on the market. These guides give advice and helpful hints *on taking* care of house plants, similar to the guides that give advice *on taking* care of pets. In fact, just as many people consider their pets part of the family, some people consider their plants part of the family. So don't be surprised if, when you visit an American home, you are introduced to the plants.

Special Case: *to*

To can occur either as part of a main verb or adjective phrase:

She *looks forward to* gardening every weekend.
He is *accustomed to* smoking.

or as the first part of an infinitive construction:

He wants *to see* a movie.
Ferns tend *to grow* better in damp climates.

In the first case, *to* is part of the first verb form, not the second. Because *to* is a preposition in such cases, and therefore not part of a second verb form, it must be followed by a verb-*ing* (gerund) form. Here are the most common verb phrases with *to*:

Jim is used to being careful with money.
His wife is getting used to being thrifty.
He is opposed to buying on credit.
Jim objects to having dozens of plants around the apartment.
He isn't accustomed to sharing his living room with ferns and ivy.
They are looking forward to having their own house and garden some day.

Practice 8

Complete this paragraph by inserting the correct verb form.

Yesterday Don had quite a few things on his mind. Although he thought he had succeeded in (get) _____ settled before classes began his first quarter, several things continued to (upset) _____ his schedule. First, one of the courses he wanted to (enroll in) _____ was cancelled, so he had to think about (enroll in) _____ another one. Besides (look) _____ in the want ads for a used car, and (straighten out) _____ an error in his checkbook, he was trying to (get) _____ used to (have) _____ to ask where things were. By the time Don got back home all he wanted to do was to (forget) _____ about his problems, so he tried to (relax) _____ by (listen) _____ to records and (write) _____ letters.

Practice 9

Using some of the following phrases, write a paragraph on *one* of the following:

STRUCTURAL AIDS TO WRITING

1. arriving at an airport in a foreign country;
2. studying and taking a test;
3. participating in an event such as a soccer match, a frisbee contest, or a table tennis tournament.

used to reading/playing
able to find out
afraid of being
warned about cheating
unable to concentrate

worried about
interpreting
interested in
figuring out
pleased to notice/find

Add other phrases or change parts of these if you wish.

Practice 10

Incorporate some of the following phrases into a paragraph on *one* of the following topics:

1. reform of your country's secondary school system;
2. attitudes toward sex education;
3. attitudes toward public transportation.

be in favor of
be accustomed to
be interested in
be opposed to
be planning on
be used to
prevent from

be concerned about
discourage from
approve of
object to
get tired of
worry about

Verb-*ing* Structures with Possessives

Earlier in this lesson you reviewed the structure of a verb or verb phrase followed by a gerund:

They favor taking a vacation in June.
(They favor the action of taking a vacation in June.)

She disapproves of buying on credit.
(She disapproves of the action of buying on credit.)

I remember doing it last week.
(I remember that I did it last week.)

Now compare these sentences and explanations to the above sentences.

They favor my taking a vacation in June.
(I plan to take a vacation in June. They favor my plan.)

She disapproves of their buying a car on credit.
(They plan to buy a car on credit. She disapproves of their plan.)

I remember his doing it last week.
(He did it last week. I remember that he did it.)

In formal English, when the action of the gerund is performed by someone other than the subject of the main verb, the possessive form is generally used. Discuss these sentences:

I recall his telling me about the special concert.

Kay appreciates Jane's staying late to help her correct the mistakes in the paper.

Dan's adviser is in favor of his taking a semester off to recover from his illness.

They couldn't imagine his not wanting to participate in the pizza-eating contest.

Practice 11

Combine the sentences so that the first sentence is the object of the second sentence. Thus, the subject of the first sentence becomes a possessive pronoun followed by a verb-*ing* noun clause.

Examples

You sent a quick reply. I appreciated it.
I appreciated *your sending* a quick reply.

Jack told me he would come. I remember it.
I remember *his telling me* he would come.

1. He mentioned that he would arrive a little late today. I remember it.
2. Sue barged in halfway through the meeting. The other members disliked her behavior.
3. John phoned Rose at 4:00 A.M. She resented it.
4. The students attended a conference out of town. The students' adviser consented to it.
5. Jason is applying for a grant to study in Indonesia. His mother approves of it.
6. He practices the tuba in the shower. I don't mind.
7. She gets very sleepy. Her roommate worries about it.
8. The professor said that we should read two chapters. I don't recall it.
9. Sonny wanted to pass up the party. I couldn't imagine it.
10. Ken and Gary are taking some evening classes. Their wives are in favor of it.

Negative Second Verb Forms

When the second verb is negative, *not* is placed between the main verb and the second verb. For example,

She promised *not* to miss her next appointment.
Most people like *not* getting up early on weekends.
Elizabeth suggested *not* leaving before Sunday.
Peter learned *not* to volunteer for anything.
We hope Jim and Shirley won't mind our *not* stopping by tonight.
The fans pretended *not* to care when their team lost.

Practice 12

What advice would you give to a student planning to study in another country? Complete the following phrases.

Examples

Plan to *spend as much time as you can getting to know people.*
Avoid *spending all your time with students from your country.*
I recommend not *taking too many classes the first quarter.*

1. Get used to _____

_____ .

2. Arrange not to _____

_____ .

3. Remember _____

_____ .

4. I hope you've decided not _____

_____ .

5. I don't think you'll mind not _____

_____ .

6. Keep _____

_____ .

Practice 13

Fill in the blanks with the appropriate verb forms.

Product Marketing

Marketers have found that it is worth spending substantial amounts of money to find out what attracts people to new products. The study of consumer behavior is an interesting aspect of marketing.

By (study) _____ human behavior, sociologists, anthropologists, psychologists, economists, statisticians, and even mathematicians have something to tell the marketer. In (purchase) _____ a product the consumer exchanges his money for an object he expects (be) _____ useful to him. But what is useful to a customer is a complicated matter. The marketer's interest lies in (fulfill) _____ the consumers' needs, which vary from inescapable requirements to whims. Generally the greater the need, the more the consumer is willing (spend) _____ for what he needs. By (question) _____ the consumer, the marketer can get some idea of what the consumer wants and needs. If you asked Mr. Jones why he bought a four-door, low-priced station wagon, he might respond, "My wife needs a station wagon for (shop) _____ . With rising gas prices I want (buy) _____ a car which will get good gas mileage. My son dreams about (take) _____ the car camping, but I don't want (buy) _____ a van." Besides attempting (satisfy) _____ all the preferences which his family expresses, he hopes (get) _____ a car which is safe on the road and has a reputation for low frequency of repair. In (plan) _____ any large purchase, any intelligent, responsible consumer goes through an elaborate decision-making process.

Marketers have found that because it is almost impossible to intervene in the consumers' decision-making process, they are better off (supply) _____ what the customer wants.

Before (introduce) _____ a new product, the

STRUCTURAL AIDS TO WRITING

marketer arranges (conduct) _____ a variety of quantitative and qualitative marketing research tests, and tries to determine which advertising approach and what prices would give the company the greatest profits. If the sample population seems not (like) _____ (use) _____ it, the marketers will recommend (improve) _____ it to meet consumer taste. Sometimes this means (reduce) _____ the price, thus appealing to "bargain hunters." Or they may recommend (change) _____ the packaging. Research has shown how important this aspect of product marketing is to the consumer. Good packaging is economical, functional, and attractive. An important aspect of attractiveness is the choice of colors used. The dominant colors for (package) _____ are bright reds and yellows. These seem (be) _____ most easily seen by the customer. Interestingly enough, in lab tests most people report (see) _____ red first. However, all that they notice is the red color. If they are expected (identify) _____ the product and the brand name, they cannot remember them. Red is still seen first but it is not associated with any brand name. One study showed that people are able to identify product and brand name when green is the dominant color.

Although marketers cannot control the needs and wants of the consumer, they can control the stimuli to which the consumer responds. By (develop) _____ and (advertise) _____ products which appeal to those needs and wants, they can be successful and at the same time satisfy consumers.

Practice 14

Write a ten-line conversation *or* a fairly long paragraph about one of the following trends in your country. Use verb-*ing* or *to* + verb in at least five of the phrases in your conversation or paragraph:

1. a hobby which has become extremely popular;

2. some people I know are interested in . . . ;
3. a successful advertisement;
4. a sport that is growing in popularity.

1.9 THE PASSIVE VOICE

This lesson reviews the formation and use of verbs in the passive voice, and the balancing of passive and active voices in writing. Passive constructions are frequently used in academic writing, which often emphasizes a resulting action rather than the agent that performs the action. Passives are also frequently used in official correspondence and in instructions. It is therefore important to know how to form the passive and to know when its use is appropriate.

Contrast of Active and Passive

Active: *subject agent + verb action + object receiver*
Robert Frost wrote "The Road Not Taken."

Passive: *object receiver + form of be + past participle*
"The Road Not Taken" was written

+ by + agent
by Robert Frost.

A passive construction includes the following elements in this order:

1. an object receiver in subject position;
2. a form of *be* in the same tense as the verb in the active sentence;
3. the past participle of the verb;
4. optional: *by* + agent.

Examples of corresponding active and passive forms:

Present

Active: Two million people watch the program every week.
Passive: The program is watched by two million people every week.

Present Continuous

Active: Someone is introducing a resolution tonight.
Passive: A resolution is being introduced tonight.

Future

Active: The university will hold commencement in the park.

Passive: Commencement will be held in the park.

Past

Active: The jury convicted the two men.
Passive: The two men were convicted by the jury.

Present Perfect

Active: The personnel director has sent all applications to the screening committee.
Passive: All applications have been sent to the screening committee by the personnel director.

In informal writing and in conversation *get* is often used rather than *be* in passive structures:

Hassan got accepted to the University of Michigan and Penn State.

When Daylight Saving Time began, Ellen got mixed up and went to class an hour too early.

Last year she got so involved in student committee work that she had a hard time keeping up with her classes.

Uses of the Passive in Different Contexts

Passive is used when the agent is unknown or unimportant (a "nonessential agent")—that is, when the action is more important than the agent.

English is used in many international business transactions.
10.7 ml of NaCl was added to the solution.
A book order will be submitted next Monday.
Little pop music has been played on FM radio.
Oranges and lemons are grown in California and Florida.

Passive is used when the object receiver is being emphasized.

A few years ago a "Stone Age" tribe was discovered in the Philippines by a member of another tribe in the area.
Six cars were overturned by a tornado in Florida last week.
A Nobel Prize was awarded to a young professor at Princeton.

Passive is used when a writer wants to make a statement sound objective. Notice that in this use the subject may often be *it*.

Juvenile delinquency is considered by many experts to be a major factor in rising crime rates.
It is assumed that you understand the terms of the agreement.
It is widely believed that he will announce his candidacy this weekend.

Passive is used when a writer wants to be tactful, to avoid naming someone who has made an error or taking sides in a controversy.

Work has not been completed on the underground transit system.
Based on the total figure, it appears that an error was made in last week's inventory.
No agreement has been reached on the critical issue of seniority.
Two cases of cheating were reported during the examination.

Passive is used in newspaper headlines; see the lesson on newspaper vocabulary.

Practice 1

Read the statement and answer the question to practice emphasizing the actor.

Examples

The budget was prepared by the governor last week. (What did the governor do?)
The governor prepared the budget last week.

Mini-calculators are being bought by many students. (What are many students doing?)
Many students are buying mini-calculators.

1. He is being charged higher rent this year by his landlord.
   (What is his landlord doing?)

2. He is often scolded by his parents for not returning library books on time.
   (What do his parents do?)

3. Your request has been considered by the committee members, and a decision will be announced by them tomorrow.
   (What have the committee members done and what will they do tomorrow?)

4. What games are played by children in your country?
   (What do children in your country play?)

5. James Frenzel was elected president of a labor organization by the delegates.
   (What did the delegates do?)

6. Bicycles are used only by the people who live outside the capital city.
   (Begin with *Only*.)
   (What do people outside the capital use?)

STRUCTURAL AIDS TO WRITING

Practice 2

Circle the essential agents in the passive sentences below, and cross out the non-essential agents.

Example

The music for *West Side Story* was written (by Leonard Bernstein). The movie version was filmed ~~by the crew~~ at four different locations.

1. The letter has already been signed by ten members of our consumer group.
2. Spanish is spoken by people in many parts of the world.
3. The documentary was prerecorded by NBC.
4. In the United States a great deal of food is wasted by people every day.
5. A committee is being set up by the mayor to study the city's housing problem.
6. Many sophisticated and expensive research techniques are being used by researchers.
7. Money for a recreation center will be raised by local residents.
8. Luxury cars are usually purchased by people in high income brackets.
9. "Several serious complaints concerning the rising rate of unemployment have been brought to my attention by some people from my office," the governor said.
10. The revised edition of that dictionary will be published by the company next year.
11. He was treated in a hospital by a doctor and released.
12. It has been shown by scientists that coffee drinking and sleeplessness are related.

Practice 3

Change these sentences to passive in order to place greater emphasis on the object receiver. Keep the same verb *tense* and omit any non-essential agents. Follow any specific instructions given for a particular sentence.

Examples

Frank Lloyd Wright designed that building.
That building *was designed* by Frank Lloyd Wright.

Someone is going to introduce the guest speaker in a few minutes.
The guest speaker *is going to be introduced* in a few minutes.

1. Someone has made a mistake in calculating the bill.
2. Economic instability follows a major war.
3. The university expelled him for cheating on the exam.

4. Many people across the country will need instruction in the use of the new tax form.
5. People abandon dozens of pet cats and dogs daily.
6. Someone must judge the results with respect to the original goals.
7. Yesterday's rain cleaned the air, so today there is no smog. (Change only the first clause.)
8. The staff filed a complaint two months ago but has received no reply. (Change both clauses.)
9. A language reveals the culture of the area where people speak it. (Change only the wh- clause.)
10. Newspapers have been predicting a shakeup for several days.
11. People recognize that he is having a difficult time coming to a decision. (Change only the first clause.)
12. The public hopes that someone will discover the cause of cancer soon. (Change both clauses.)
13. In the past twenty years people have invented numerous fast means of transportation such as the jumbo jet and automated mass transit systems.
14. The police know that someone is smuggling contraband across the border. (Change both clauses.)
15. This author feels that extrasensory perception is worthy of scientific study.

Practice 4

To practice using passives, rewrite the passage below, changing the underlined structures from active to passive. Omit non-essential agents.

Examples

Bears can injure people.
People can be injured by bears.

You should report any signs of disruptive bears to a park ranger.
Any signs of disruptive bears should be reported to a park ranger.

Bears in the National Parks

Bears are a common sight in many national parks in the United States, and the National Park Service allows them to wander freely throughout the parks. It is easy for people to forget that bears are wild animals which can be a nuisance or even cause injury if people try to feed them or are careless with their food. Accordingly, the National Park Service has issued a list of suggestions for campers and travelers:

1. You should not encourage bears to come near your picnic site.

2. You should select food which does not have strong smells. Airtight containers reduce food odor.
   3. You should not leave food on your table when the meal is over.
   4. You should throw away all trash in containers which the Park Service provides.
   5. You should wrap leftover food carefully. Generally food will be safe if you store it in the closed trunk of your car.
   6. Finally, whenever you are traveling in an area of a national park where there may be bears, you should keep all car windows closed.

Practice 5

To practice using passive constructions, rewrite the passage below, changing from active to passive wherever possible. Omit non-essential agents.

How to Make a Bookcase

Many stores sell elaborate, expensive wood or metal bookcases, but you can construct a durable, nice-looking bookcase for very little money.

Buy boards of the required length and width. You can make your choice from pine, fir, redwood, and other types. Usually you can purchase precut lumber, but sometimes a lumberyard employee may have to cut it to the desired size. He will charge you 25 to 50 cents per cut.

Bricks are the second essential item. Often the same place will carry both lumber and bricks so that you don't have to make a separate trip for each thing. You can buy bricks in many colors, qualities, and price ranges. Many stores sell spare cinder blocks as well as regular fireplace bricks. You should decide on the height to have between the shelves to determine how many bricks to buy.

Then you go home with your boards and bricks and build your bookcase. You put one board on the floor along a wall and then stack an equal number of bricks on each end. You push each pile of bricks into a stable column. Then you put another board on top and continue as before.

At long last you put some books on each shelf and then sit back to admire your handiwork. You have finished your useful, inexpensive bookcase!

Active/Passive Verb Choice

In academic writing there are very few verbs which are used only in passive or in active voice. Examples of the most common ones follow.

Passive Only

to be composed of	A whole is composed of its parts.
to be known for	Einstein is known for his theory of relativity.
to be noted for	Jonas Salk is noted for developing a polio vaccine.

Active Only

to consist of	The Micron Corporation presently consists of one major plant and three small branches.
to stem from	The company's success in the transistor market stems from innovative design.
to result in	Better working conditions and profit-sharing have resulted in increased productivity.

Some verbs which occur frequently in academic writing are used in passive much more frequently than in active:

Usually Passive

to be based on	Scientific plant breeding is still based on Mendel's observations.
to be classified	Plants are classified according to structure.
to be comprised of	The evergreen group is comprised of plants which do not lose their leaves in autumn.
to be derived from	Domesticated horses are derived from the extinct wild horses of Asia.
to be distributed	These modern horses are distributed all over the world.
to be made up of	They are made up of a number of distinct breeds.

Practice 6

In class read this passage about the study of the universe; for each verb, determine:

1. whether the verb is active or passive;
2. what its possible synonyms are.

Theories of Astronomy

Ptolemy, who lived in ancient times, is noted for his theory that the universe was composed of heavenly bodies which revolved around the Earth. In the fifteenth century Copernicus theorized that our solar system was made up of planets which revolved around the sun. Modern astronomy is based on this theory. Today, as a result of sophisticated techniques and space exploration, we know far more about the universe, especially about our own solar system. The universe consists of planets, stars, comets, "black holes," and other phenomena. Continuing analysis of lunar rocks and planetary data may reveal when our solar system was formed and what natural materials it contains. These studies will in turn lead to more questions for astronomers to answer.

Practice 7

Complete each sentence with the appropriate form of the verb in parentheses.

Examples

(result in)   Volcanic action sometimes _results in_ the formation of craters.

(classified)   The sun _is classified_ as a star.

1. (noted for) Fleming _____ the discovery of penicillin.
2. (make up of) The United States _____ fifty states.
3. (base on) The director's final decision will _____ the consensus of his staff and his own investigation.
4. (known for) Mexico _____ its ancient ruins.
5. (comprise) Greater New York City _____ five districts.
6. (consist of) The exhibit _____ eight scale models of space stations.
7. (classify) Members of the animal kingdom _____ into families.
8. (derive from) Plastics _____ petroleum.
9. (stem from) The severity of the housing problem _____ a shortage of space and lack of funds.
10. (composed of) An anthology _____ numerous articles or essays.
11. (distribute) Fertilizer should _____ evenly over the soil.
12. (result in) A disclosure made last week _____ a renewed investigation. (Use past tense.)

Practice 8

Write a sentence for each verb introduced in the previous section, Active/Passive Verb Choice.

Balanced Use of Active and Passive

In academic writing a balance between active and passive is considered good style. There are times when an agent is unknown or unimportant, but there are other times when the agent must be mentioned. The following section provides practice in recognizing balanced use and in developing skill in achieving balance in writing.

Practice 9

Study the balance of active and passive in the two selections below. Discuss the reasons for choosing passive or active structures.

Testing for Water Leaks in New Cars

An unusual method <u>has been devised</u> by auto manufacturers to determine whether or not a new car leaks. The car <u>is subjected to</u> a deluge of water similar to a heavy rainstorm. The water <u>contains</u> a chemical dye which glows in "black light" (ultraviolet light). After several minutes, the water <u>is turned off</u>. The technician <u>opens</u> the doors and trunk and, using a black light, checks to see if there <u>has been</u> any water leakage. Thus a trouble area <u>can be located</u> so that the defect <u>can be corrected</u>.

Alga[2] Powder—A New Food Supplement

In Peru for the past two years a group of Peruvian and West German scientists <u>have been</u> jointly <u>conducting</u> an agricultural experiment of potential significance in improving nutrition and helping solve the world's food problem. The experiment is one of the first major algae-cultivation projects which <u>has been attempted</u>. The technique is relatively simple. The alga <u>is spread</u> in shallow trays of water and <u>left out</u> in the sun to grow. Carbon dioxide and a mineral fertilizer <u>are added</u> to the alga. Every four days researchers <u>harvest</u> a crop with a centrifuge, which <u>recycles</u> the water back to the trays for the next planting.

Practice 10

Rewrite the following passage in order to achieve a better balance of active and passive. This passage is a continuation of the passage on alga powder found in Practice 9. Where appropriate, change verbs from active to passive; leave some other verbs in the active form. In class, discuss the reasons for choosing active or passive in each case.

[2]Alga (plural—algae): a small, often microscopic, green plant which is generally found growing in water.

STRUCTURAL AIDS TO WRITING

Continuation of Alga Powder[3]

The researchers dry the alga into a powder which people can add to food to increase the nutritional value of the food significantly. People can use the versatile powder in everything from soup to cookies, and the powder does not change the flavor or color of the food. Nutritionists have prepared many meals of alga-fortified foods, and the scientists report that consumers have readily accepted the foods. Key advantages of the alga are that people can cultivate it very economically, that growing it uses up few natural resources such as water and energy, and that it provides far more protein per acre than wheat or soybeans do. The researchers have shown that the product is commercially feasible and publicly acceptable. The future of the alga powder now depends on whether health departments of countries around the world promote its production and use.

Practice 11

Write a one- or two-page composition on one of the following topics:

1. How has your country been affected by the recent realignment of control of energy resources?
2. What effects has television had on your country (education, social interaction, health, mobility, public information, entertainment)?
3. What effects have other communications media had on your country?
4. Describe how regional customs in your country have been influenced by geography.

Practice 12

In a textbook or journal frequently used in your field, find a paragraph or two illustrating a balanced use of active and passive constructions. Using it as a model of academic writing, write a paragraph or short composition on a related topic.

1.10 SPELLING

English writing has a very confusing spelling system, based as much on word origin as on sound. There is not a clear relationship of one sound to

---

[3]Adapted from David F. Belnap, "Scientists Cultivate, Study 'Food of Future,'" *Los Angeles Times,* 24 February 1974.

one symbol. After spending hundreds of hours studying spelling in school, many Americans still have considerable difficulty with spelling. Therefore, foreign students can anticipate difficulty with spelling too.

In this lesson there are four rules with exercises. If you learn these rules and words, you can overcome part of the difficulty. Above all, when you want to be sure that words you have written are correctly spelled, look them up in an American English dictionary, as native speakers of English do.

Doubling Consonants

-ing, -ed, -er. You have to double the last consonant if you add -ing, -ed, or -er to a verb that has:

1. one syllable;
2. one (and only one) vowel letter (a, e, i, o, u) and one consonant letter at the end.

Do *not* double the last consonant if there are two vowel letters or two consonant letters at the end. For these purposes, *y* and *w* after vowels are considered vowels, and *qu* is considered a consonant.

Examples

	Verb Forms		Noun Forms
	-ing	-ed	-er
run	running	—	runner
wash	washing	washed	washer
hit	hitting	—	hitter
stop	stopping	stopped	stopper
help	helping	helped	helper
join	joining	joined	joiner

Practice 1

Write the following words with the -ing, -ed, and -er endings.

		-ing	-ed	-er
1.	pin	_____	_____	xxx
2.	plan	_____	_____	_____
3.	sign	_____	_____	_____
4.	read	_____	xxx	_____
5.	spell	_____	_____	_____

STRUCTURAL AIDS TO WRITING

6.	shop	_____	_____	_____
7.	show	_____	_____	xxx
8.	burn	_____	_____	_____
9.	rub	_____	_____	_____
10.	scrub	_____	_____	_____
11.	play	_____	_____	_____
12.	slip	_____	_____	_____
13.	swim	_____	xxx	_____
14.	build	_____	xxx	_____
15.	drum	_____	_____	_____
16.	wrap	_____	_____	_____
17.	mean	_____	xxx	xxx
18.	snow	_____	_____	xxx
19.	stay	_____	_____	xxx
20.	loan	_____	_____	xxx
21.	send	_____	xxx	_____
22.	sleep	_____	xxx	_____
23.	tell	_____	xxx	_____
24.	spot	_____	_____	_____
25.	watch	_____	_____	xxx
26.	point	_____	_____	_____
27.	rent	_____	_____	_____
28.	quit	_____	xxx	_____

In words of two or more syllables, the basic rule applies only if stress is placed on the final syllable.

Examples

	-ing	-ed	-er
begin	beginning	—	beginner
permit	permitting	—	—
refer	referring	referred	—
order	ordering	ordered	—

Practice 2

Write the following words with the -ing, -ed, and -er endings.

		-ing	-ed	-er
1.	occur	_____	_____	xxx
2.	control	_____	_____	_____
3.	transfer	_____	_____	xxx
4.	travel	_____	_____	_____
5.	allow	_____	_____	xxx
6.	discover	_____	_____	_____
7.	propel	_____	_____	_____
8.	borrow	_____	_____	_____
9.	maintain	_____	_____	xxx
10.	develop	_____	_____	_____
11.	admit	_____	_____	xxx
12.	accept	_____	_____	xxx
13.	account	_____	_____	xxx
14.	benefit	_____	_____	xxx
15.	enter	_____	_____	xxx
16.	repair	_____	_____	xxx
17.	return	_____	_____	xxx
18.	employ	_____	_____	_____

Words that End in -y

When you add -s or -ed to a word that ends in a consonant + y, change the y to i and then add the ending. To add -s you must write -ies.

Examples

Nouns	-s	-ed	-ing
city	cities	—	—
factory	factories	—	—
country	countries	—	—

70   STRUCTURAL AIDS TO WRITING

Verbs

carry	carries	carried	carrying
cry	cries	cried	crying
study	studies	studied	studying

Practice 3

Add *-s* to the nouns. Add *-ies, -ed,* and *-ing* to the verbs.

Nouns   -s

army   _____

lady   _____

Verbs	-s	-ed	-ing
marry	_____	_____	_____
apply	_____	_____	_____
study	_____	_____	_____

When you add an ending to a word that ends in a vowel + *y*, do not change the *y*.

Examples

Nouns	-s	-ed	-ing
day	days		
driveway	driveways		

Verbs	-s	-ed	-ing
stay	stays	stayed	staying
enjoy	enjoys	enjoyed	enjoying
play	plays	played	playing

Practice 4

Add *-s* to the nouns. Add *-s* and *-ed* to the verbs. This exercise includes both consonant + *y* and vowel + *y* words.

Nouns

1. freeway   _____
2. joy   _____
3. relay   _____

4. valley   _____

5. delivery   _____

6. birthday   _____

7. community   _____

8. battery   _____

9. salary   _____

10. industry   _____

11. grocery   _____

12. activity   _____

13. disability   _____

14. property   _____

15. opportunity   _____

16. injury   _____

17. story   _____

18. century   _____

Verbs	-s	-ed
1. destroy	_____	_____
2. occupy	_____	_____
3. spray	_____	_____
4. hurry	_____	_____
5. delay	_____	_____
6. buy	_____	bought
7. say	_____	said

Words that End in -e

When you add an ending that begins with a vowel, drop an unpronounced final *e*.

response   responsible, responsibility
move   movable, moving
admire   admirable, admiration

When you add an ending that begins with a consonant, retain an unpronounced final e.

Examples

achieve	achievement
move	movement
nine	ninety, nineteen
same	sameness

Exceptions:

1. If c or g precedes a final e, retain the e before vowels to keep the pronunciation of c or g the same as it is in the verb form.

trace	-able	traceable
notice	-able	noticeable
manage	-able	manageable
courage	-ous	courageous

2. If u precedes e, drop e before -ing, -ed, or noun suffixes.

argue	arguing, argued, argument
true	truly, truth

Practice 5

Rewrite these words, adding the endings in the second column.

come	-ing	_____
advise	-able	_____
believe	-able	_____
hope	-ing	_____
fame	-ous	_____
imagine	-able	_____
encourage	-ment	_____
compare	-able	_____
compare	-ative	_____
love	-able	_____
love	-ing	_____
change	-able	_____

desire	-able	_____
achieve	-ing	_____
scare	-ing	_____
like	-able	_____
like	-ing	_____
like	-ness	_____
slice	-ing	_____
judge	-ing	_____

ie and ei

There is a rhyme which helps English-speaking people remember when to use *ie* and when to use *ei*.

i before *e*
except after *c*
or when sounded like *a*
as in *neighbor* and *weigh*.

ie [i][4] as in *meet*	*ei* [i] as in *meet*	*ei* [ei] as in *mate*
achieve	ceiling	freight
believe	conceive	neighbor
brief	deceive	reign
chief	perceive	veil
field	receive	weight
niece		
piece		
relieve		
thief		
yield		

The rule above applies only to syllables pronounced [i] as in *meet* or [ei] as in *mate*; it does not apply to the following words which have different pronunciations:

conscience	mischievous
friend	science
their	sovereign
foreign	view
height	weird

[4]Phonemic symbols from the International Phonetic Alphabet.

STRUCTURAL AIDS TO WRITING

Practice 6

Add *ie* or *ei*.

rec____ve	f____ld	p____ce	y____ld	r____gn
br____f	consc____nce	sc____nce	v____l	dec____ve
misch____vous	for____gn	c____ling	fr____ght	n____ce
v____w	perc____ve	h____ght	th____r	

Unusual Plurals

Plurals of most nouns are formed by adding -s. The following groups have other plural endings.

Nouns which end in -s, -sh, -ch, -x, -z

bus	buses
bush	bushes
match	matches
box	boxes
buzz	buzzes

Other plural forms

alga	algae	formula	formulas
analysis	analyses		formulae
appendix	appendixes	hypothesis	hypotheses
	appendices	index	indexes
axis	axes		indices
bacterium	bacteria	man	men
basis	bases	matrix	matrices
child	children	memorandum	memoranda
crisis	crises	parenthesis	parentheses
criterion	criteria	phenomenon	phenomena
datum	data[5]	stratum	strata
emphasis	emphases	thesis	theses
erratum	errata	tooth	teeth
foot	feet	woman	women

1.11 PUNCTUATION

The following sections provide the basic rules of punctuation for your reference.

[5]*Data* is sometimes used for singular as well as plural.

Period (.), Question Mark (?), Exclamation Mark (!). A complete sentence requires a period, question mark, or exclamation mark at the end. The exclamation mark is used very seldom in academic English. However, you will see it occasionally in informal writing such as advertisements and letters.

Semicolon (;). A semicolon may be used to connect two closely related statements (independent clauses). The statements are usually short, and there is no coordinating conjunction *(and, or, but, nor)* between them.

Will took his bike to the repair shop; then he walked home.

First a researcher states his hypothesis; next he plans an experiment to test it.

Two students chose to write theses; another decided to take a comprehensive oral examination.

A semicolon is used to connect two closely related statements when the second one begins with a conjunctive adverb or transitional phrase such as *nevertheless, therefore, on the other hand.*

I will attend the meeting; however, I have to leave by 4:00.

The policeman rescued a drowning child; as a result, he was given a special service award.

Below is a list of some common conjunctive adverbs and transitional phrases which may be used after semicolons:

accordingly	in addition	nevertheless
as a result	in other words	on the contrary
consequently	in the meantime	on the other hand
furthermore	likewise	therefore
however	meanwhile	thus

A semicolon is used to separate items of a series when the items are long or complex. Commas may be used within an item. Notice that if a semicolon is used after one item, it is used between *all* major items in the series. Do not mix commas and semicolons to separate items.

The results of the vote in the United Nations were the following: nine nations voted for the resolution; two nations, Canada and Mexico, voted against it; and three nations abstained from voting.

Five men were found guilty of the crime: two were given the maximum sentence of five years; two were sentenced to one year in jail; and one was given a sentence of six months.

After registering there were several things I had to do: buy the rest of my books; get an I.D. card, a meal ticket, a parking sticker; and cash a traveler's check.

Colon (:). A colon is used immediately before a list or a special explanation. Many writers prefer to use the expression *as follows* or *the following* preceding a colon.

The three major factors are: size, weight, and cost.
The three major factors are the following: size, weight, and cost.

Dr. Fuller defined the phenomenon as follows: a sonic boom is the interfering sound heard when. . . .
The following areas were included in our tour: the research lab, computer center, library, and assembly plant.

A colon is used in academic writing to introduce a long quotation (usually five or more typewritten lines). In this case, quotation marks are not used, and the text is single-spaced and indented.

In his article on animal behavior, a psychologist from the University of Chicago states:

> Students of behavior generally agree that the early experiences of animals (including man) have a profound effect on their adult behavior. D. O. Hebb of the University of Montreal goes so far as to state that the effect of early experience upon adult behavior is inversely correlated with ego.

One form of the influence of early experience of animals is known as "imprinting." This phenomenon contributes. . . .

A colon is used after the salutation in a formal letter.

Dear Mr. Whillen: Dear Sir:
Dear Mrs. Thompson: Gentlemen:
Dear Ms. Graham: Friends:
Dear Miss Paige:

Comma (,). The best overall guide to the use of commas is this: a comma is generally used at a major break, a point where a reader would pause when reading aloud.

A comma is used between two complete statements connected with a coordinating conjunction *(and, but, or, nor)*.

Alan would like to buy a used bike, *and* he is looking on bulletin boards around campus to find an ad for one.

He's been looking in the want ads, *but* he hasn't seen a bike for sale.

A comma is used to separate items (words, phrases, or short clauses) in a series. The comma before the final item in a series is still recognized as correct for formal writing, though in journalism or informal writing it is sometimes not used.

Comedies, detective stories, game shows, and occasional documentaries are scheduled on commercial television between 7:00 and 9:00 P.M.

The horror movie on TV last Friday frightened children, bored adults, and intrigued teenagers.

A comma is used after introductory units which come before the main or independent clause. It is infrequently used when a dependent clause or phrase comes after the main clause.

adverb clauses	Although he owns a car, he prefers to ride a bike to work.
	He prefers to ride a bike to work although he owns a car.
	He wanted to go by plane; however, because he didn't have enough money, he took a bus instead.
	Obviously, that was the only thing he could do.
participial phrases	Lost in the city, tourists often pull into a gas station to ask directions.
	Advised to turn left at the next stoplight, they thanked the attendant and pulled out of the station.

A comma is used to indicate an inverted structure—that is, a structure that can be placed at the end of a sentence but may be placed at the beginning.

dependent clause	As soon as the sale was announced, thousands of people flocked to the store.
	(Thousands of people flocked to the store as soon as the sale was announced.)
	Before he took the examination, he reviewed his lecture notes and the assigned problem sets.
	(He reviewed his lecture notes and the assigned problem sets before he took the examination.)
prepositional phrase	From 1972 to 1976, Karen Perry attended Caltech.

(Karen Perry attended Caltech from 1972 to 1976.)

In the case of Mr. Addison, the tax exemption did not apply.

(The tax exemption did not apply in the case of Mr. Addision.)

purposive phrase
(*to* + verb)

In order to see the library, it is necessary to walk across the campus.

(It is necessary to walk across the campus in order to see the library.)

To ensure good results, begin with high-quality ingredients.

(Begin with high-quality ingredients to ensure good results.)

A comma is used to set off a nonrestrictive, nonidentifying clause or phrase, which carries additional information not necessary for understanding which noun you are referring to. Restrictive clauses are not set off with commas because they are necessary to the basic meaning of a sentence.

Nonrestrictive

Karen Ferguson, an independent candidate for the congressional seat, hopes to spend the Christmas holidays with her family.
(Karen Ferguson hopes to spend the Christmas holidays with her family.)

Her mother, who lives in Palm Springs, has offered to help Karen organize her campaign.
(Her mother has offered to help Karen organize her campaign.)

Her first speech will be delivered in Campton, which is a pleasant residential district in the western part of this city.
(Her first speech will be delivered in Campton.)

Restrictive (The clause cannot be eliminated without changing the meaning.)

Many people who don't get enough physical exercise are prone to heart attacks.

The park that my roommate jogs in is quite far from our house.

The equipment which we need is available in any good sporting goods department.

Contrast Between Restrictive and Nonrestrictive

My sister who is working on a Ph.D. in psychology has a research grant for next year.
(I have more than one sister. I am making it clear which one I am referring to.)

My sister, who is working on a Ph.D. in psychology, has a research grant for next year.
(I have only one sister.)

The rescue team helped the tenants who had jumped out of the windows of the burning building.
(Some tenants jumped. Others did not.)

The rescue team helped the tenants, who had jumped out of the windows of the burning building.
(All of the tenants jumped.)

Hyphen (-). A hyphen is used in fractions and in compound numbers up to ninety-nine when they are written out.

five-eighths   seventy-three
three-fourths   thirty-eight

A hyphen is used to identify an adjective unit which is made up of two or more words:

a well-defined goal
a well-thought-out proposal
a step-by-step procedure
a two-year-old child
the Polish-American vote
their clearly profit-oriented system

A hyphen is used to indicate that a multisyllable word has been divided on two consecutive lines on a page. Native speakers avoid dividing words whenever possible, because the English writing system makes it particularly difficult. Some guidelines follow; if you are not sure how to divide a particular word, check your dictionary.

1. The hyphen should come after a syllable of two or more letters.
2. The part of the word on the next line should be more than two letters long.
3. If a word is already hyphenated, for example, *self-control,* divide it at the hyphen, or not at all.
4. If there is a double consonant in the syllables to be divided, break between them, such as *commit-tee* and *control-ling.* For exceptions, check your dictionary.

After a brief glance at the surrounding area, he guessed that it would be possible to walk across the sand.

When he found out that the examination had been rescheduled, he was very pleased.

Dash (—). A dash is used in informal writing, particularly in friendly letters, to show an interruption in thought or to give non-essential information.

Let's meet at 11:00—no, wait—make that 10:00 on Tuesday.

Jerome Goldburg—the only candidate for judge—is campaigning throughout the district.

Apostrophe ('). An apostrophe is used in a contraction to indicate that one or more letters have been omitted. Contractions are used in informal writing, but not in formal writing such as academic papers.

Informal

If you don't hurry up, you'll be late.
You're always the last one ready.

Formal

Recent experiments do not corroborate his findings.
The exact procedure will be outlined in the following section.

An apostrophe is used with a noun or indefinite pronoun (for example, *nobody, someone, other*) to express possession by human beings and, in a few cases, by inanimate objects. Put an apostrophe after *-s* for plural nouns (voters' responsibilities). The *of* form of possession is preferred for possession of a more abstract nature. In order to avoid long possessive phrases, however, writers often use adjectives rather than possessives.

Someone*'s* coat is on the chair; maybe it is *Mary's*.

Although the committee*'s* resolution was quite specific, *the recommendation of the Board of Trustees* was vague.

Further funding is necessary for *the completion of this research*.

Corporate resistance to *consumer* demands stimulates *government* action in establishing stricter standards.

Notice the differences in meaning in these four pairs, which sound alike:

1. *It's* customary for a ship to blow *its* whistle as it comes into port.
   (it + is)   *(possessive pronoun)*
2. *Who's* the visitor *whose* car is parked out front?
   (who + is)   *(possessive pronoun)*

3. When *you're* sure that *your* paper is ready, turn it in.
    (you + are)   *(possessive pronoun)*
4. *They're* confident of success in *their* new enterprise.
    (they + are)   *(possessive pronoun)*

Capitalization

Capitalize the first word of a complete sentence, including sentences in quotation marks.

Harry Truman, speaking about the presidency, said, "The buck stops here."

"No matter how time-consuming it will be," she insisted, "it has to be done."

Capitalize the first word and every content word in the title of a written work, such as a book, paper, or document.

System Analysis by Digital Computer

"Digital Filter Structures Related to Classical Filter Networks"

The New York Times

Capitalize every important word in major headings or subheadings of divisions of a work.

Chapter Three: Approaches to the Approximation Problem

Recommendations for Further Research

Capitalize the following:

1. the name of a person
2. a geographical feature or location—including a city, state, country, region, continent; the name of an island, mountain, body of water; the name of a street or highway; the name of a building or institution.

San Francisco, Asia, the Northeast, the Pacific Ocean, Skyline Drive, Wells Fargo Bank, the Minneapolis-St. Paul Airport.

Contrast these examples:

He lives in the *Southwest.*
He lives in the *southwest(ern)* part of the United States.
He drove *southwest* for ten miles.

Adjectives and compass directions are not capitalized.
Names of languages, nationalities, races as nouns or adjectives are usually capitalized.

Black English
Afghan Farsi
Spanish-speaking students
Native Americans
the Mexican government

Italian-Americans
Japanese cameras
Persian carpets
Latin American textiles
French cuisine

Days of the week, months, festivals, holidays, major events are capitalized.

Monday
Saturday
March
September
Sunday, January 3

Easter
the Fourth of July
Thanksgiving
the Bicentennial
the Olympics

The title of a course and name of a degree are capitalized.

Economics IA
Computer Science 236
Bachelor of Science
Master of Arts

A title or group affiliation is capitalized.

John Fredericks, Professor and Chairman of the Department of Civil Engineering
President-elect Fitzgerald has been a member of the Rotary Club for fifteen years.
His dentist, Dr. Steward, is a registered Democrat.

Capitalize abbreviations based on proper nouns:

the U.S.
Mt. Everest
Psych. 50
Prof. Leonard

35 Adams Ave., N.W.
Dr. Steward
M.B.A.
Ph.D.

For correct bibliographical referencing, see the section on documentation of sources. See Section 3.7 for a list of frequently used abbreviations and acronyms.

Practice 1

Correct punctuation wherever necessary in the following passage.

Young People's Preferences in the Arts

In the years since 1970 young people in the United States have developed some characteristic preferences in the arts, particularly in the fields of music literature and movies

The music preferred by many young people which has grown out of the rock music of the fifties and sixties is a combination of the direct, dance-based sound of rock combined with the traditional lyricism of the traditional ballad. it is interesting that the reemergence of the lyric as a primary element in popular music in the united states was to a large extent based on the popularity of a british group the beatles which became popular in the 1960s.

The literature preferred by many young people can be described as a kind of writing of discovery. in recent years the most dramatic development in american literature has been the rise of women's literature in fiction in non-fiction and in poetry More and more insightful women writers are being published among the more famous are Joyce Carol Oates, Dorothy Sayers, Erica Jong, and Maya Angelou. Another strain of popular literature includes satire and fantasy. There seems to be less emphasis now than in past years on the development of character in ordinary circumstances. Novels and short stories by such writers as Kurt Vonnegut Ralph ellison Ken kesey and Jerzy Kosinski have been brilliant strange and very funny. such writers are making important modern statements on human conflict and confusion. Perhaps their popularity is based on the characteristic of young people in this country which some call honesty and others self consciousness

u.S. taste in movies has become distinctly international such movies as the following have been quite popular in recent years The Seventh Seal, directed by Bergman Amarcord by Fellini the last picture made by DeSica a brief vacation and the british production of King of Hearts. Some American pictures that have been well received are The French Connection, 2001: a space Odyssey and easy rider. But perhaps the best reflection of the taste of young people in this country is the solid popularity of the satires of Woody Allen Sleeper, Bananas, Love and death and Mel Brooks The Twelve Chairs, young Frankenstein, and Blazing Saddles

    We can expect these trends to continue into the 1980s. If they do we may well see an extended period of intense creativity. Accordingly attention will be directed at the young and intelligent artists who will produce the music movies and literature of tomorrow.

Vocabulary Development

2

2.1 INTRODUCTION

The following explanations and practices are designed to provide you with useful tools for expanding your vocabulary. The first part discusses criteria for deciding what vocabulary to learn and presents various methods of recording and practicing new vocabulary. The other parts of this section provide practice with three vocabulary structures which occur frequently in academic contexts: negative prefixes, noun agent suffixes, and verb-forming suffixes.

Chapter Outline

Expanding Your Vocabulary
Negative Prefixes
Noun Agent Suffixes
Verb-forming Suffixes

2.2 EXPANDING YOUR VOCABULARY

Vocabulary learning is a continuous process for all educated people. There are hundreds of thousands of English words; an educated native speaker uses approximately 40,000 words. A foreign student cannot expect to match this number within a few years. Clearly, every foreign student has to be selective. You need to determine which will be the most useful of the words you encounter; that is, whether a word is useful for your passive reading vocabulary or for your active speaking and writing vocabulary. There are three criteria to consider in making your choices: frequency, range of usage, and connotation.

Frequency

Frequency is the first and easiest basis for choice. How often do you hear the word and how often do you read it? During your first few months in an English-speaking country, you will pick up many words that native speakers use every day. You will continually learn vocabulary needed for various activities: academic work, student life, sports, mass media, and the arts. This section and the following section present lessons on vocabulary which is useful in some of these areas.

Range of Usage

In addition to observing how often you encounter a word, you need to notice when and where you find it. Does it occur in a formal situation such as a rental agreement or a commencement speech, or does it occur in a student newspaper or in conversation around a dormitory? The situation in which a word occurs is its *context*. Everyone adjusts his use of language as he moves from situation to situation; that is, he has variations of language appropriate for given situations such as speaking with his superiors, with his peers, with children, with loved ones; writing a formal request, a homework assignment, an interdepartmental memo, a friendly letter. Vocabulary is the part of language that a speaker most often adjusts, according to the situation.

Present-day English vocabulary is derived from two primary sources: Anglo-Saxon and Latin (via French).[1] More Latin-based words than Anglo-Saxon-based words are used in formal speech and writing; and more Anglo-Saxon than Latin-based words are used in less formal conversation and semiformal writing. The fact that Latin-based words are used in more formal situations than Anglo-Saxon ones does not imply that they are "better." In informal conversation, Anglo-Saxon-based words are generally preferable. Each type has its appropriate use. Consider these parallel examples:

Anglo-Saxon origin   *Latin origin*

find out   ascertain
call off   cancel

[1] A considerable number of technical and literary English words are derived from Greek. However, a distinction between Anglo-Saxon-based and Latin-based vocabulary is sufficient for the purposes of this lesson.

88   VOCABULARY DEVELOPMENT

understanding	comprehension
make up	constitute
hard	difficult
twist	distort
hand out	distribute
point out	indicate
put off	postpone
pay back	reimburse
look like	resemble
breathing	respiration
like	similar
strained	tense
put up with	tolerate
sight	vision

In the list you will notice that many of the Anglo-Saxon words are "two-word verbs," which are very numerous in English. A two-word verb is a verb plus a preposition, forming a meaning unit which is often different from the meanings of the separate parts. For example, there is a difference between these two:

Look up in the air.   (verb + prepositional phrase)
Look up the word.   (two-word verb + object)

The verb in the second sentence means *find or locate;* it is not related to looking in an upward direction. As you gain experience using English, you will see how many two-word verbs there are like *look up* and the ones in the list above. You will gradually learn when it is more appropriate to use two-word verbs.

Connotation

A literal dictionary definition or *denotation* is limited. It does not cover the possible range of meanings of a word, those associations that native speakers have from their experience with the word. This additional meaning is called *connotation*. When you communicate your ideas and attitudes in English, you need to be aware of connotation, because it affects the way a native speaker interprets what you are saying. Without looking, how do you think a dictionary would define these words? What do you mean by them?

fun
to take advantage of
aggressive

Using an "English-English" dictionary[2] is an essential first step, but it is not enough. To have a full understanding of the meaning of a word, you have to listen, read, and ask a lot of questions. The Americans that you meet are sources of information who can help you understand words more completely.

Because meaning varies according to context, or situation, it is much more productive and efficient to learn vocabulary as you listen and read instead of studying words out of context. It is impossible to learn how to use words appropriately by studying word lists, or relying exclusively on a bilingual dictionary.

If a word you do not understand occurs in conversation, ask the person who used it to explain it to you. When you do not understand a phrase that an instructor uses in class, ask someone what it means. Most instructors want to help foreign students with English, but often they do not know which vocabulary is unfamiliar.

With practice you will learn to understand the meaning of a word from its context; that is, from structure, from prefixes and suffixes, and from situation. When you first read any assigned reading, always go through it completely without stopping to look up words in the dictionary. On the second reading, get as much meaning as you can from the context; put a check mark in the margin next to key words you still cannot comprehend. After you finish reading, look the words up in a dictionary before you close the book. By all means, use a dictionary written entirely in English. Ideas, attitudes, terms, value judgments, and other abstractions do not have exact translations.

Recording and Practicing New Vocabulary

There are many systems and styles of learning vocabulary. If you do not already have a method, you need to develop a systematic way of recording phrases that you have decided to incorporate into your active vocabulary. Consider the following three techniques.

Vocabulary Cards

1. Buy a packet of three-by-five-inch index cards and carry some blank cards with you every day.
2. When you hear or read a word or phrase that you need to learn, write it and if possible, write down the sentence which contained the word. At the very least, write down the situation in which you heard or saw it:

[2]The following are three standard college desk dictionaries:

Webster's New World Dictionary of the American Language, 2nd college edition. Collins and World, 1974.

Webster's New Collegiate Dictionary, 8th edition. G. & C. Merriam, 1975.

The Random House College Dictionary, revised edition. Random House, 1975.

sign, newspaper, magazine, textbook, academic journal, conversation, lecture, movie.

3. Later, if necessary, look up the words on your cards in an English-English dictionary. Write the words in syllables and mark the stressed (accented) syllable. Also, write down related forms of the word.
4. Relate the dictionary meaning to the meaning of the word in the source sentence. Write down the key words from the dictionary definition that will help you remember its basic meaning. To test your understanding of the meanings and uses of the words, ask a native speaker of English to go over your cards with you, as you try to use each word in an original sentence.
5. Every few days, take out a group of cards and look at the top one. Ask yourself what the word means in the sentence. Pronounce the word and its related forms.
6. Turn the card over to see if you were correct. If you were right, put the card in a separate pile. If you were not, put the card at the bottom of the stack and go on to the next card.
7. As soon as possible, try to use the word in conversation or in writing. If you do not practice it soon, you may forget it.

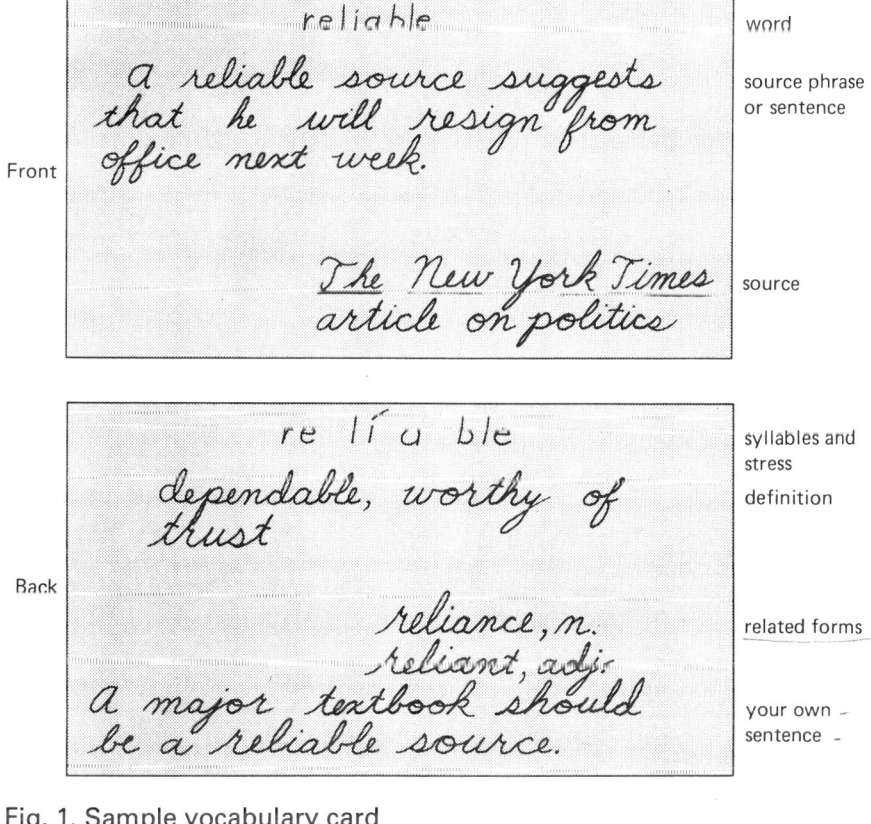

Front:
- reliable — word
- A reliable source suggests that he will resign from office next week. — source phrase or sentence
- The New York Times article on politics — source

Back:
- re lí a ble — syllables and stress
- dependable, worthy of trust — definition
- reliance, n. reliant, adj. — related forms
- A major textbook should be a reliable source. — your own sentence

Fig. 1. Sample vocabulary card

Vocabulary Notebook

1. Buy a small pocket-size notebook which you can carry with you every day.
2. When you hear or see an unfamiliar word which seems important, write it down. Write down the sentence or at least the situation next to it.
3. Later, look up the words and write down their definitions, stress, and related forms. A notebook entry might look like figure 2. You may want to write an original sentence using the word.
4. Ask a native speaker of English to go over your notebook with you.
5. Every few days, take a card or piece of paper and cover all of the information except one word and its context. Ask yourself to define and pronounce it, as well as give related forms. When you are sure of a particular word, put an asterisk (*) next to it.
6. As soon as possible, try to use the word in conversation or writing.

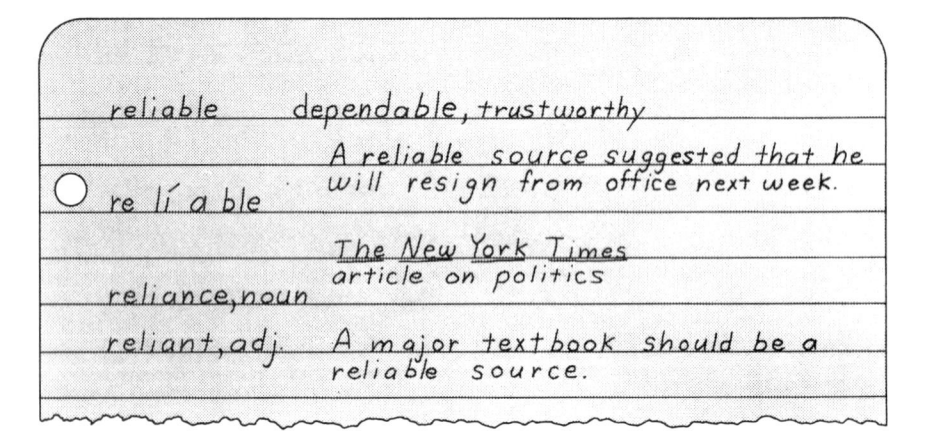

```
reliable      dependable, trustworthy

              A reliable source suggested that he
○ re lí a ble   will resign from office next week.

              The New York Times
              article on politics
reliance, noun

reliant, adj.  A major textbook should be a
              reliable source.
```

Fig. 2. Sample notebook entry

Daily Journal

Keep a journal or diary account of your experiences and impressions. Incorporate words that you are learning, and question those you are unsure of so that a native speaker can discuss them with you.

Practice 1

For homework, find out what these words and phrases mean and when it is appropriate to use them. Later, discuss them in class.

VOCABULARY DEVELOPMENT

1. bruise
2. come up with
3. convene
4. cram
5. gadget
6. goof off
7. hit the books
8. matriculate
9. to make a dent
10. libel
11. off the top of my head
12. procrastinate
13. scan
14. stingy
15. quibble

Practice 2

Many two-word verbs have related nouns. Generally the verbs are stressed on the second word, while the nouns are stressed on the first word. Study these examples:

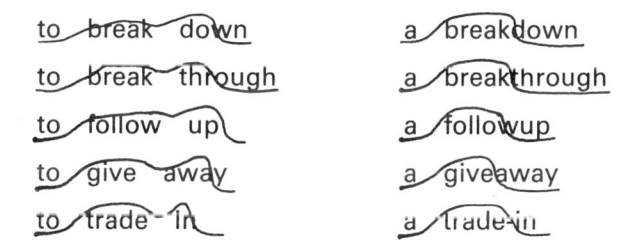

to break dówn   a bréakdown
to break thróugh   a bréakthrough
to follow úp   a fóllowup
to give awáy   a gíveaway
to trade ín   a trádein

In class, pronounce the following nouns and write down their related two-word verbs. Mark stress, find out what each one means, and then use it in a sentence.

Example

a breakthrough   to break through

The Salk vaccine was a major breakthrough in the fight against poliomyelitis.

A sonic boom is caused by a plane breaking through the sound barrier.

a sellout _____   a standby _____

a playoff _____   a backup _____

a turnoff _____   a make-up _____

a letdown _____   a setup _____

a mix-up _____   a drive-in _____

a flashback _____   a turnover _____

a blackout _____   a turnout _____

a pushover _____   a cutback _____

a pullover _____

Practice 3

Choose five words that you have learned within the past week. Prepare a vocabulary card for each one, including comments on context and connotation. Go through the cards in class.

1. See if any words were selected by more than one student;
2. See how many of the words are new to everyone;
3. Decide which words should be incorporated into each student's active vocabulary;
4. Make a master list of the words that the class agrees on, including the following information:
   a. stress
   b. appropriate situations
   c. a sentence.

2.3 NEGATIVE PREFIXES

Words with negative prefixes are keys to the interpretation of ideas. Since such words occur frequently, it is important to understand their precise meanings and to incorporate them into your active vocabulary. This lesson distinguishes among the most common negative prefixes and provides vocabulary-building practices. The last section discusses the use of negative prefixes with other negatives for emphasis in writing.

The following passage contains a variety of words with negative prefixes. Underline each negative prefix.

Recycling

Many recycling programs have been established in the United States in recent years to prevent waste of irreplaceable resources. Some states have passed anti-litter laws which make the sale of nonreturnable bottles illegal so that consumers will have a financial incentive to take reusable bottles back to the store rather than throw them away. Many communities have recycling centers where people can turn in glass, metal, and paper. Some companies pay ten or fifteen cents per pound for returned aluminum cans. Recycling reduces littering as well as excessive use of raw materials. In the same way more and more home gardeners are using compost piles, in which vegetable wastes gradually decompose into soil-enriching organic matter.

In spite of these benefits, some people say that recycling is impractical because it takes a lot of time and labor to recycle and reprocess materials. Although recycling is not unpopular—most people say they want to help preserve the environment—it would be an overstatement to say that they "practice what they preach." Critics claim that up to now recycling programs have been relatively ineffective, since only a small percentage of Americans are participating in recycling plans.

Un-; in- and variations; non; a-

The most common negative prefixes are *un-* and *in-*, which both mean *not*. There are three variations of *in-* related to the sounds which follow: *in-* becomes *im-* before *b, m, p; il-* before *l;* and *ir-* before *r*.

un-

unaware (adj.)
unlocked (adj.)
unpopular (adj.)
unreliable (adj.)

in-

inaccuracy (n.)
inadequate (adj.)
inconsistent (adj.)
insufficient (adj.)

im- before b, m, p-

imbalance (n.)
immature (adj.)
improper (adj.)
impractical (adj.)

il- before l-

illegal (adj.)
illegible (adj.)
illegitimate (adj.)
illiterate (adj.)

ir- before r-

irrational (adj.)
irregularity (n.)
irrelevant (adj.)
irresponsible (adj.)

Non- and *a-* are other prefixes which indicate *absence of.* Of the two, *non-* is much more common.

non-

nonconformist (n.)
nonfiction (n.)
nonprofit (adj.)
nonviolent (adj.)

a-

amoral (adj.)
apolitical (adj.)
atypical (adj.)
asymmetrical (adj.)
asexual (adj.)

Practice 1

Fill in the blank with the correct negative prefix: *un-*, *non-*, or *a-*. Do not use a hyphen after the prefix. Use a dictionary if necessary.

Examples

The (identified) *unidentified* plant turned out to be (poisonous) *nonpoisonous*.
The (profit) *nonprofit* corporation held an (planned) *unplanned* meeting.

1. Often a(n) (known) _____ writer writes a(n) (fiction) _____ book which becomes a best seller.

2. (Smokers) _____ are often (comfortable) _____ when heavy smokers are smoking nearby.

3. The future of the (aggression) _____ pact between the two countries is (certain) _____ .

4. (Skilled) _____ laborers make up a big part of most (employment) _____ lines.

5. Some paramedics made a(n) (successful) _____ attempt to revive the (conscious) _____ man.

6. A (partisan) _____ committee voted on a(n) (conventional) _____ plan to increase the city's revenues. A very conservative member voted for it, which was (typical) _____ of his voting behavior.

7. (Commercial) _____ TV, which began with (even) _____ programing and which initially received a(n) (favorable) _____ response, now has a large supportive audience.

8. (Allergenic) _____ pillows and (toxic) _____ color crayons are two products which were developed as a result of consumer pressure.

9. Previously (political) _____, John developed strong views on (violence) _____ and subsequently joined a student political organization.

10. A travel agent said that economy class seats were (available) _____ for that flight, but when the plane took off, there were several (occupied) _____ seats.

Practice 2

Fill in the blank with the correct negative prefix: *in-, im-, il-,* or *ir-*. Do not hyphenate the prefix. Use a dictionary if necessary.

1. For many years _____literate people in the U.S. were not allowed to vote because of their _____ability to sign their name.

2. The _____experienced driver caused an accident which did _____reparable damage to the other person's car. (Note: the opposite of _____rep\arable is re/pair\able.)

3. There is a difference between _____regulars and "seconds," two types of sale items often seen in stores. The former have _____perceptible flaws whereas the latter have more obvious defects.

4. I find it _____conceivable that he is _____capable of meeting the deadline. I am sure he can do it if he tries.

5. Though a former president is _____eligible for the presidency if he has served two terms, it is not _____legal for him to seek another position in the government.

6. The _____accurate statistics, _____appropriate language, and the _____legible handwriting in this paper are _____excusable. The paper must be rewritten.

7. Because the couple thought there were _____reconcilable differences between them, they went to a marriage counselor. The counselor was of _____measurable help in leading them back to a close relationship.

Dis-, anti-, de-, counter-, contra-

This group of negative prefixes means *actively doing the opposite* of the base word, whether or not the action is intentional. The sounds *de-* are found in many verbs which are not negative; for example, *decide, declare*. The following examples show contrasts between prefixes in this category and *un-* in the previous category. Discuss the difference in meanings in class.

Contrasting Examples

uninterested
disinterested
The public is generally uninterested in labor-management conflicts.
A disinterested person is generally called in to settle a lengthy strike.

unsatisfied
dissatisfied
The researcher's desire to solve the problem is still unsatisfied after a year's work.
He is dissatisfied with the experimental findings to date.

unclassified
declassified
Document A is unclassified.
Document B has recently been declassified.

unproductive
counterproductive
A procedure which does not increase output is unproductive.
A procedure which decreases output is counterproductive.

Study the following examples.

dis- *total lack of, or actively doing the opposite*

disapprove (v.)   dishonest (adj.)
disagreement (n.)   disintegrate (v.)

anti- *doing the opposite or being against*

antiaircraft (adj.)   antisocial (adj.)
antimagnetic (adj.)   antitrust (adj.)

de- *do the reverse*

decelerate   de-emphasize
decentralize   devaluation

counter-, contra- *work against or stop the action of*

counterclockwise   contraceptive
counterproductive   contradiction

Practice 3

Fill in the blank with the correct negative prefix: *dis-, anti-, de-,* or *counter-* or *contra-*. Do not hyphenate the prefix. Use a dictionary if necessary.

1. When you go hiking in a remote area, you should carry a canteen of water. _____hydration can not only cause _____comfort, but it can also be dangerous if it is prolonged.

2. The government recently filed an _____trust suit against a large corporation. If the company loses, it may have to _____continue making several of its major products.

3. A new _____aircraft weapon was used in a surprise _____attack near the _____militarized zone.

4. The sudden _____appearance of the town's most respected banker has had a _____moralizing effect on its residents.

5. The official _____closure of the reasons for the basketball team's _____qualification from the tournament was _____climactic, since most people had already learned the details from the press.

99

Mis-, mal-, under-, over-

A third group of negative prefixes adds a negative connotation to the base word. These prefixes suggest doing something incorrectly, insufficiently, or to an inappropriate degree. Discuss the meanings of these words:

misuse	overuse
disuse	underuse

Study the following examples.

mis- *incorrect action*

misconduct (n.)	mispronounce (v.)
misplace (v.)	misrepresentation (n.)

mal- *incorrect or insufficient action*

maladjusted (adj.)   malpractice (v.)
malfunction (n.)   maltreat (v.)

over- *excessive or careless use or action, with negative results*

overdo (v.)   oversight (n.)
overemphasize (v.)   oversimplify (v.)

under- *insufficient or incomplete action*

underachieve (v.)   underestimate (v.)
underdeveloped (adj.) underprivileged (adj.)

Practice 4

Fill in the blank with the correct negative prefix: *mis-, mal-, under-,* or *over-*. Do not use a hyphen after the prefix. Use a dictionary if necessary.

1. _____nutrition and _____population are two common problems in _____developed, developing, and even in some developed countries.

2. _____management of the firm and _____use of its profits eventually led the company to bankruptcy.

3. If a(n) _____ambitious doctor takes on more patients than he has time for, he may become careless and end up involved in a(n) _____practice lawsuit.

4. A faculty advisor told one of his students: "Please don't _____understand me. I'm not being critical of what you have done so far. I just don't want you to _____look other factors as you continue your project."

5. It would be a(n) _____simplification to say that the computer operator's _____calculation caused the _____function of the computer, but it undoubtedly contributed to the breakdown.

6. It is a mistake to _____rate his ability to gain public support, but it is equally dangerous to _____estimate his capabilities.

Practice 5

Fill each blank with an appropriate negative prefix word which corresponds to the underlined word in the sentence. If the underlined word is a noun, you will need a noun; if it is a verb, you will need a verb. This practice reviews all of the negative prefixes presented in this lesson. Be sure to check verb tense and agreement, as well as noun plurals. Note on style: writers occasionally use contrast of affirmative and negative forms for emphasis; such use is stylistically acceptable, but overuse is undesirable.

Examples

He does not <u>like</u> spicy food. He *dislikes* spicy food.

The business was not <u>profitable</u>. It was a(n) *unprofitable* business.

1. The date of the picnic is not <u>definite</u>. The date is _____ .

2. A system which does not have many <u>advantages</u> may have many _____ .

3. If you don't <u>judge</u> someone's character correctly, you _____ the person.

4. The reasoning was not <u>logical</u>; it was extremely _____ .

5. Is that quantity <u>sufficient</u> for your needs, or is it _____ ?

6. This chair is not very <u>comfortable</u>. It's _____ .

7. He didn't <u>calculate</u> the solution correctly. He _____ and had to do it again.

8. If a type of paint is not <u>toxic</u>, it is labeled "_____."

9. The lack of <u>regularity</u> in the trial disturbed people. There were many _____ in the trial.

10. They do not <u>approve</u> of her being out late. They strongly _____ .

11. Are you _____ about the answer, or are you <u>certain</u>?

12. If the hand on a dial moves the reverse of clockwise, it moves _____ .

13. If you do not obey their wishes, you _____ them.

14. A person who is insufficiently nourished may have mental as well as physical problems because he is _____ .

15. Some medicines are supposed to act against cold symptoms; that is, they _____ the symptoms.

16. He didn't have the appropriate answer. His answer was _____ .

17. It is not typical of him to be late; in fact, it is very _____ .

18. A coupon which is attached to the center of a magazine often says, "_____ and mail today!"

19. When you have been connected with the party you are calling, sometimes you get _____ by mistake.

20. If a student is not achieving on his potential level, he is _____ .

21. The pet cat was badly treated by the child. The cat was _____ , so the child's parents took the pet away.

22. The mayor will make an official statement tomorrow, but the _____ word is that he will give his approval to the new transit system.

23. A car accelerates when you push down the gas pedal; it _____ when you release your foot.

24. The politician was so confident of his reelection that he stopped campaigning. He lost the election because he was _____ .

25. Is any other planet in our solar system inhabited, or are they all _____ except for earth?

Practice 6

Fill in the blank with an appropriate negative prefix word related to the underlined word in the sentence. In other words, if the underlined word is a noun, you may need a verb, adjective, or adverb. Be sure to use a word which fits the sentence structure. Use a dictionary if necessary, and check verb tense, agreement, and noun plurals.

Examples

They do not agree on the method. They are in *disagreement*.

Many people felt the report was not fair, that is, that the information had been presented *unfairly*.

1. It is not convenient for me to see them this noon. In fact, it would be a great _____ .

2. His homework was not completed; he turned in _____ homework.

3. If you make an incorrect interpretation of a question, you _____ the question.

4. Did the spray have an effect, or was it _____ ?

5. To prevent his car's engine from freezing in the winter, he put in _____ .

6. We can't predict whether or not it will rain; the weather is _____ .

7. The department decided not to continue Chemistry 221. The course was _____ .

8. If you have too much anxiety, you will be _____ and may not do well on the test as a result.

9. He was not very patient. He displayed great _____ .

10. Can you walk outside safely at night, or are the streets _____ ?

11. The plane goes from here to Boston without making any stops. It is a _____ flight.

VOCABULARY DEVELOPMENT

12. Something which is not suited to a particular purpose is _____ for that purpose.
13. A word which you spell wrong is a _____ word.
14. She does not do the gardening in an efficient way. She does it very _____ .
15. His lawyer said he was not sane and entered a plea of _____ . (You must put a noun in the blank.)
16. He was not satisfied with the solution and expressed his _____ .
17. Not all new techniques produce good results; some actually turn out to be _____ . (Use an adjective.)
18. This information does not lead the reader to the correct conclusion. It is _____ information.
19. If someone does not consider the wishes of other people, he is _____ .
20. An agent which works against foreign bodies (bacteria, for example) in the bloodstream is called an _____ .
21. If a person tries to take on too great a load, he may _____ himself with responsibilities.
22. His comment does not adequately state the complexities of the situation. It is a gross _____ .
23. His business did not succeed. It was an _____ business.
24. Because of their nutritional value, peanuts in the diet may help reduce the level of _____ among children in that country.
25. Deep-sea divers use compressed air when they are underwater. When they return to the surface, they go through a gradual process of _____ to get accustomed to normal air pressure.

Practice 7

Choose any twenty negative prefix words in this lesson which are new to you. Use each word in an original sentence.

Example

It is unwise to <u>overstate</u> your qualifications.

Practice 8

Write a paragraph or short composition on one of the following topics. Try to use five negative prefix words, each one beginning with a different negative prefix if possible:

automobile safety
consumer protection
small business management
urban water supply

camping in the wilderness
use of natural vs. synthetic materials
gourmet dining vs. "fast food" drive-ins

Using Negatives to Emphasize a Positive Condition

To emphasize the positive aspect or importance of something, both a negative word or phrase *(not, no, not at all, no longer)* and a negative prefix word are used in a sentence. You will find this pattern in your reading. If you want to use it in your writing, use it sparingly. A person usually includes only one or two sentences of this type in a speech or paper.

Solving the problem is possible.
Solving the problem is *not impossible.*

It is familiar now.
It is *no longer unfamiliar.*

The tax increase is a necessary step.
The tax increase is *not an unnecessary step.*

You may also hear and read a similar usage, *no* + adjective + noun. For example, "He denounced the policy in no uncertain terms."

Practice 9

Change each sentence to the affirmative pattern. In this practice, do not use any negative words or negative prefixes.

Example

With new detection methods, the movement of major storms is no longer unpredictable.

With new detection methods, the movement of major storms is _predictable_.

1. Experimenting with various life styles is not an uncommon practice among young people today.
2. It took no inconsiderable effort on the part of officials to make people aware of the impending energy shortage.
3. It is not at all unlikely that a new sea-level canal will be built in Central America before the year 2000.
4. Entrance should not be permitted to those who are unidentifiable as members of the group. (Put _only_ after _permitted_ in your sentence.)
5. Researchers have found that in many cases it is no longer unessential for two members of a family to hold jobs.
6. The change in the rats' behavior was not an insignificant result of the experiment, though physical changes were what the scientists had been examining.
7. The foundation's decision to deny funding is not irreversible; if new data is submitted, it will reconsider the proposal.
8. He does not feel the seminar should be discontinued.
9. The school's annual budget contained no unnecessary expenditures, yet the school still spent more than it had. (Put _only_ after _contained_ in your sentence.)
10. No longer is there an indecisive chairman of the committee, as a result of last week's election. (Put _now_ after _is_ in your sentence.)

Practice 10

To emphasize the positive aspect of the idea, rewrite these sentences using both a negative and a negative prefix word.

Example

It is usual for symphony concerts to be sold out.

It is _not unusual_ for symphony concerts to be sold out.

1. The police determined that the two reports of the shootout were consistent.
2. To his surprise the student learned that the course was structured after all.
3. It is wise to reread the chapter before taking the test. (Use _not at all_ as the negative phrase.)
4. Turning off the lights at night made a significant dent in the company's electricity consumption. (Use _no_ as the negative word.)
5. The agreement is an important milestone in international relations.
6. After looking in a dictionary, the critical viewer found that the broadcaster had pronounced the word correctly.

2.4 NOUN AGENT SUFFIXES

A noun agent is a person or thing which is suited to a particular action or task. The following suffixes are used to form noun agents. All of these are used for humans, and all except -ian are used for objects; -er and -or are most often used for tools and instruments.

-er	employer, adviser, eraser, recorder, cleanser
-or	investor, sailor, instructor, projector
-ent	president, correspondent, deterrent, referent
-ant	accountant, occupant, deviant, depressant
-ist	artist, geologist, leftist, nationalist
-ian	guardian, librarian, politician, statistician

Sample sentences:

An *eraser* is an object which *erases* pencil or chalk marks.

An *investor* is a person who *invests* money in a bank, stock, or property.

A *deterrent* is something that *deters* a future action.

An *accountant* is a person who keeps business *accounts*.

A *physicist* is a person who works in the field of *physics*.

An *electrician* is a person who installs and repairs *electrical* wiring.

Practice 1

Fill in the blanks with the noun agent related to the underlined word. Consult a dictionary as needed. Spelling changes are sometimes required.

Example

A machine which records sound is a tape recorder.

1. A person who commutes to work is called a _____ .
2. A _____ is a machine which projects an image on a screen.
3. Coffee is considered a _____ because it stimulates the nervous system.
4. One who challenges a champion is called a _____ .
5. A _____ is a person who conforms to a fashion, way of thinking, or lifestyle.

VOCABULARY DEVELOPMENT

6. A _____ is a machine which generates electricity.
7. A _____ is someone who is trained in the law.
8. A _____ is a person who resides in a particular locale.
9. Anyone who consumes goods or services is a _____ .
10. A traffic _____ is a person who violates the laws of vehicular traffic.
11. An _____ is a person who works in the field of economics.
12. Any substance which pollutes the environment is called a _____ .
13. A _____ is a person who subscribes to a magazine, journal, or newspaper.
14. Someone who analyzes the structure of systems is called a systems _____ .
15. _____ are people who collaborate on a project.
16. Because he writes about the future, Isaac Asimov is called a _____ .
17. A _____ is a person who survives a plane crash or other disaster.
18. A person you would consult about a business problem is called a _____ .
19. An _____ is a piece of equipment which amplifies sound waves.
20. A _____ is a person who has an advanced degree in mathematics.

Practice 2

Fill in the blanks with appropriate noun agents.

1. Not every _____ can type faster than 60 words per minute.
2. Did the stain _____ work for removing the stain in your carpet?

3. People who are <u>defeated</u> before they even try are justifiably called
   _____ .

4. For <u>manufacturing</u> a defective toy, the _____ was fined $20,000.

5. Because of the popularity of <u>ecology</u>, there has been a dramatic increase in the number of _____ .

6. If cars didn't have _____ , even small <u>bumps</u> with other cars would be more serious than they are.

7. When soap gets in your eyes and <u>irritates</u> them, it becomes a dangerous _____ .

8. Does everyone accused of being a _____ have <u>left-wing</u> political views?

9. Are _____ the only people who <u>theorize</u> about things?

10. There are many types of _____ used to <u>disinfect</u> germ-ridden places.

11. _____ from four countries met to <u>negotiate</u> a peace settlement.

12. Today most university _____ have a <u>Library</u> Science degree.

13. People who merely watch sports are called spectators, whereas those who <u>participate</u> are called _____ .

14. Not every _____ succeeds in <u>managing</u> a large store efficiently.

15. Spaceships are <u>boosted</u> into outer space by means of _____ rockets.

Practice 3

In class, discuss what each of the following does. If necessary, review the examples at the beginning of this lesson.

Example

a faculty adviser   An adviser is a faculty member who helps a student decide which courses to take.

1. a metal detector
2. a dissenter
3. a politician
4. a cyclist
5. a flame retardant
6. a windshield wiper
7. a psychiatrist
8. an opponent
9. a dietician
10. an environmentalist

2.5 VERB-FORMING SUFFIXES

One of the ways in which English verbs are formed is by the addition of certain endings to nouns and adjectives. This lesson focuses on three frequently used suffixes. Notice the underlined verbs in the following paragraph:

Small-Town Fire Departments

Many small-town fire departments have made efforts to establish cooperative relationships with other nearby fire departments. The chief of one small department recently <u>emphasized</u> how these efforts to improve protection have been <u>intensified</u>. "When there is a fire in a nearby town, we send units which stay there until the situation is <u>stabilized</u>. If we have a fire, the other towns <u>reciprocate</u>. We have <u>standardized</u> our equipment and <u>formalized</u> our reciprocal arrangements." This kind of cooperation has <u>vitalized</u> and <u>solidified</u> rural fire protection in the United States.

The words underlined in the passage contain suffixes frequently found in English:

-ize   found in academic and nonacademic contexts, frequently used to create new verbs
-ify   often found in technical vocabulary
-ate   found with Latin-based words in academic contexts

All three of the suffixes mean "to cause to be, to make into."

noun	+	*suffix*	=	*verb*
item	+	-ize	=	itemize
class	+	-ify	=	classify
origin	+	-ate	=	originate

111

adjective	+	suffix	=	verb
civil	+	-ize	=	civilize
solid	+	-ify	=	solidify
active	+	-ate	=	activate

Other nouns may be formed by adding *-ation*, *-cation*, or *-tion*. This noun is "the act of" or "the result of" the verb.

verb	+	suffix	=	noun
civilize	+	-ation	=	civilization
classify	+	-cation	=	classification
motivate	+	-tion	=	motivation

Practice 1

Fill in each blank with the verb form of the underlined word. Spelling changes are necessary for some of the words; look up the spellings of words you are unsure of.

Example

He put a lot of emphasis on it. He *emphasized* it.

1. Roxanne made some formal statements. She _____ her ideas.

2. The fighting became more intense. It _____, and the _____ was considered serious.

3. In a reciprocal trade agreement, both countries agree to _____ commercial advantages.

4. The new government achieved greater economic stability. The economy _____.

5. Water becomes solid at 0°C. It _____.

6. Every language has a standard form. Mass communication tends to _____ the way people speak. Some people don't like this kind of _____.

7. A group of engineers felt that their project was not very vital, so they made plans to re- _____ it.

8. The graph contained some symbols which _____ various resources.

VOCABULARY DEVELOPMENT

9. The <u>active</u> ingredient is _____ by warm water.
10. Mark needed a <u>simple</u> sentence, so he _____ a complex one.

Practice 2

Complete each paragraph by filling in the blanks, using a dictionary as needed. Read the idea expressed in parentheses, and then for each space select a single word which expresses that idea *and* is related to the word within the parentheses. Spelling changes are required for some words.

Income Tax Deductions

(make a careful list of <u>items</u>)   People who _____ deductions on their income tax form generally end up paying less or getting a bigger refund than they would otherwise. It's one way to

(be more <u>economical</u>)   _____ on the personal budget

(get the <u>maximum</u>)   and to _____ one's gain or to

(keep to a <u>minimum</u>)   _____ one's losses.

The Equal Rights Amendment

(the act of <u>equalizing</u>)   To promote _____ of job opportunity for women and minorities, a new amendment to the U.S. Constitution has been proposed. The proposed amendment attempts to satisfy women's rights groups, to

(make <u>neutral</u>)   _____ their arguments. If the amendment is ratified, it will make it illegal *not* to give women equal treatment. Law or no law, it is up to women to have enough

(the act of being <u>motivated</u>)   self-_____ to seek jobs actively.

A City Councilman

(make clear) "Gentlemen, I wish to clar-_____ my point. I feel it is extremely important that we do not

(general statements) make sweeping _____ about our local issue, because then we will be in danger of losing sight of the purpose which

(made necessary) _____ this council meeting."

Becoming Western

(the act of becoming like Western society) _____ results in different actions in different societies. It may include

(the act of becoming urban) _____ and

(the act of organizing) _____ of the middle class,

(the act of becoming mechanical) and/or some _____ of industry.

(create a fantasy) In some countries, leaders _____

(the act of making a duplicate) about the possibilities of complete _____ of Western life, and neglect their nation's unique characteristics.

(make radical) Such efforts tend to _____

(make active) political parties and to _____ dissidents in the country, who

(use as capital) _____ on the opportunity to point out faults in both developing and developed countries.

Forms of Learning

Education involves many mental processes.

(commit to memory) Sometimes students must _____ information; other times they must

VOCABULARY DEVELOPMENT

(make a summary) _____ material. On more

advanced levels students often need to

(develop a formula) _____ or

(make a synthesis) _____ new ideas.

Practice 3

Read a journal article or a magazine article of interest to you. Make a list of the *-ize, -ify,* and *-ate* verbs and their related nouns in the article. Write original sentences for five or six of the words.

Practice 4

Write a paragraph in which you use several of the verbs and related nouns you learned in this lesson and some of the words you have collected on your own. The paragraph may be on one of the following topics, or on another topic of your own choice:

1. education
2. recent developments in your field of study
3. economic changes in your country
4. bargaining between labor and management
5. negotiations for a treaty or other political agreement

Frequently Used Word Groups

3

3.1 INTRODUCTION

These sections provide contexts for vocabulary words which are used to describe appearances, actions and behavior. All of the words presented here in word groups come up frequently in students' lives. As you study these lessons, pay particular attention to the use of words which may be familiar but which may be used with different meanings or different connotations.

Chapter Outline

Do and *Make*
Adjectives
Health
Insurance
Newspaper Language
Useful Abbreviations and Acronyms
Politics and Government
Glossary of Political Terms
Legal Vocabulary
Verbs Expressing Attitudes
Evaluative Vocabulary

3.2 DO AND MAKE

Do and *make* are verbs used very frequently, and they occur in many idiomatic expressions. Therefore, it is particularly important to understand the general difference in their meanings.

do to perform, work, accomplish routine tasks; relates to job-oriented behavior

make to create, construct, develop something new; relates to object-oriented or product-oriented behavior

Contrasting Examples

do Frank Jordan has to do homework almost every night. Stephanie Jordan is doing research on energy conservation. Frank does the cooking on Tuesdays and Thursdays, and Stephanie does it on Mondays and Wednesdays.

make Stephanie is making a survey of attitudes towards the use of nuclear energy for heating. Frank made a report in his economics class last Friday. Last Sunday, when they had guests for dinner, they made meat loaf, mixed vegetables, and chocolate cake.

Practice 1

Read the following passage on the changing roles of men and women in the United States. After you read it through completely, go back and underline each use of the verbs *do* and *make*.

Roles of Men and Women in the United States

Now that nearly half of the women aged sixteen or older are in the work force and the average number of children per family is between one and two, it is not surprising that the roles of men and women in United States society are being reexamined.

The traditional division of responsibilities in the home assigned most household chores to women, from doing the cooking and doing the dishes to making the beds and cleaning the floors. Women who took care of a house full-time have been called "housewives" or, more recently, "homemakers." Men have been expected to do heavy work and make household improvements. There is an old saying about the unequal distribution of work: "Men work from dawn 'til set of sun, but a woman's work is never done." With more and more women working outside the home full-time, the old division of chores doesn't seem to make much sense any more. As a result, in many homes men and women both do housework and share child care.

While division of responsibilities within the family is an individual family decision, what people do outside the home is controlled by the society. For years American parents have told their children that they could do whatever they wanted with their lives, if they made up their minds to work for their goals: "You can be president if you want to." But in fact, society has trained men for certain occupations and women for certain others. Many companies have put men into management training programs, while women with equivalent degrees have been hired to do routine clerical work—typing, filing, and record-keeping. Some women particularly object to being expected to do errands, make coffee, make social appointments, and make sure that everything is in order. A secretary who does everything she can to please may be appreciated, but is rarely promoted to a decision-making position. In the mid-seventies only one out of twenty women who held full-time jobs was in an executive or middle-management position in private business. Not only do women face more obstacles in doing what they would like to do, but also they are paid less than men. Employed American men make an average of 43 percent more money than employed American women.[1]

Both men and women want to do something important and make contributions to society. Why should sex make a difference? Why shouldn't a man be a secretary and a woman be a politician? Federal law has made it illegal to discriminate in hiring. In fact, any corporation which wants to receive federal funding has to prove its intention to consider hiring women and minorities. This practice, "affirmative action," requires a business or educational institution or union to make an effort to identify women and minority people who qualify for their jobs, and to make their final choices without regard to race or sex. Even employers who want to "do the right thing" are often not able to achieve a balance in hiring.

Progress is being made in the campaign for equal treatment. The Equal Rights Amendment, passed by Congress in 1972, declares that men and women shall be treated equally under the law. The long struggle to get the ERA ratified (approved) by the states has forced women's groups to become much better organized, and it has done more than any other single issue to focus public attention on women's rights. By December 1975 over ninety nationally based women's groups were able to agree on a list of objectives which they would work for in the coming years; the introductory statement of the "U.S. National Women's Agenda" defines its overall objective:

> Although our programs and goals may vary, still we have agreed on issues which must be addressed as national priorities so that women will play a full and equal role in this country.

[1] *U.S. News and World Report*, Vol. 79, 8 December 1975, p. 58.

Sure, you can call me a little homemaker. I've been vice-president of a home construction company for four years.

Practice 2

Complete the following statements made recently by leading professional women in the United States by adding *do* or *make* in the blanks. Be sure to check verb tense.

Example

Women, who until this century were barely legal persons, have *made* their way into most areas of social life.

(Jeane Kirkpatrick, political scientist)

FREQUENTLY USED WORD GROUPS

1. It never occurred to me that I couldn't _____ or be anything I wanted.

   (Mary Calderone, physician)

2. A woman who has no purpose of her own in society, a woman who cannot think about the future because she is _____ nothing to give herself a real identity in it, will continue to feel a desperation in the present.

   (Betty Friedan, writer)

3. So few grown women like their lives. So many are miserable and whining, for want of a continuous occupation to excite them, to keep them learning and growing. Not that those who want to stay home should be _____ to feel guilty, but even those who aren't widows must face the moment when their children are grown and they'll have to figure out what they want to _____ .

   (Katharine Graham, newspaper publisher)

4. The charge has been _____ that the movement is just for white, middle-class educated women. It may have been that once, but it certainly isn't now.

   (Jessie Bernard, sociologist)

5. Black women have _____ significant contributions to struggles against the racism and dehumanizing exploitation of a wrongly organized society.

   (Angela Davis, college instructor)

6. The claim is often _____ , and without the slightest justification, that even women with more than adequate training and knowledge lack the ability to assume higher level positions in industry.

   (Shirley Chisholm, congresswoman)

7. If you are a woman twenty years old, you can expect to _____ more than six job changes during the remainder of your working life.

(Sylvia Porter, business writer)

8. I've always been a woman and I've never been an imitation man. I've _____ things in my work only a woman could _____ .

(Margaret Mead, anthropologist)

9. There have been times in my life when I've thought, wouldn't it be great to have a man at home who would be faithful, be there all the time, and I could run around and _____ what I wanted and still come back to this person.

(Erica Jong, novelist)

10. Women went through a period of believing they had to behave like men in order to _____ it in society . . . now we want to celebrate womanhood, and _____ it our own way.

(Gloria Steinem, editor)

11. The U.S. National Women's Agenda is significant, not only because of the demands it _____ , but because it establishes the minimum objectives for change that a majority of American women can readily support . . . whether the Agenda remains an attractive red, white, and blue declaration or is translated into reality depends on what women and their organizations _____ with it.

(Bella Abzug, congresswoman)

Practice 3

A student learns to do a lot of things in college. The expressions below which begin with *do* or *make* describe some of the tasks. Fill in each blank with *do* or *make,* and then add as many phrases of your own as you can. In class, share your additions.

Example

A student may *make* progress in learning English.

A student may . . .

1. _____ enough homework to fill several volumes.
2. _____ an effort to psych out professors.
3. _____ research in his major field.
4. _____ requests for a library book on reserve.
5. _____ appointments to see a professor.
6. _____ up his mind without anyone's guidance.
7. _____ without sleep to finish assignments.
8. do _____ .
9. make _____ .
10. _____ .
11. _____ .
12. _____ .
13. _____ .
14. _____ .
15. _____ .

Practice 4

To complete this conversation between Ed and Cathy, choose the correct form of *do* or *make* for each blank.

A Dialogue

"I know you're busy, but we have to eat somewhere, so please _____ up your mind," Ed said. "Choose a restaurant and I'll _____ reservations."

"Would you _____ me a favor and leave me alone until I've _____ my homework?" Cathy answered. "Tomorrow I have to _____ a speech about the research I _____ last quarter and right now none of it _____ much sense."

"_____ your best and you'll _____ a good impression," Ed argued. "Anyway, what you _____ now won't _____ much difference. You've already _____ everything you can, so forget about it until tomorrow."

"O.K., you win," she agreed. "Let's _____ plans. I want to eat Chinese food. What would you like to _____ afterwards?"

Practice 5

Choose *do* or *make* for each blank.

If you want to get a job, first you've got to _____ a favorable enough impression on people in the personnel department to get an application. When you fill it out, you have to _____ sure that you haven't _____ any mistakes and that you've filled it out completely.

In your interview, you have to _____ everything you can to impress the interviewer with your qualifications and your potential, while suggesting that you will learn a great deal from the company. From the time you walk in the door until you sign a contract, you've got to _____ every effort to convince people of your value as an employee.

Practice 6

In class, divide up in pairs. In each pair, one student can play the role of a personnel interviewer, and the other can play the role of a job applicant. Practice some job interview situations and present them for the class.

Practice 7

Write a one-page composition on one of the following topics, using examples of *do* and *make* when appropriate.

1. Describe the daily life of your mother when she was your age.
2. Discuss the roles of men and women in your country.

3.3 ADJECTIVES

As a rule, beginning and intermediate textbooks of English for foreign students do not devote much attention to the study of adjectives, because students on those levels need to master other areas of English. However, students who intend to live in the United States for a time, to enroll in university courses, and to participate in formal discussions and informal conversations need to become familiar with the adjectives most commonly used in speech and writing. Evaluative adjectives are covered in the lesson at the end of this chapter titled Evaluative Vocabulary.

This lesson provides practice with adjectives used to describe objects and people.

Description of Objects

In this section there are three reading passages. Read each passage and do the practices which follow.

Pizza

Pizza is one of the most popular foods in the United States and is, in fact, a genuine American invention despite its close association with Italy. A pizza is basically a round piece of dough, covered with a layer of mild, stringy cheese and spicy tomato sauce, along with one or more toppings such as sliced fresh mushrooms, sausage, olives, and onions. It is freshly baked, cut into pie-shaped wedges with a sharp knife or pizza cutter, and served piping hot. Each person helps himself to a piece and eats it with his fingers.

When people go out for pizza, they have to make a lot of choices. First, they must decide if they want to eat it in a pizzeria or order it "to go." If they do want to eat in a pizzeria, they can choose from a variety of places. Some pizzerias are tiny, dimly lit spots which seat only a few dozen. Others are big, bright places which have loud, live entertainment and seating for hundreds. Regardless of size, places that serve good pizza are usually so crowded that people have to wait for an empty table. Once seated, they have to decide what kind of pizza to get—pepperoni, a "half and half" (for example, half salami, half mushroom), or a "combination" with everything. Next, they have to decide on size—two medium pizzas, a large and a small, or maybe an extra large?

There are other considerations too. Some people like a thin, crisp crust, while others prefer a thicker, softer crust. According to some people, soft drinks go well with pizza; others say nothing goes better than light or dark beer, or wine. Pizza is a group experience, and part of the fun is making choices.

Practice 1

The passage about pizza contains many descriptive adjectives. Some of them you already know; others may be unfamiliar. As a class, make a list of the unfamiliar adjectives in the reading. Discuss synonyms of the adjectives that you or your classmates think of.

Examples

Phrase   *Adjective Synonyms*

genuine American invention   authentic, real
a *crisp* crust   hard, firm, brittle, dry

Practice 2

Each of the following words is an opposite of an adjective in the passage. Find the word and discuss the meanings of the pair of opposites.

Example

immense is an opposite of *small* in the passage.

blunt	dull	immense	soggy
canned	fake	minute	spoiled
crunchy	full	occupied	tasteless
dim	hard	phony	tiny
disliked	huge	recorded	thick
distant	gigantic	remote	tough
		soft (music)	wet

FREQUENTLY USED WORD GROUPS

Practice 3

Describe in class each of the following types of food in class members can help each other find words.

Example

An apple   An apple is a round red or yellow fruit.
outside. On the inside it is soft and white, with small brown seeds in the center. When you bite into an apple, it is crunchy and sweet.

1. a potato
2. a banana
3. a raisin
4. a hamburger
5. a cucumber
6. a slice of bread
7. rice
8. lettuce
9. a chicken drumstick
10. your favorite food

Practice 4

Describe a meal you recently had at home, in a dorm dining hall, or at a restaurant. Include details about the place where you ate the meal. Use appropriate adjectives in your description.

Roads

The United States is criss-crossed with a network of major highways designed to help a driver get from one place to another in the shortest possible time. Although these wide modern roads are generally smooth and well-maintained, with few sharp curves and many straight, even stretches, a direct route is not always the most enjoyable one. Large highways often bypass scenic areas and interesting small towns. Furthermore, these highways generally connect large urban centers, which means that they become clogged with heavy traffic during rush hours, when the "fast, direct" way becomes a very slow route.

Unless time is short, there is almost always an alternate route. Not far from the relatively new "superhighways," there are often older, less heavily traveled roads (sometimes marked as "scenic routes") which go through the countryside. Some of these are good two-lane roads; others are quite bumpy, with one winding gravel or dirt lane curving through the country. These secondary routes may go up steep slopes, along high cliffs, or down frightening inclines to towns lying in deep valleys. Though these less direct routes are usually longer and slower, they generally go to places where the air is clean and the scenery is beautiful. The driver may have a chance to get a fresh, clear view of the world and wonder why he spends five mornings and five afternoons a week inching along on a smelly, dirty, noisy freeway.

Practice 5

Each of the following words is a synonym of an adjective in the passage on roads and could be substituted for it. Find each synonym in the reading and as a class discuss the unfamiliar adjectives.

Example

pure is a synonym of *clean* as in *clean, fresh air*

broad	fun	precipitous	subsidiary
chief	intriguing	principal	substitute
congested	jammed	pure	sudden
crawling	level	rough	swift
crooked	loud	rugged	terrifying
crowded	lovely	scary	tiny
dense	minor	severe	towering
filthy	nice	sluggish	twisted
flat	pleasant	speedy	unobstructed

Practice 6

To build your active vocabulary, give the related noun and verb for each adjective listed below. Use a dictionary if necessary. Practice using the nouns and verbs in sentences.

long	narrow	smooth
short	deep	flat
high	shallow	sharp
low	straight	modern
wide	clear	
broad	clean	

Practice 7

Describe one of the following routes. Include characteristics of the road and of things along the route in your description.

1. the road you take to get to campus
2. a route you took in your country to get from home to school, to a job, or to some other place
3. a scenic walk you would recommend to tourists

Practice 8

Describe one way of getting from one specific place to another specific place, and then describe an alternate route. Point out similar and different characteristics of the two routes. Explain which route you prefer and why.

Endangered Species

Many kinds of animals are endangered by human beings. The United States government list of endangered species includes alligators, tigers, grizzly bears, some kinds of whales, and over three dozen species of butterflies. What has led to the scarcity of these animals, which may become extinct without vital protection?

One important factor is that many animals have been widely hunted and killed for food (as in the case of whales), or for their beautiful skins (as in the case of tigers and alligators). In accordance with the Endangered Species Act, it is illegal in the United States to hunt, sell, or collect endangered species. Thus, an expensive fur coat made from a tiger killed in Asia cannot be legally sold to a wealthy matron in New York or San Francisco.

Some predators, such as eagles or wolves, which kill useful, more common animals are threatened by ranchers who are concerned that predators will carry off chickens and young sheep, and use this fear to justify trapping or killing them.

Perhaps the saddest cases involve species which are endangered only because humans are successfully competing with them for the use of environmental space. The territorial range of the huge, powerful grizzly bear, once seen in many parts of the American West, is now quite restricted. Polar bears are killed in arctic regions when they come too close to towns that were built in the middle of their natural territory.

The butterfly is an accidental victim of man's effort to control his environment. For a long time collectors have searched for unusual specimens for their colorful butterfly collections; now, there is an additional, more serious threat—widespread use of dangerous pesticides which farmers apply to their crops to control harmful insects.

With various animals being killed for food, for decoration, and for the protection of domesticated animals, or dying because of unfortunate contact with human environments, it is not surprising that some are becoming scarce, that the number of species on the endangered list is growing every year. Man is discovering that his world includes the other animals in it, and one can only hope this discovery is not coming too slowly or too late.

Practice 9

There are more than twenty adjectives in the reading, "Endangered Species." Underline them and compare your list with your classmates. See if you can name a synonym and antonym (opposite) for each underlined word. Have one student make a list on the blackboard.

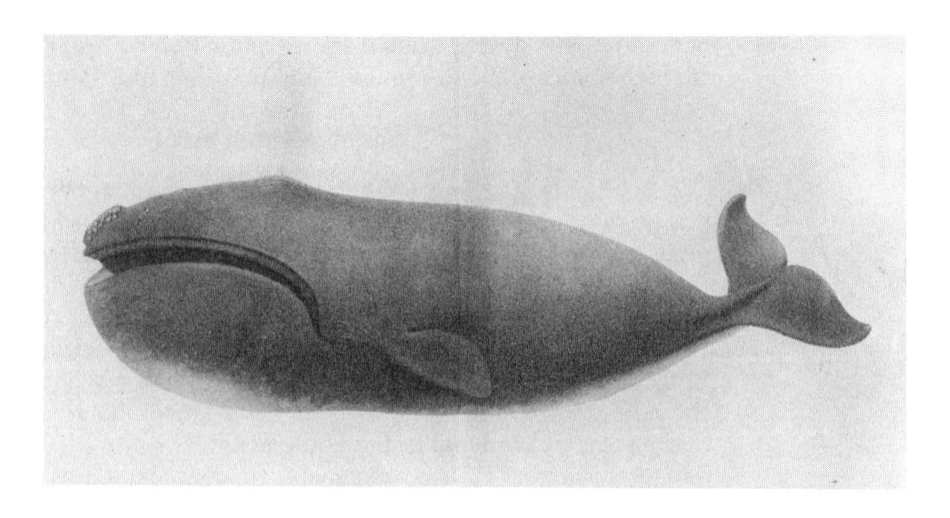

Right whale of the northwest coast. *California Academy of Sciences.*

Example

adjective	*synonyms*	*opposites*
huge	gigantic	tiny
wealthy	prosperous	poor

Practice 10

Some of the words in the following list are synonyms of words in the passage. Others are opposites. Put each word in the appropriate column on your list. Some of the words fit in several places. Notice that the synonyms do not necessarily substitute precisely for corresponding words in the passage. After arranging the words, discuss unfamiliar words and distinctions in class.

Examples

In the passage	*Synonyms*	*Antonyms*
accidental	unplanned	
scarce		abundant

abundant	deliberate	beneficial	extensive
advantageous	deprived	cheap	further
affluent	drab	critical	gigantic
artificial	enormous	customary	gorgeous

FREQUENTLY USED WORD GROUPS

injurious	plentiful	threatened	vast
limited	savage	unlawful	vivid
minute	scarce	unintentional	wild
numerous	tame	valuable	worthless

Practice 11

For more practice, use the words from Practices 9 and 10 in full sentences. Create a sentence and ask a classmate to substitute an opposite for the adjective in the sentence. If the resulting sentence does not make sense, the second student must make a new sentence using an *opposite* of the first student's adjective.

Examples

cheap

first student: Some grocery items are cheap.
second student: Some grocery items are expensive.

domesticated

first student: Domesticated animals are often found on farms.
second student: Wild animals are kept in zoos.

Practice 12

Describe a change that has occurred in the natural environment in your country. Use some of the adjectives you have learned in the three passages.

Further Practice

Meanings of adjectives, like shades of color, are different to different speakers. Five people may agree that a piece of cloth is green, but they may call it different names for green: Kelly green, bright green, chartreuse, apple green, or grass green. Similarly, people may agree that the ground outside has moisture in it; that is, that it is "wet." However, depending on their perception of the degree of "wetness" and their attitude toward the "wetness," they may use different adjectives to describe it: wet, damp, moist, soggy, soaked, squishy, mushy, saturated.

Practice 13

To practice words you have learned and to learn new ones, read and discuss each of the following situations in class. As a class, think of three additional adjectives; if you use a word which some of your classmates do not know, explain it to them.

Example

Noun	Descriptive Adjectives
a small car	compact, cramped, economical, sensible, unsafe, reasonable
a chocolate cake	rich, delicious, tasty, fattening, moist, scrumptious

1. a house — cozy, spacious, poorly designed . . .
2. the Empire State Building — massive, impressive, towering . . .
3. Disneyland or Disney World — delightful, disappointing, expensive . . .
4. the Concorde airplane — vital, huge, unnecessary . . .
5. a basketball game — exciting, close, sloppy . . .
6. an abstract painting — shocking, appealing, incomprehensible . . .
7. a marble sculpture — lovely, priceless, disproportionate . . .
8. a self-cleaning oven — convenient, extravagant, time-saving . . .
9. a fruit salad — luscious, sweet, colorful . . .
10. American food — tasteless, varied, starchy . . .

Practice 14

Choose an object which is familiar to everyone in your class. Describe it without saying what it is and have the class guess what you are describing.

Example

I'm thinking of a long white object. It may be smooth or rough on the outside and is sometimes very squeaky. It's powdery when you write with it.

Practice 15

Describe a specific place or event in your country or in the United States, for example, a market place, a festival, a beach, a cafeteria, your house. Use at least ten adjectives in your description.

Physical Descriptions of People

How often have you been asked to describe someone you know, for example, your parents, your brother or sister, your roommate, your spouse? You may be asked, "Tell me about him. What does he look like? What is he like?" This lesson gives you practice in answering the first question.

Some of the descriptive vocabulary you have practiced with objects applies as well to physical descriptions of people. The introductory passage contains several physical descriptions of people. Notice how the descriptions are made so that you can describe people later in the lesson.

The Party

Recently I went to a party at the home of a person I work with. There were quite a few people there, but since I live in another city, I didn't know many of them. Being a stranger didn't bother me because it gave me a chance to practice one of my favorite hobbies—"people-watching."

The woman who opened the door when I arrived was tall and slender. She was wearing a loose dress made of sheer silk. Her hair, long, straight, and blonde, was tied back with a brown velvet ribbon. She spoke in a low, husky voice with a trace of a European accent. She said, "Come in."

I went in. She floated away from me toward a handsome young man wearing a tie-dyed T-shirt. He was tall and athletic. I have never seen such a powerful-looking man. His face was deeply tanned and his smile showed brilliant white teeth. I made my way through the crowd to the punch bowl.

There was a knock on the door. A man with a dark complexion came in. He was slightly bald, with graying hair which made him look distinguished. His thick moustache and heavy-rimmed glasses gave him a scholarly, mature appearance. After a few minutes of small talk, he tried to sell me some insurance.

There was a drab-looking man with pale eyes and damp hair standing near a wall, appearing shy and timid. When an elegant young woman spoke to him, he became embarrassed and tongue-tied. I walked toward him, but he edged away, so I concentrated on eating a cracker and tried to look nonthreatening. He left very early, after murmuring to the hostess, "Thank you. I had a wonderful time, but I have to go home to watch my goldfish."

Not more than a half hour later, the elegant young woman had an argument with the handsome young man, and she left the party. I left soon afterward.

Practice 16

To help you practice giving physical descriptions of people, consider these words and some synonyms: *height, weight, build,* and *age*. Add words. Discuss differences between the various words in class.

Height, Weight, and Build. A person may be (very) tall, (very) short, or of medium height. Often height is specified: *She's about five two (five feet, two inches); He's over 6 feet tall.* Tact is very important when one describes a person's weight and build, particularly if the person has an unusual build. For example, a person may be thin, slender, skinny, underweight, fat, plump, chubby, heavy, stocky, overweight. Which have the most positive connotations?

Age. A person may be described as young, old, middle-aged, elderly, around thirty-five, in her early forties. Some people are very sensitive about their age and prefer that it not be known or given to other people.

Other Features. A person's eyes may be described in terms of color, size, shape, and intensity (for example, bright, penetrating). A person's hair may be described in terms of length, color, and texture (curly, thin, straight). A person's voice may be high or low in pitch, and loud or soft in volume. In addition, it may be gentle, harsh, soothing. A description of a person may also include one or more of the following features: nose (small, straight, prominent), face shape (oval, square), forehead (high, broad), mouth (small, full), posture (good, poor, erect), and hands (rough, slender, large).

Overall Description. A person may be described as beautiful, ugly, handsome, attractive, not bad-looking, good-looking.

Practice 17

Give a physical description of the person sitting on your left.

Practice 18

Give a physical description of someone outside the classroom who is attractive.

Human Characteristics

Adjectives dealing with human characteristics are subjective and often do not have precise meanings; which ones a person chooses depend on what he thinks of himself and of other people. Opinions about people tend to be evaluative (that is, positive or negative), but there are few characteristics which are exactly opposite. Only pairs of words which include negative prefixes, such as *efficient* and *inefficient,* are exact opposites.

Two Types of Drivers

There are two extremes of drivers behind the wheel today. The first type is the unsafe driver, the one who disregards traffic regulations and makes life difficult for pedestrians and other drivers. He is impatient and honks his horn or blinks his lights unnecessarily. He is also inconsiderate; he takes two parking places, tailgates[2] other cars, and slows down or speeds up just to annoy other drivers. Above all he is reckless, taking risks and causing accidents. In sharp contrast is the safe driver. He obeys traffic regulations and practices the courtesy of the road. Aware of the rights and desires of others, he is always considerate of pedestrians and of other drivers. He is a careful driver, one who signals, plans ahead, and does not

[2]Follows other cars so closely that he might cause an accident.

take chances. Often it is the alert driver who, through quick action, is able to prevent a dangerous situation from turning into a bad accident.

Practice 19

Give the adjective forms for each of the following nouns.

patience	help	responsibility
tolerance	sensitivity	carelessness
consideration	care	recklessness
thoughtfulness	caution	safety
respect	conscientiousness	
courtesy	competence	

Practice 20

Add the negative prefixes to these adjectives.

Examples

<u>un</u>reasonable
<u>dis</u>interested

1. _____patient
2. _____considerate
3. _____aware
4. _____tolerant
5. _____thoughtful
6. _____respectful
7. _____courteous
8. _____competent
9. _____responsible
10. _____sensitive

Practice 21

For each of the following items, write a complete sentence using a variety of adjectives to describe each kind of driver. When you finish the ten below, add five more questions of your own for other students to answer.

How would you describe a driver who . . .

Example

doesn't change lanes when a car wants to pass?

He is an inconsiderate driver.
A person who drives like that is unthoughtful.

1. goes slowly when the road is wet?
2. signals whenever he turns?
3. honks his horn repeatedly?
4. lets a pedestrian cross?

5. dims his lights when there is an oncoming car?
6. takes two parking places?
7. swerves to avoid a child's ball in the street?
8. follows another car too closely?
9. helps a motorist change a flat tire?
10. deliberately forces another car off the road?

Practice 22

Discussion:

1. Is it possible for a driver to be too cautious or too considerate?
2. How would you describe the average driver in your country? (Use adjectives describing human characteristics.)

Profile of a National Leader

What characteristics do Americans feel a president should have? In a 1975 poll[3] conducted in California, the following qualities emerged as those considered most desirable: honesty, fairness, and concern for people. The respondents wanted a national leader who is candid and trustworthy, even more than they want someone who can deal effectively with Congress or who can handle fiscal policy. A president should be responsive to the needs of the people, and compassionate when they need help. Many of the respondents prefer an able, intelligent leader between forty-five and fifty-five years old who is capable of handling the complexities and pressures of the position.

Practice 23

Below are some adjectives related in meaning to each of five human characteristics. What other synonyms can you think of? Discuss the differences between words.

honest	frank, open . . .
fair	decent, moral . . .
kind	concerned, compassionate . . .
unkind	unsympathetic, cruel . . .
intelligent	smart, bright . . .

Practice 24

Match each characteristic on the left with a description on the right, creating sentences which begin, "A person who is . . ."

[3]Public opinion poll conducted by the Field Research Corporation, reported in *The Los Angeles Times* (20 April 1975), pp. 1, 16.

Example

A person who is <u>honest</u> tells the truth.

1. cruel _____
2. responsive _____
3. candid _____
4. unreliable _____
5. generous _____
6. sharp _____
7. deceitful _____
8. trustworthy _____
9. uninformed _____
10. capable _____

a. gives of his time, energy, and/or money to others, especially those in need
b. is intelligent and gives perceptive answers
c. does not have the necessary knowledge to make a decision
d. listens to people's wishes and tries to do something about them
e. can be depended upon to do what he says
f. is able to handle a job
g. is willing to tell someone the truth, whether it is good or bad
h. ignores or deliberately hurts a person or animal
i. tells only part of the truth or distorts the truth
j. cannot be trusted to follow through on an assignment

Practice 25

Prepare five questions about human characteristics for your classmates to answer.

Example

Question: What kind of person disregards other people's needs?
Answer: an inconsiderate or unsympathetic person

Practice 26

Student A gives a generalization about a person. Student B gives a specific example to agree or disagree.

Example

Student A: Charley is *friendly*.
Student B: Yes, when I first arrived, he introduced himself and offered to help me get settled. He has invited me to his house several times.

1. compassionate
2. ruthless
3. open
4. dependable
5. bright
6. blunt

7. obnoxious
8. inexperienced
9. concerned
10. knowledgeable

Practice 27

Ask three American friends what characteristics they feel a national leader should have. Compare their opinions with the results given in the passage and explain the similarities and differences to the rest of the class.

Practice 28

Describe the characteristics you feel are most desirable for a national leader in your country.

What Today's Single Woman Looks For in a Man

When a number of career-oriented American women between the ages of twenty and forty were asked what characteristics they were looking for in a man, they used words like "gentle, warm, sincere, mature." They do not like a man who is self-centered or threatening. They want someone who is both aware of his potential and also willing to respect a woman's desire to fulfill her potential as well. They tend to prefer an outgoing man who has a zest for life. All of the women want someone they can respect.[4]

Practice 29

Discuss the characteristics which are listed in groups below. Which are considered "positive" in your country?

1. friendly, cold, unfriendly, warm, tender, indifferent, contemptuous, amiable
2. shy, withdrawn, outgoing, talkative, reticent, gregarious
3. content, optimistic, sad, downcast, unhappy, pessimistic, cheerful, happy, despondent
4. sophisticated, mature, naive, green, worldly, immature
5. unpretentious, modest, self-centered, arrogant, conceited, humble, egotistical, proud
6. self-conscious, relaxed, high-strung, nervous, tense, easy-going, calm

Practice 30

Complete each sentence with an appropriate human characteristic adjective. There are many possibilities for each sentence. Change *a* to *an* when necessary. Compare your sentences with those of your classmates and discuss differences.

[4]Based on Bess Winakor, "Pursuing Careers, Not Husbands," *The Los Angeles Times* (13 April 1975), p. 20.

Example

A *shy* person does not often speak up in class.

Next, change each sentence to the opposite characteristic, adding or deleting negatives when necessary.

Example

A *talkative* person often speaks up in class.

1. _____ people think only of themselves and not of others.
2. A(n) _____ person does not act grown-up when the situation requires it.
3. _____ people focus on the joys rather than the heartaches of life.
4. A(n) _____ person is not bothered by little things.
5. A(n) _____ person likes to be with other people in a social setting.
6. A(n) _____ person does nothing to help others out of their troubles.
7. A person may become _____ when everything seems to be going wrong.
8. _____ people may show their uneasiness by chewing their fingernails, chewing gum, or smoking too many cigarettes.
9. A(n) _____ person is willing to listen to others' problems and may help them find solutions.
10. _____ people generally do not find it hard to make new acquaintances.

Practice 31

How do people with the following characteristics act? Create a sentence with each adjective.

Example

A *talkative* person often does not give other people a chance to say anything.

1. warm
2. immature
3. withdrawn
4. easy-going
5. indifferent
6. cheerful
7. unpretentious
8. relaxed
9. supportive
10. sophisticated

Getting Ahead

To get ahead in business, it is usually not enough to be intelligent, capable, and dependable. Certainly those qualities help, but other characteristics are more important. How efficient and versatile an employee is may make a lot of difference. Employers favor a productive, hard-working employee who not only does not waste time, but also actually saves the company time and money. An employee has an even greater chance of getting ahead if he or she is ambitious and resourceful. The person who suggests new practical approaches to increase quality and quantity will be remembered by a wise employer when it is time for promotions.

Practice 32

Discuss the characteristics which are listed in the groups below. Which are considered "positive" in your country?

1. efficient, diligent, negligent, incompetent, conscientious, meticulous, inefficient, disorganized
2. uncreative, unoriginal, clever, resourceful, enterprising, unimaginative, imaginative
3. open-minded, perceptive, foolish, intuitive, unwise, silly, skeptical, gullible, wise

Practice 33

Choose any five adjectives you have learned in this part of the lesson and use them in sentences.

Example

A *resourceful* person suggests new approaches which increase production.

Practice 34

Discussion: What qualities does a person need to get ahead in business in your society?

Practice 35

Read and discuss each of the following situations in class. Try to figure out precisely what each adjective means and whether it is culturally positive or negative. Add other adjectives that you can think of. After discussing these with each other, choose several words and ask three Americans how they interpret those words.

Example

A student who studies late before a test may be called: hard-working, worried, panicky, competitive, overworked.

1. A person who really tries to succeed might be called ambitious, aggressive, hard-working, . . .
2. A politician might be called: dynamic, fair, opportunistic, . . .
3. A person who hesitates a long time before making a decision might be called: cautious, judicious, indecisive, . . .
4. A job recommendation might describe an applicant as: conscientious, careless, reliable, . . .
5. A teacher's attitude toward students in class might be called: indifferent, concerned, condescending, . . .
6. Parents may think their daughter's decision to move away from home at age eighteen suggests that she is: independent, ungrateful, rebellious, . . .
7. Negative attitudes toward marijuana smoking might be called: justified, unwarranted, alarmist, . . .

Practice 36

Describe several famous people. Use at least three adjectives in each description.

Pre–twentieth century

Napoleon Bonaparte
Abraham Lincoln
Simon Bolivar
Meiji
Machiavelli
Hernan Cortez
Confucius
Joan of Arc

Twentieth century

Mahatma Gandhi
Martin Luther King
Joan Baez
Mao Tse-tung
Fidel Castro
Pelé (Edson Arantes do Nascimento)
Anwar Sadat
Louis Armstrong
Golda Meir
Toshiro Mifune
Andres Segovia
Henry Kissinger
Shah Reza Pahlavi

Practice 37

Americans love to rate themselves on various social and psychological characteristics. Many popular magazines such as *Esquire, Psychology To-*

day, and *Ms.* as well as the magazine sections of Sunday newspapers, often include articles which ask the readers to rate themselves in order to find out how "modern," or sociable, or well-rounded they are. The self-rating scale[5] included below will help you gain familiarity with the American English connotations of some important emotional adjectives. A similar test was first presented to the public on national television and is a typical example of the kind of test Americans like to take.

For each adjective in the following chart, answer the question: "How _____ are you?" according to this scale:

1. usually not
2. sometimes
3. often
4. almost always

Put the number in column A.

Example

Happy
How *happy* are you?   3

Write 3 if you consider yourself happy often.

	A	B
Happy	3	+
Warm		
Loyal		
Aggressive		
Dominant		
Conceited		
Affectionate		
Conscientious		
Understanding		
Sympathetic		
Willing to take a stand		
Compassionate		

[5] Based on research done by Sandra Bem, a psychologist at Stanford University.

FREQUENTLY USED WORD GROUPS

Conventional Loving toward children Tactful		
Ambitious Gentle Moody		
Sensitive to others Adaptable Self-reliant		
Competitive Forceful Sincere		

Practice 38

For each adjective which is considered a positive attribute in your country, put a + in Column B. For each adjective which is considered a negative attribute in your country, put a − in Column B.

Practice 39

Compare the results in Column B with those of your classmates and your teacher.

Practice 40

Discuss the qualities you look for in the following:

1. a spouse
2. a professional athlete
3. a friend

3.4 HEALTH

Take the following true-false test. Circle T for those statements which you think are true and F for those which you think are false. Discuss unfamiliar vocabulary in class and then check your answers with the information given in the reading selections below.

T F 1. You can avoid colds by staying away from people who have colds.

T	F	2.	Headaches are caused by eyestrain.
T	F	3.	Poison oak can cause a rash.
T	F	4.	A vitamin deficiency can cause a cold.
T	F	5.	Decongestants are available without prescription.
T	F	6.	You can avoid colds by not going out with wet hair.
T	F	7.	Respiratory illness increases as education level increases.
T	F	8.	Every few years a new strain of flu virus shows up.
T	F	9.	You can get the flu through contact with people who have the flu.
T	F	10.	Too little exercise can make you susceptible to a cold.
T	F	11.	A headache may signal a serious infection.
T	F	12.	Hay fever is an allergy.
T	F	13.	People who have allergies cough.
T	F	14.	A person with a viral infection may have a headache and fever.
T	F	15.	Sooner or later everyone gets the flu.

According to "People Should Feel Good," a bulletin of Stanford Health Services (Third Edition, 1973), the common cold, headaches, hay fever, and poison ivy and oak are the most common ailments that students suffer from. Read the following explanations and discuss them in class.

The Common Cold

Colds are caused by infection with one of fifty or more viruses. Symptoms vary with the age of the individual, whether or not he has previously been infected with the same or a closely related virus, how much he has been exposed to the virus, and, to a very limited degree, climatic conditions.

There is no definite evidence that one's susceptibility to colds is influenced by not getting enough sleep, too much or not enough exercise, vitamin deficiency, or too many alcoholic beverages. There seems to be no dependable way of avoiding colds except by staying away from people who have colds.

Treatment of a cold is aimed primarily at relieving symptoms, by the use of a variety of medications. Antibiotics should *not* be used in the treatment of the common cold, but only in the treatment of complications such as bacterial infection of the middle ear, the sinuses, or the bronchial tubes. Fever, headache, and muscle aches can be controlled with aspirin. Some decongestants are available without prescription. Sore throats can be treated by taking nonprescription anesthetic lozenges and by gargling warm salt water (two tablespoons of table salt to one glass of hot water).

Headaches

Most students have occasional headaches which have no obvious cause and are not associated with known diseases. Contrary to public opinion, headaches are rarely if ever caused by eyestrain or chronic sinus trouble. Headaches often occur with fever; this is particularly true with certain viral infections such as influenza (flu). Aspirin is frequently used, as it tends to bring down the temperature in addition to relieving pain. Headaches may signal more serious infections or internal problems, but if so, they are usually accompanied by other symptoms and signs which call immediate attention to the severity of the condition.

Hay Fever

Next to colds, hay fever is the most common cause of nasal obstruction. Most people who suffer from allergies have symptoms for several weeks or months, especially during the spring and summer when pollens are in the air. When a person's skin contacts pollen or dust repeatedly, inflammation results in the nasal passages and eyelids. A person usually complains of itching at the corners of the eyes, sneezing, and sometimes coughing and difficulty in breathing. Over 60 percent of allergy patients respond well to treatment with antihistamines.

Poison Ivy and Poison Oak

During the spring and summer months some people find that their skin is sensitive to poison ivy or poison oak plants which grow wild in wooded areas. Material from the leaves which contacts the skin tends to cause an itchy, red rash which is quite uncomfortable for five or more days, and which may require consultation with a doctor in some cases. Learn to recognize the plants and avoid them. Cover your arms and legs when walking in the woods, and afterwards wash your face and hands with soap and warm water as soon as possible.

Practice 1

Practice this conversation:

Ron: You're sneezing. What's the matter, do you have a cold?
Judy: Well, I guess so. It started a couple of days ago and at first I thought it was an allergy. Now I'm beginning to wonder. It feels more like a cold.
Ron: Why? Does your head hurt? Are you feeling tired?
Judy: Yeah, I've been feeling really run-down lately. I feel achy and I've got a stiff neck. Too much work and too many late nights, I guess.
Ron: That's a myth—you've just caught a virus, that's all. My mother would tell you to go to bed and stay there, but I don't think that makes any difference.
Judy: Well, I can't stay in bed, anyway. My paper is due tomorrow.

Poison Oak

Practice 2

The most common phrases to describe pain or discomfort are these:

I have a _____ ache. (for example, stomachache, headache, earache, toothache, backache)

My _____ hurts. (stomach, arm, leg, foot, thumb, ear, jaw)

I have a sore _____ . My _____ is sore.

(throat, knee, ankle, toe, wrist)

Use the above expressions when appropriate for the following:

1. Describe how you might feel after a particularly rough game of soccer.
2. Describe how you might feel after spending four or five hours on an airplane reading in poor light.
3. Describe how your friend felt after spending an "all-nighter" studying for an exam.
4. Karen has the flu. Describe how she feels to one of your classmates.
5. Douglas fell off his bicycle. Describe how he looks and feels to one of your classmates.
6. Robert went walking in the woods and thinks he may have contracted poison ivy. What are his symptoms?

Practice 3

Read and discuss the following article in class.

Flu Gets Us All, Eventually

This winter, the National Center for Disease Control in Atlanta reported flu outbreaks in 34 states, most recently in New England, the South Atlantic and the West Coast.

But this year, as in every flu year, there are those who don't get sick at all.

Are there really people who always escape? The answer is: "no." Not everyone gets the flu every time it strikes, true. But what's equally true is that not everyone who has the flu knows he has it.

"Sooner or later, over the period of years," says New York City's First Deputy Commissioner of the Department of Health, Dr. Pascal J. Imperato, "everybody gets flu in some form, unless he's been immunized with a vaccine that happens to work."

The reason some people think they can't get the flu: flu can be a fooler. It can cause chills, fever, sore throat, headache, muscle aches; or such a mild illness that victims think they have a cold, or mild bronchitis. Or it may produce no symptoms at all.

The telltale sign of infection is the presence in the blood of antibodies, the specific proteins produced by the body to defend against specific invading organisms, such as viruses. Dr. Edwin D. Kilbourne of the Mount Sinai School of Medicine in New York says, "You can do antibody studies before and after a flu epidemic and show that 60 or 70 per cent of the subjects were infected, but not all had any illness." In such a group could be those who claim they never get flu.

Contact with people who have the flu matters. Their coughing and sneezing transmits flu viruses through the air, though the dose varies with distance and direction, and not all doses are infectious. Recently, Dr. J. Owen Hendley of the University of Virginia Medical School found that rhino-viruses, the major cause of upper respiratory infections, such as the common cold, are actually found more frequently on an infected person's hands than in his sneeze.

They survive three hours on any non-porous surface he touches (a glass, for example), and can be picked up by another person who can then give himself an infection by touching his now contaminated finger to his eye or nose. Flu viruses, some scientists suggest, may be transmitted the same way.

What's called host resistance counts, too. General good health is known to favor antibody production, and so resistance to viral infections.

Does stress impede it? "I think probably it does," says Dr. Kilbourne. "But investigators have worked like hell to prove it without yet producing much evidence. They've chilled, fatigued, shouted at and otherwise abused volunteers before and after inoculating them with viruses, but found no significant difference in disease incidence. Yet we know that in people under physical or emotional stress many things happen that should interfere with antibody response." Among the physical changes produced by stress situations are ups and downs in the secretion of adrenalin and other hormones. Since the rate of hormone secretion is known to affect the metabolism, it's therefore assumed to affect antibody response.

New and Puzzling Data

New and puzzling data comes from Drs. Arnold Monto and Betty Ullman of the University of Michigan. They have found that the incidence of flu and other respiratory illnesses increases as educational level increases, and also as income level decreases. Income level generally goes up with educational level. But the Michigan results imply that to have the lowest frequency of respiratory illness one should be poorly educated but have high income. A particularly unhappy combination would be to be highly educated and have low income. Why? Drs. Monto and Ullman aren't sure.

There is better news, though, on the vaccine front.

Finally, after years during which flu viruses have driven vaccine scientists to distraction, yes. (sic) Vaccines use a weak type of a specific virus to stimulate antibody protection and so resistance to the "wild" or stronger type of that virus. But antibodies for one kind of virus are powerless against another. Flu viruses not only come in three major classes, A, B, and C (B is causing this year's outbreak). They have an uncanny survival mechanism: they mutate, or recombine into new forms. Every few years a new strain turns up, and scientists rush to produce a specific vaccine.

After years of research, workers at Mount Sinai, the National Institute of Health, University of Michigan and elsewhere have finally been able to turn the viruses' unique ability to mutate to use. By introducing different strains simultaneously into the same cultured cells to encourage recombinations, they've produced temperature-sensitive viruses that grow well only between 90 and 97 degrees Fahrenheit. Wild flu viruses flourish between 90 and 103 degrees. The new viruses can be simply sprayed or dropped into the nose (temperature, 90–94) where they can grow and stimulate antibody production locally, but can't survive and possibly cause trouble in the lungs (temperature, 98.6).

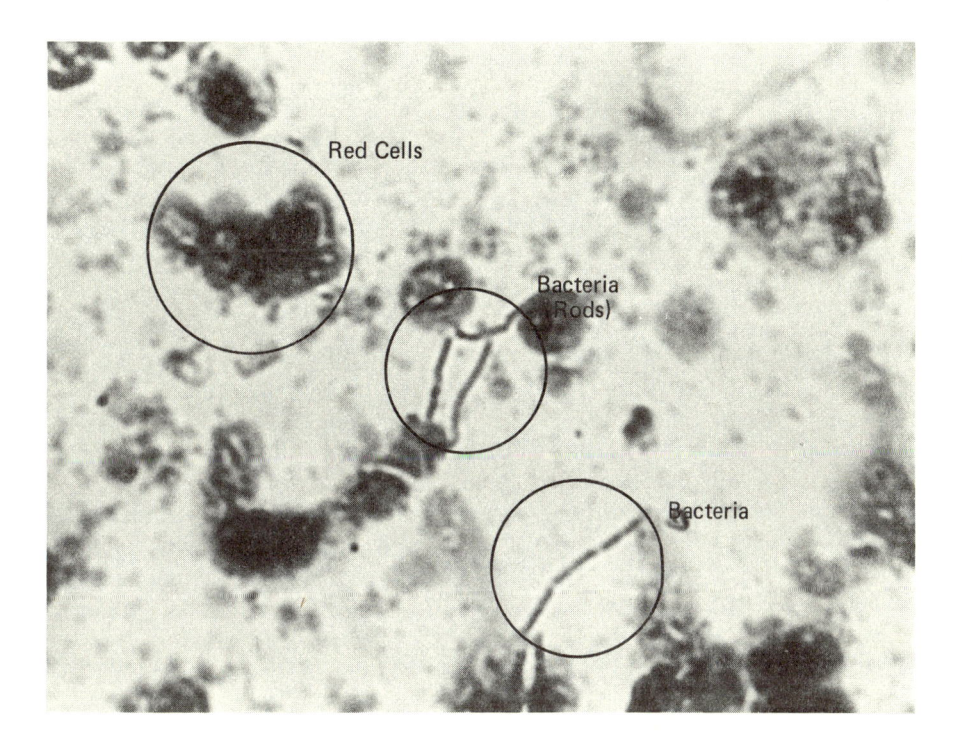

Early this year, researchers at the University of Michigan, for example, reported the successful combination of the new viruses with the Hong Kong 1968 and London flu viruses, and prototypes of vaccines that appear effective against both types of flu.

Field tests are now under way. If they are successful, vaccine-producing techniques will finally have been proven to be as shifty as the viruses themselves. And the day when, in reality, nobody gets the flu could be at hand.[6]

Practice 4

Some of the vocabulary in this lesson may be new to you. See how many of the following words you already know by matching the word with its definition. Look up the words you don't know in a dictionary or ask a friend. Check your answers in class.

[6]By Lawrence Galton. Copyright 1974 by The New York Times Company. Reprinted by permission. March 24, 1974.

1. cough
2. immunize
3. interfere
4. turn up
5. sore
6. infected
7. mild

8. abuse
9. shout at
10. strike
11. claim

12. drive to distraction
13. shifty
14. stress (noun)
15. chills
16. survive

a. not strong or sharp
b. hit, affect a group or population
c. shows up, reveals itself; is revealed
d. treat badly, mistreat, hurt
e. confuse, mix up or upset someone
f. yell at
g. feeling of coldness which may be accompanied by shivering
h. live
i. pressure
j. state as a fact; say
k. a sharp, short noise made when pushing air out of the lungs
l. changeable, tricky
m. give the ability to resist disease
n. contaminated with disease germs
o. clash, enter into someone else's affairs
p. painful, sensitive, tender

Practice 5

Discussion topics:

1. According to the article, "Flu Gets Us All, Eventually," what is the best way to avoid getting the flu?
2. According to the article, what kinds of research have been done so far on flu?
3. For what reasons do you agree or disagree with Galton's conclusion?

Practice 6

Discuss health problems using these questions and the words below as starting points:

1. What is _____ ?
2. How serious is it in your country?
3. How is it treated in your country?

the common cold   mumps   arthritis   mononucleosis (mono)
a headache   cancer   tuberculosis (TB)   tonsillitis
an allergy   heart disease   venereal disease (VD)   smallpox
poison ivy   a stroke   pneumonia   cholera
obesity   emphysema   chicken pox   strep throat
diarrhea   a nervous breakdown   acne

Practice 7

Look for a current newspaper or magazine article about health or nutrition. Present a summary of the article to your classmates.

3.5 INSURANCE

There are numerous types of insurance. Those which you will be most concerned with are medical, automobile, and renters' insurance. Renters' insurance protects a person's property in case of theft or fire. Automobile insurance is essential if you buy a car; in many states you are required by law to have liability insurance if you own a car. It is important to shop around carefully for car insurance, to compare *rates* and types of *coverage,* and not to be pressured by an ambitious *agent* who wants to make a "quick sale." Your age, the make and model of car, and where you live are some of the factors that will affect the rate you have to pay.

Medical insurance is an absolute *must,* particularly if you have *dependents.* Only you, the student, are entitled to free medical care at the student health center, and this care does not extend to long hospital stays or serious illness. Thus, it is extremely important to select a health insurance plan to cover you and your family's medical needs. One common plan for coverage in case of illness or serious injury is called a *major medical plan.* Generally such *policies* contain a *"deductible clause,"* usually about $50.00, which means that you would pay the first $50 of your medical bills for a given year. Other plans have 100 percent coverage but require the *policyholder* to use medical facilities operated by the company.

A health plan has many *benefits,* but there are also things that are excluded; for example, eye and dental care are generally not covered. It is up to you to read the *terms* or *provisions* of an *insurance contract* carefully so that you know what is and is not covered. If you or your family become ill, and the services rendered by a doctor or hospital are covered in your contract, you will need to *file a claim* with the company.

In general, when you have decided what insurance to get and have applied for it, you will receive a full contract and a *premium notice,* and be notified of your *effective date of coverage.* When the expiration date of your policy is near, you will be given an opportunity to *renew* your policy and will be told of any change in the premium rates for the following period.

Remember—if you buy a car, you must buy auto insurance. More important, everyone needs medical insurance. You may feel that health insurance is expensive—but even *one* day in a hospital costs more than $100. It is important to be prepared in case something happens.

Insurance Terms	Explanation
an agent	A sales representative of an insurance company. Generally medical insurance companies do not have agents but have large centrally located offices which are staffed by people who can give you information about insurance policies and answer questions.
benefits	Amounts that the company will pay if you have an accident that is covered by your policy.
a contract	A legal document. By taking out an insurance policy, you agree to the terms of a contract.
coverage	The conditions for which benefits may be paid; for example, $35,000 liability coverage means that that amount is the maximum a company would pay for personal injury and property damage. Medical coverage may also include a maximum on time, for example, 100 days of hospitalization in a year.
to cover the cost	(The company) pays for the total expense of the policyholder's claim.
a deductible clause	A statement in a contract which sets an initial amount to be paid by the policyholder before the company pays the remaining costs.
dependents	Generally one's spouse (husband or wife) and children. Some medical plans have different benefits for the principal policyholder and for dependents.
effective date	The beginning date of a policy.
exclusions	Conditions which the company will *not* cover.
to file a claim	To submit an application for payment, including bills, receipts, and other evidence of costs to be paid by the company, within the terms of the contract. A hospital or doctor's office always asks for your insurance card or policy number so that a claim can be completed.
an insurance policy	Insurance contract with a statement of the benefits and the cost.
liability	Responsibility for another person's injury or property damage when you are at fault.
a major medical plan	Also may be called "extended plan"—a plan which covers infrequent but possible conditions such as injury and illness, which require a doctor's care and/or hospitalization.

a policyholder	The person who takes out the insurance policy (who agrees to the contract).
a premium	The partial or total amount paid for an insurance policy, for example, a monthly premium, a semiannual premium, an annual premium.
provisions (terms)	The exact specifications in a contract regarding benefits, exclusions, and compensation by the company.
rate	The amount you must pay for the insurance, generally an annual rate divided into three or four payments.
renters' insurance	A policy that protects against loss of property in case of a robbery or a fire; the minimum coverage is $4000, which costs $60 or more per year.
to renew	To sign up for another period of time with the same policy in the same company. If you choose to discontinue your policy, you *cancel* it.

Practice 1

On the following pages is an advertising letter like those sent to students on college campuses. Fill in the blanks with items from the list below. Use each term only once. One word is not used.

agent	dependents	policy
benefits	exclusions	policyholder
coverage	effective date	premium
covered	claim	rates
deductible	major medical	

CAMPUS INSURANCE, INC.
P.O. Box 3550
Chicago, Illinois 60651

New Students September 10, 1977
Central University
Barnesville, Illinois 62980

Dear Student:

Don't delay! Hospital costs are going up, up, up––and now is the time to be sure you and your family are adequately _____ in case a medical problem arises.

Let us tell you about our plan for students, the A100 plan. Under the A100 _____ plan, you as policyholder would have 100% _____ including up to 100 days of hospitalization; in addition your _____ would have 80-90% coverage, depending on the type of conditions. (Please read the attached brochure for a list of _____ and a partial list of _____.) This coverage applies after an initial _____ amount has been paid. All this for less than $400 a year!

We invite you to compare our _____ with others, to talk to your friends, and to come to a decision with care. We think you'll agree that we offer a plan that is adequate for <u>your</u> needs, at a _____ you can afford to pay.

As a special bonus to early subscribers, we will give you an additional thirty days' grace before you have to make your first payment. Yet the _____ of coverage will be the day we receive your application in the mail. With our new computerized system, we can process your application within forty-eight hours; the same system can efficiently process any _____ that you file as well.

No _____ will call. We urge you to give our plan your full consideration and to act before the deadline printed below. Simply fill out the enclosed form and drop it in the mail. That's all there is to it. In a few days you will receive your _____ .

Protect yourself and your loved ones—you will be glad you joined the A100 plan.

Sincerely yours,
William Jackman
William Jackman, Agent

Practice 2

In class, explain what type of coverage you need in the United States and which policy you have bought or plan to buy. For more information on insurance policies, read a consumer publication such as *Consumer Report*.

Practice 3

In class, explain what type of insurance people usually have in your country. Include cost, benefits, and exclusions.

3.6 NEWSPAPER LANGUAGE

Headlines

To save space, newspapers abbreviate article titles and use short terms which are understandable to native speakers, but which may be unfamiliar to non-native speakers. Understanding these conventions will help to make newspaper headlines more comprehensible.

The passive voice is used without the appropriate form of *be*. Because of this deletion, the tense of the verb is often not clear in the headline. To avoid thinking that the object is the agent, the reader has to supply the missing form:

PG&E Granted Rate Increase	(PG&E has been granted a rate increase.)
3 Freed in Diner Shooting	(Three people involved in a shooting at a small restaurant were released.)

For a more complete description of passive constructions, see the lesson on passives on pages 58–67.

PG&E Granted Rate Increase

Broker-Loan Rates Boosted by Chase, Morgan Guaranty

Cattle Sales Off Drastically in Cal.

Royals eye a throne *

Dinner to Bar Some Reporters

Abreast of the Market

Dams Linked to Quakes

Eastern Air Posts Loss for February, 2nd Month in a Row

Boycott Urged To Protest Seal Slaughter

FHA to push * **farm housing**

Flimsy Excuses Cause Blood Donation Lag

Meat Boycotters Vow to Persist

Continental Airlines Slips Into Red; 10% Cost Hike Blamed

Power bills spark revolt *

Port Delays Blamed on City

Nevada Will Crack Down on Pushers

FCC to Study Complaints Alleging Airwave Pollution

3 Freed In Diner Shooting

PROBE OF LAND SALE ASKED

Headlines from the following American newspapers reprinted by permission: *The Los Angeles Times, The San Francisco Sunday Chronicle and Examiner, The Wall Street Journal,* and *The Christian Science Monitor.*

FREQUENTLY USED WORD GROUPS

To + verb represents the future tense, "is going to":

Dinner to Bar Some Reporters	(is going to bar)
FCC to Study Complaints	(is going to study)
FHA to Push Farm Housing	(is going to push)

Articles are often deleted:

Boycott Urged	(a boycott)
Probe of Land Sale Asked	(a probe, a land sale)
Power Bills Spark Revolt	(a revolt)

The following verbs and related nouns are frequently used:

to bar	prohibit, prevent
to boost, a boost	increase, support
to eye	look at eagerly, as an objective, or to investigate
to hike, a hike	increase, especially in costs
to lag, a lag	delay, slow down
to be off	decrease, appear less than expected
to probe, a probe	investigate
to push, a push	encourage, support, exert pressure
to seek, sought	look for, try to obtain
to slash	reduce, cut to an extreme degree
to spark, a spark	cause, initiate, like the beginning of a fire
to urge	insist, strongly encourage or request
to vow, a vow	promise in a formal sense

Notice how the conventions are employed in the following headlines. Cover the right column with your hand; try to understand the headline before you read the explanation.

Dams Linked to Quakes	(Dams have been causally associated with earthquakes.)
Cattle Sales Off Drastically in California	(There is presently a marked and significant decrease in the volume of sales of cattle in California.)
Continental Airlines Slips into Red; 10% Cost Hike Blamed	(Continental Airlines is losing money; analysts attribute the loss to a ten percent increase in costs.)
Probe of Land Sale Asked	(Someone has requested an investigation of a land sale.)
Meat Boycotters Vow to Persist	(The people who are refusing to buy meat promise to continue their organized protest.)

3 Freed in Diner Shooting	(Three people who have been accused of involvement in a shooting at a small restaurant were released.)
Flimsy Excuses Cause Blood Donation Lag	(Insubstantial claims or reasons are creating a delay or decrease in the amount of blood given by volunteers.)
Dinner to Bar Some Reporters	(A group planning a banquet will prohibit the attendance of some news reporters.)
FCC to Study Complaints Alleging Airwave Pollution	(The Federal Communications Commission is going to analyze complaints which charge that radio and TV stations broadcast poor quality programs.)
Broker-Loan Rates Boosted by Chase, Morgan Guaranty	(Interest rates for broker loans have been increased by Chase Manhattan Bank and the Morgan Guaranty.)
Port Delays Blamed on City	(Some people are charging the city government with responsibility for lack of progress in changing or modernizing its facilities for ships in the harbor.)
FHA to Push Farm Housing	(The Farmers Home Administration is going to put pressure on for more money to construct houses for farm laborers.)
Eastern Air Posts Loss for February, 2nd Month in a Row	(Eastern Airlines announced that it lost money in February for the second consecutive month.)
Boycott Urged to Protest Seal Slaughter	(A group strongly recommends that the public stop buying seal skins in order to stop the killing of seals.)
Nevada Will Crack Down on Pushers	(The Nevada state government plans to enforce its narcotic laws more effectively, putting more pressure on narcotics sellers.)
Abreast of the Market	(Keeping informed about the current situation in the stock market.)

Power Bills Spark Revolt	(Recent high utility bills are causing homeowners to protest and sometimes to refuse to pay.)
PG&E Granted Rate Increase	(The utilities commission has decided to allow Pacific Gas & Electric Company to raise its charges for utilities services.)
Royals Eye a Throne	(The Kansas City Royals baseball team hopes to win the championship this year.)

Practice 1

Write explanations for these fictitious headlines:

1. Boycott Blamed for Sales Dropoff
2. Flimsy Excuses Bar Environmental Protection
3. Jail Budget Slashed; Pushers Freed
4. Probe of Interest Rate Hike Urged
5. FCC Vows to Crack Down on TV Profanity
6. Shortages Spark Imports; Govt to Push Production

Practice 2

Choose two or more headlines from a newspaper you read. Explain them to the class if possible; ask for explanations if you cannot understand them.

Vocabulary in News Articles

There are many verbs which express meanings closely related to the verb *to say*. Notice the use of the underlined verbs in the following paragraph:

Speculation about both political parties' nominees for president in the next election begins almost as soon as the current president takes office. Once in a while a major candidate <u>declares</u> his intention to seek nomination, but often a major contender <u>maintains</u> that he has no plans beyond his present position, waiting to be "drafted" by his party. In fact, a prospective candidate is usually careful about <u>mentioning</u> the future because newsmen will <u>report</u> any suggestion that he is "testing the waters," whether or not he has shown clear intent. If he <u>alleges</u> that the incumbent has failed the voters in one way or another, he can be sure that the media will comment on his criticism and <u>remark</u> that he is showing more and more interest in the office. Naturally, the incumbent will <u>claim</u> that his record demonstrates what a responsible and effective leader he has been. As the campaign progresses, investigative reporters and columnists may try to divulge little-known facts from the candidate's past. To say the least, a well-known politician does not have to disclose his plans to be in the public eye; the public is constantly watching him.

to allege	express the fact that a person has been accused by someone, but not by the writer because he has no proof
to assert	state with confidence, but possibly without proof
to claim	assert, state with confidence, defend
to comment	interpret, illustrate, observe; may be subjective or objective
to declare	express formally, state publicly
to disclose	announce something that was private; used in politics, and on the society pages to announce a couple's engagement
to divulge	tell a secret, often something surprising; suggests intimate knowledge of the situation
to maintain	claim, insist; defend in argument; subjective
to mention	express casually, without emphasis; to refer to something incidentally
to remark	express a brief casual observation, usually spontaneous
to report	give a factual account; objective
to state	express clearly, definitely

When reporters refer to their sources of information, they often use phrases that indicate which type of report it is. Jack Anderson's famous syndicated column, "Merry-Go-Round," often contains such phrases in order to avoid naming confidential sources.

direct quotation	the official has given the reporter permission to repeat his exact words
paraphrasing	the official has told the reporter to re-word the information
"a reliable official" "a government spokesman" "persons close to the president"	all of these mean that the official did not allow any name to be used, but quotations may be used
"informed sources" "off the record"	the official asked the reporter to promise not to reveal the story, or at least not to reveal the source

Practice 3

Be prepared to explain the meaning of these sentences in class:

1. Federal prosecutors now have evidence linking Johnston and Fredrickson to illegal activities, sources close to the investigation have disclosed.
2. Informed sources reported that the president has decided to reorganize his executive staff.
3. Despite growing charges against the director, his staff maintains that he is innocent.
4. When he came home he remarked that there had been a fair turnout at the reception.
5. Matthew's administrative assistant commented that his superior has genuine convictions, but little political clout.

Practice 4

During the next two weeks, find five examples of newspaper vocabulary in American papers or magazines; write a short explanation of each sentence.

3.7 USEFUL ABBREVIATIONS AND ACRONYMS

International Agencies

EEC	European Economic Community
FAO	Food and Agriculture Organization
IDA	International Development Association (a World Bank agency)
IIE	Institute of International Education
IMF	International Monetary Fund
NATO	North Atlantic Treaty Organization
OAS	Organization of American States
OPEC	Organization of Petroleum Exporting Countries
SEATO	Southeast Asia Treaty Organization
UNESCO	United Nations Educational, Scientific, & Cultural Organization
UNICEF	United Nations Children's Fund
WHO	World Health Organization

United States Government

AID	Agency for International Development
CIA	Central Intelligence Agency
ERDA	Energy Research and Development Agency
EPA	Environmental Protection Agency
FAA	Federal Aviation Agency
FBI	Federal Bureau of Investigation

FCC	Federal Communications Commission
FTC	Federal Trade Commission
FDA	Food and Drug Administration
HEW	Department of Health, Education, and Welfare
IRS	Internal Revenue Service (tax office)
NASA	National Aeronautics and Space Administration
NIH	National Institute of Health
NSF	National Science Foundation
NTIS	National Technical Information Service
SEC	Securities and Exchange Commission

Labor Unions

AFT	American Federation of Teachers
AFL-CIO	American Federation of Labor–Congress of Industrial Organizations
UAW	United Auto Workers
UFW	United Farm Workers

Mass Communication

AP	Associated Press
UPI	United Press International
ABC	American Broadcasting Company
CBS	Columbia Broadcasting System
NBC	National Broadcasting Company
PBS	Public Broadcasting System

General

TGIF	Thank God It's Friday!
AAA	American Automobile Association (Triple A)
AAUP	American Association of University Professors
ACLU	American Civil Liberties Union
ERIC	Educational Resources Information Center
PTA	Parent Teacher Association
AA	Alcoholics Anonymous

3.8 POLITICS AND GOVERNMENT

Students who are interested in learning more about United States politics and government need to become familiar with basic terms before doing extensive reading. This lesson provides three passages for study and discussion, some suggestions for practice, and a glossary of terms you can refer to as you read more about politics and government.

Levels of Government in the United States

Students all over the world have studied the balance of power among the three branches of the national government of the United States: the executive, the legislative, and the judicial. What has been studied less, but what has been discussed more by the United States public, is the balance of power among the various levels of government from national to local. The following chart shows official titles on the various levels; there is a great deal of regional variation in the titles of local officials and governing bodies.

	Federal	*State*	*County*	*City*
Executive	President	Governor	Board of Supervisors	Mayor
Legislative	Congress	Legislature		City Council
Judicial	U.S. Supreme Court; Federal Courts	State Supreme Courts	Superior Courts	Municipal Courts

The Constitution of the United States limits the powers of the federal government to regulation of foreign affairs and interstate activity. State and local governments have powers and responsibilities concerning everyday affairs, including intra-state business, law enforcement, transportation, education, labor, and public welfare. Since the Civil War (1861–65), the U.S. Supreme Court has interpreted the Constitution to give power to the federal government to assume national control in state and local matters which affect all U.S. citizens. Thus, in the twentieth century the original decentralization of control has gradually given way to greater federal authority in some areas, particularly transportation, civil rights, education, and welfare.

Transportation. Each state has its own system of highways, supported by state tax dollars. In recent years, with construction of superhighways costing over a million dollars per mile, states have asked the federal government to share the cost, and more and more highways have been federally funded. The federal government has also supported research and development of high-speed mass transit systems.

Air transportation has come under the jurisdiction of federal agencies as well. Airplane safety is supervised by the Federal Aviation Agency (FAA), and airport security inspection is regulated by the federal government.

Transportation has become such a national concern that the Department of Transportation was established (in 1966) as a major department of the federal administration. The secretary of transportation is a member of the president's cabinet.

Civil Rights, Education, and Welfare. The federal Civil Rights Act of 1964 guarantees certain individual rights to all citizens, regardless of race or belief. Federal enforcement of this act has led to greater uniformity in voting eligibility and educational opportunity.

Traditionally, educational structure, curricula, and budgets have been determined by each state, and there has been considerable resistance to federal involvement in public or private education. At the same time, however, individuals at schools on every level have applied for funds from the federal government for pilot programs and research. This federal grant money is a substantial source of support for graduate students.

In 1953 the Department of Health, Education, and Welfare was added to the administration. Since that time it has grown tremendously in power and influence, with particular emphasis on help for the disadvantaged, for minority groups, and for the aged.

Recently a revenue-sharing program was established to allocate federal tax money to local areas, providing funds for local projects under local control. It is an attempt to put a greater amount of control over spending in the hands of local governments.

Some people argue that the federal government has assumed too much control over everyday affairs, while others argue that only the federal level can administer necessary programs equally.

Practice 1

Compare and contrast the degree of centralization of power in the United States with that in your own country.

A Timetable for the Presidential Election. A United States president serves a four-year term and may be reelected to a second term. Elections are held during leap years: 1976, 1980, 1984, 1988, 1992, 1996. As you can see in Table 1, the presidential campaign and election are spread over a year's time.

The Declaration of Candidacy. Each person who wants to enter the campaign has to file his intention and his political party for each state primary in which he wants to compete.

The Primary Elections. Some states have elections in which voters in each political party indicate their preference for candidates; the types and dates of primary elections differ from state to state, but they are generally held sometime between February and June.

The Nominating Conventions. Each political party has a week-long convention during which representatives from each state nominate a pres-

Table 1

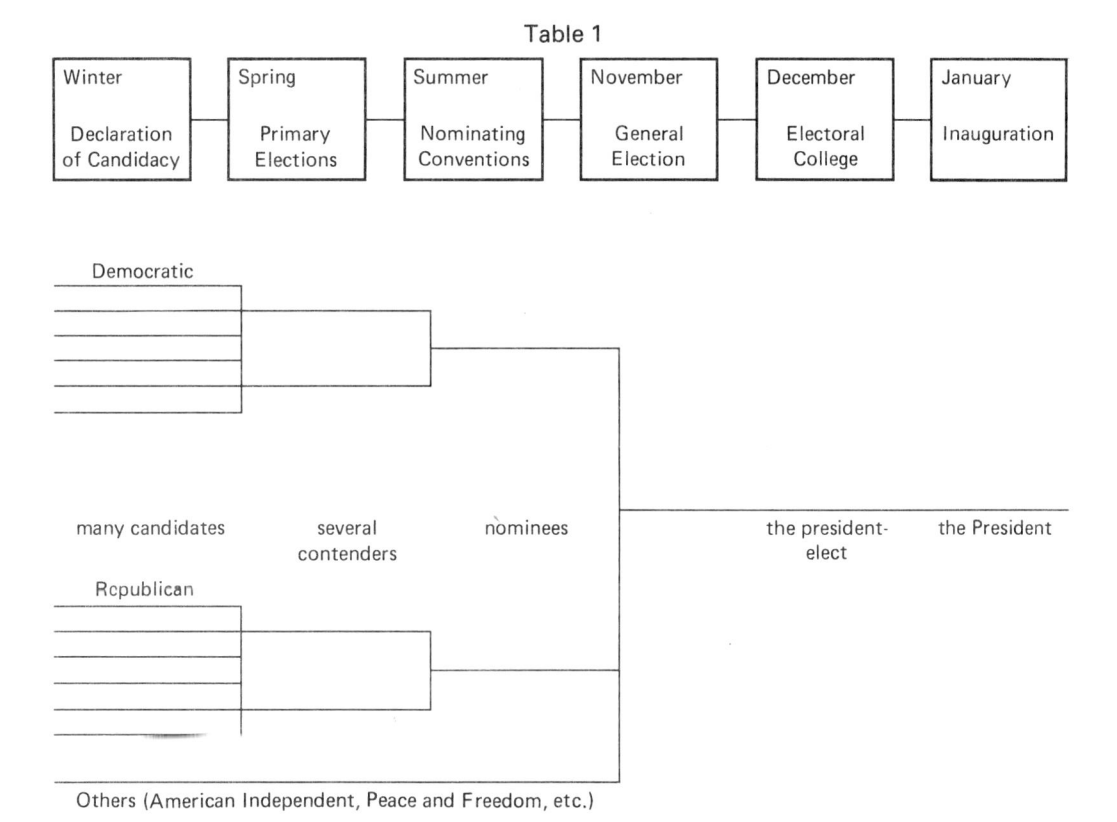

Winter	Spring	Summer	November	December	January
Declaration of Candidacy	Primary Elections	Nominating Conventions	General Election	Electoral College	Inauguration

Democratic

Republican

many candidates — several contenders — nominees — the president-elect — the President

Others (American Independent, Peace and Freedom, etc.)

idential and a vice-presidential candidate and write a party platform as well.

The General Election. On the first Tuesday in November, all registered voters may go to the polls and mark their choices on the ballot. The ballot states that the voters want their state's electors to vote for the candidates of their choice.

The Electoral College. In December the official votes of the state electors are counted. This is usually only a ceremony; however, if no candidate receives a majority, the House of Representatives has to determine the winner.

The Inauguration. On January 20, the new president takes the Oath of Office and begins his four-year term.

A United States Senator. As you read the following passage about a former United States senator, consult the Glossary of Political Terms (section 3.9) and a dictionary.

The Defeat of a Senator

May 1974 marked the virtual end of the thirty-two year congressional career of Senator J. William Fulbright. Although known internationally, Senator Fulbright was defeated in his home state by a fellow Democrat, just as the polls had predicted several months before.

To understand Fulbright's role more clearly, it is necessary to understand the committee structure in Congress. Within Congress and state legislatures, much of the preliminary legislative work is done in committees governed by seniority; committee chairmen wield a tremendous amount of power by screening what will be debated by the committee, and by determining when measures will reach the main floor for a vote. As chairman of the Senate Foreign Relations Committee for fifteen years, Fulbright was a powerful figure in foreign affairs, often voicing dissent against administration policy. A liberal Democrat, Fulbright often expressed distinctly nonpartisan views, as in the case of his criticism of Democrat Lyndon Johnson's Vietnam policy. He continually questioned U.S. foreign involvement and foreign aid, so much so that he was called an isolationist. Well-known for his role in the Senate hearings on the Vietnam war—hearings which influenced U.S. public opinion—he is probably best known for his sponsorship of the bill to authorize international fellowships, later called the Fulbright-Hays Act.

In the United States political system, candidates within a party first compete against each other for their party's nomination. The first election is called a primary and is held in each state five months or more before the general election; the winners in each party face each other on the November ballot. Senators serve six-year terms, staggered so that only one-third are up for reelection each two years. The man who challenged Fulbright's bid for reelection was Dale Bumpers, the young moderate-to-liberal governor of Arkansas, whom Fulbright had endorsed in the 1970 campaign for the Arkansas governorship. The two differed on relatively few issues.

Given the above, it might seem improbable that Fulbright would be defeated. His defeat was caused by several factors. One was his record of "no" votes on civil-rights legislation. Another was his age. Quite important in his state was the public's feeling that he had grown "aloof," that the only time he paid attention to his home state was during his campaign once every six years, and that he no longer maintained an official residence in Arkansas. Some analysts feel that the most important factor was a general dissatisfaction with elected officials in Washington. Many incumbents were defeated in the 1974 elections.

In an editorial following the primary, *The Christian Science Monitor* stated that although it had often disagreed with Fulbright, it recognized the value of "articulate dissent" and respected him as a "thorny independent citizen."[7] Using the occasion of Fulbright's defeat for editorial com-

---

[7]*The Christian Science Monitor,* Vol. 66, No. 130 (30 May 1974), p. F8.

ment, the *Monitor* suggested that the United States develop some means of utilizing the talents of elder statesmen, so that the country could continue to benefit from their expertise whether or not they were members of Congress. Fulbright decided to devote one of his early post-congressional years to international education, traveling abroad as a special representative of the Institute of International Education.

Practice 2

Read a news article about a political figure and explain it to the class.

Practice 3

Discussion topics:

1. Compare the campaign and election procedures in various countries.
2. Discuss the roles of women and men in politics.
3. Discuss the relationship between business and government.

3.9 GLOSSARY OF POLITICAL TERMS

The following is a list of terms frequently used in discussions about elections and government. Do not attempt to learn every word. Use this as a reference when you read newspapers and magazines.

Verbs	*Definitions*
to appropriate	to set aside for a particular purpose; synonym of *allocate*
to campaign	to attempt to get votes through publicity and public appearances
to concede	to publicly admit defeat in an election, usually "to concede defeat" or "to concede the election"
to convene	to begin a legislative session
to draft a proposal	to write a piece of legislation
to draft someone	to gather support for a person and ask him or her to be a candidate
to drum up support	to attract, seek, get interest by campaigning
to enact	to make a law; to pass through a legislature a bill which then becomes a law
to endorse	to announce support for a candidate or a bill
to lobby	to try to persuade legislators to vote for a bill by legal persuasion of many types
to override	to oppose and counteract a request or an objection; specifically, Congress has the power to override a presidential veto

to pay off	1. to bribe; 2. to get the desired effect from a lot of effort—"Spending all that time really paid off in benefits."
to reform	to change, remove the corrupt and bad; cleanse, improve
to repeal	to withdraw, revoke, call back a law that was passed, annul, nullify
to run for office	to campaign for election
to sponsor a bill	to propose, support a new piece of legislation
to veto	to refuse to sign a bill which has passed in the legislative branch; the executive's power to stop legislation which he opposes

Nouns	*Definitions*
accountability	judgment of responsible performance by an official or employee (to be held accountable)
an act	a bill which has become law
the administration	the executive branch under each president, for example, the Ford administration
a backer	a supporter, especially a financial supporter
a ballot	a voting sheet, a list of candidates on which a voter indicates his choice
a bid for nomination	a declaration and attempt to be nominated
a bill	a proposed law, a piece of legislation from the time it is proposed until it becomes a law or is defeated
a caucus	a political party meeting, usually to set policy or choose a new candidate or nominee
civil rights	a person's individual rights, such as those listed in the Bill of Rights; often used in the same way as "equal rights"
a compromise	a decision in which each opposing party gives up part of its demands; meeting halfway
conflict of interest	the position of having interest in both sides of an issue; often refers to a politician whose business would benefit from a political decision
a congressional hearing	an investigative meeting in which many people tell what they think, held to gather information for a later trial in court or for later legislation in Congress
a contender	a person running for office, competing for a position
a dark horse	a person running for office who isn't well known or whose chances are not considered

	good, but who may surprise everyone and become very popular.
a frontrunner	the candidate who has the most support at a particular time, either early in the campaign, or immediately before the election
inauguration	the ceremony in which an executive accepts office, promises to serve honestly and faithfully, and makes his opening speech
incumbent	the person who holds an office and is running for reelection
a maverick	a political independent, one who has gone away from allegiance to the major parties, whether or not he is officially listed as a party member
nomination	a party's endorsement of a candidate, the act of choosing a party representative for an election
nominee	the man a party chooses for a particular election
a plank, a platform	an official list of the party's policy for an election, the issues on which it promises to work if elected
politicking	"playing politics," using one's influence
polls	1. the place people vote on election day; neighborhood places where people are assigned to vote, in homes, schools, churches, fire stations, garages, any public or designated private building 2. public opinion surveys
precinct	a local political unit, the neighborhood voting district; an area which consists of people who vote at one or a few polling places
primary	a preliminary election held several months before a general election, in which voters of each party decide who each party's representative will be
a rally	a meeting to show support for a candidate or an issue
a resolution	an agreement, a statement made by a legislative body
seniority	length of time in office
a slate	a party's list of candidates or nominees, sometimes called a ticket, as "a reform ticket"
social service	the agency, office, or bureau which administers welfare and government aid for health
a swearing-in	a ceremony of commitment to carry out the duties of office, a pledge, an inauguration

a task force	a group chosen to investigate or oversee a particular project; in politics, often a panel of citizens, respected and trusted, who will look for a reasonable and equitable solution to a troublesome issue or problem
ways and means	concerns finances, usually the name of the finance committee
a write-in	a person who tries to be elected at the last minute by asking people to write in his name on their ballots; usually not an organized campaign

Adjectives	*Definitions*
ad hoc	formed for a special purpose, may be temporary; for example, an ad hoc committee
eleventh hour	the last possible moment for doing something, usually after long negotiation or deliberation
extremist	politically extreme, far left or far right
leftist	politically left of center, liberal (left-wing)
middle-of-the-road	balancing liberal and conservative views
partisan	referring to political party, for example, a partisan issue, a nonpartisan office
radical	politically extreme, usually leftist
rightist	politically right of center, rightist (right-wing)
top secret	carefully guarded, confidential
underground	relating to secret political movements or nonestablishment "alternative" groups; for example, "the underground press" refers to newspapers of radical groups

3.10 LEGAL VOCABULARY

Law is an area so bound to cultural tradition that it has quite a formal language of its own. Educated Americans know and use hundreds of legal vocabulary items, yet they may have difficulty reading a legal contract or understanding the intricacies of a court proceeding. The legal terms introduced here are words that educated laymen know, the words most often used by law enforcement agencies, by the courts, and by the mass media.

Read this description of American law with the help of a native speaker of English or someone who is familiar with the United States legal system. A glossary containing some of the words in the passage follows; it is intended to serve as a general reference for your future reading of newspapers and magazines.

United States Law

The legal system in the United States originated from the English system of common law, unwritten law in which *precedent* plays an important role. However, as the United States developed, its own system of written statutes and codes evolved. American law is now based on a blend of written legal decisions and of legislation.

There are two types of American law: *civil* law and *criminal* law. Civil law covers *suits* between individuals (companies as well as people are "individuals"). Auto insurance claims, divorces, and fraudulent business practices are examples of matters handled under civil law. Criminal law covers *cases* brought by the state against individuals; criminal offenses range from traffic tickets to major crimes like hijacking and murder. The focus in the rest of this discussion will be on criminal law.

Criminal law is almost entirely under the *jurisdiction* of state governments and therefore differs somewhat from state to state. To get a clearer view of criminal procedure, read through these steps:

Warrants. Except in extreme situations, a policeman must have: (1) a *search warrant* obtained from a judge to search one's home or person for evidence which can be seized and used in court against him; or (2) an *arrest warrant* obtained from a judge, before he can arrest a *suspect* and take him into *custody*. After making an *arrest,* a policeman is required to tell the suspect that the law protects him against *self-incrimination;* the suspect does not have to answer questions and he may request a lawyer (provided at public expense if he cannot afford to hire one himself).

Booking. The official charge against the suspect is entered in the police station's book. When the suspect is *booked,* he is fingerprinted and photographed.

The Preliminary Hearing. In most states if the suspect is held in jail he must be brought before a judge within twenty-four hours. The judge may dismiss the charge, or he may set *bail,* an amount of money paid by the defendant to guarantee that he will appear in court for his trial, or he may release the person on his *own recognizance.* If the bail is paid, the defendant is released.

In the case of traffic tickets (for example, speeding, parking), a person receives a *summons* to appear in court. Before that date he obtains a statement of the bail. If he pays the bail, he is released from the necessity to appear in court, and the violation is added to his driving record. If he chooses not to pay, he must go to traffic court and fight the case.

Grand Jury. For major investigations and crimes the *prosecuting attorney* meets with a panel of citizens (a grand jury) to present his evidence; if

Courtroom scene

the panel feels that there is sufficient evidence of a crime, it votes to *indict* the defendant.

Arraignment. The judge reads the charges brought against the *defendant* and asks whether he *pleads* guilty or not guilty. If he pleads guilty, the judge sets a time for *sentencing*. If the defendant pleads not guilty, he usually asks for a *jury trial*.

Plea Bargaining. Occasionally the prosecutor, the defense lawyer, and the defendant agree that the defendant will plead guilty to a less serious charge than the one he was accused of, in order to avoid being tried for the more serious crime.

The Jury Trial. The prosecutor and the defense counsel present their cases by *examining* and *cross-examining* witnesses who have been *subpoenaed* to appear in court so that they can *testify*. The judge presides and acts as a referee, but the jury is absolutely silent. When both lawyers have finished presenting their cases, the jurors *deliberate* until they reach a *verdict*. In some states their decision must be unanimous.

The Verdict. When the jury has reached a decision, the *foreman* of the jury announces the verdict. If the members cannot agree, the jury is called a *hung jury* and the judge declares a *mistrial;* in that case, the defendant may be tried again by another jury.

Sentencing. If the verdict is "guilty," the person has been *convicted* and the judge sentences him. If the defendant has been found innocent, he is *acquitted*.

Appeal. Occasionally the defense lawyer appeals the judge's ruling to a higher court. The judge of the higher court considers the case and decides either to *uphold* or to reverse the lower court's decision.

The series of steps can become quite complex and time-consuming; it may take several years to complete the sequence for a major case.

Legal-Criminal Vocabulary

General Categories	*Definitions*
petty offenses	minor local crimes such as failing to observe building restrictions or crossing a street in the middle of a block
misdemeanors	minor crimes, including traffic violations, disturbing the peace, indecent exposure
felonies	serious crimes including such crimes as forgery, robbery, and rape

Crimes	*Definitions*
bribery (to bribe)	payment for a business or political favor. The payment is called a bribe.
burglary	breaking into and entering a building for the purpose of committing a crime. The person who breaks in is called a burglar. Colloquial verb: to burglarize
fraud	intentional misrepresentation of fact in order to get someone else's rights or property
hijacking (to hijack)	to steal while in transit, usually to force a pilot to change a plane's destination according to personal wishes
kidnapping (to kidnap)	seizure of a person for money or political demands
murder (to murder)	killing; if the act was premeditated, it is called first degree murder. There are also second- and third-degree murder charges.
rape (to rape)	sexual attack

shoplifting (to shoplift)	stealing items which are for sale in a store

Verbs and Related Nouns	*Definitions*
to accuse (an accusation)	to blame, say that someone is guilty and should be tried
to charge (a charge)	to accuse formally, state the crime for which a person will be tried. Expressions: to bring charges against someone; to drop the charges
to cite (a citation)	to summon to appear in court because of a violation
to defend (defense) (a defense lawyer)	to act on behalf of and support the accused party in court
to dismiss (charges) (dismissal)	to end court proceedings, allowing the defendant to go free
to enter a plea	to state formally that the defendant is guilty or not guilty at the beginning of a trial
to execute (an execution)	to punish by death according to law, or to carry out any court sentence
to give (oneself) up	to surrender to the police voluntarily
to imprison (imprisonment)	to confine a person (jail, penal institution, penitentiary)
to parole (parole)	to release someone from prison or punishment with the condition that he meet certain requirements of social behavior
to plead (a plea)	to argue a case; to declare oneself guilty or not guilty; "Your honor, I plead not guilty."
to preside	to occupy the place of authority in a meeting, as a judge in court or a chairman of a committee
to prosecute (a prosecution) (the prosecuting attorney)	to carry out legal proceedings against a defendant, representing the state or government
to sentence (a sentence)	to pronounce the punishment for a convicted criminal. A sentence may be suspended or may be for a short time, for a range of time (for example, a 1–5 year sentence) or for life.
to set a precedent	to declare a new interpretation of law in a particular case which will affect later cases of the same type
to subpoena (a subpoena)	to order a witness to appear in court to testify
to sue (a suit)	to take court action against; to sue is to file a suit

to take into custody	to arrest
to testify (testimony)	to act as a witness in court, to tell what you know about an event or person
to try (a trial)	to examine judicially to determine guilt or innocence; often used in the passive
to violate (a violation)	to break a law
to withhold evidence	to refuse to give information (illegal)

Practice 1

Fill in the blanks, consulting the preceding glossary.

to accuse	attorney	jury
to arrest	burglary	lawyer
to bribe	case	legal rights
to charge	crime	murder
to convict	defense	sentence
to hijack	evidence	suit
to kidnap	fraud	suspect
to plead	guilty	ticket
to sue	innocent	trial
to testify	jail	verdict
to violate	judge	witness

Twenty of the above words fit in the following situation. Look over the entire selection, then go back and fill in the blanks, consulting the preceding explanation and lists if necessary. Do not use any word more than once. Use verbs in past tense.

A Day to Remember

It was one of those days. I was finally on my way home after serving on a _____ for a week. We had deliberated for six hours that day and finally returned a _____ of " _____ " to the presiding _____ . The defendant had been _____ of the _____ of a jewelry store. Many of the jurors were influenced by the testimony given by the final _____ who was called by the prosecuting _____ .

My mind went back to earlier parts of the _____ : the defendant who _____ not guilty; the policeman who had found the _____ at the scene of the crime, had _____ him, and had taken him to _____ ; the key _____

175

witness who _____ that she had seen someone else leaving the store.

I was thinking about what it meant to be _____ of a crime, facing a three- to five-year _____ in prison, when I heard the siren and saw a red light. A quick glance at the speedometer told me the story: in my hurry to get home I had gone over the speed limit. I pulled over to the side of the road and waited for the _____ I knew was coming. I, too, had _____ the law and, if I chose, would soon have my own opportunity to plead my _____ before a judge.

Practice 2

Compare the situation described in the reading passage below with the situation on your campus. What crimes, if any, are common? What steps have been taken on your campus to reduce crime? What can you as an individual do to reduce the possibility of crime?

Campus Security

A recent report by the campus security division shows that crime is down this year both on campus and in the immediate area near campus. Some felonies are down, which the security director attributes to better lighting on campus and to increased parking lot surveillance at night. However, one type of crime is up. Theft of bicycles, of parking permits, and of items inside cars, such as cassette tape decks and radios, have all shown an increase. Students are advised to lock their cars and bikes securely to reduce the chance of theft. Also, any theft should be reported immediately to a security guard or to the campus security office. In many cases quick action by students has led to the return of stolen property.

Practice 3

Find a newspaper or magazine article which reports an arrest, court proceedings, or an appeal to a higher court. Summarize the situation reported in the article.

Practice 4

Prepare a dialogue or story about an experience you or someone you know has had with the law. Use some of the words from the list in Practice 1.

Practice 5

In class, compare aspects of the American legal system with aspects of the legal system in your country. You may want to ask Americans their views first, or to invite a number of Americans to your class to participate in the discussion. Possible areas to consider are:

1. Divisions of the court system
2. Citizens' rights
3. Procedure by which a person is found guilty or innocent
4. System of punishment for crime
5. Frequency or infrequency of certain crimes
   a. Traffic violations
   b. Other misdemeanors
   c. Business fraud
   d. Consumer deception
   e. Computer crime
   f. Juvenile crime
   g. Political crime

3.11 VERBS EXPRESSING ATTITUDES

This lesson introduces those verbs people use to express emotions and emotional attitudes about other people, ideas or actions. Since these verbs do express attitudes, English speakers choose and use them thoughtfully.

Care of the Aged in the United States

The feeling of individual independence and self-sufficiency is so strong in the United States that often either parents or their grown children choose not to live together. The establishment of the Social Security System in the 1930s and the Medicare program in the 1960s enabled more families to make this decision. Formerly the immediate family had primary responsibility for the care of the aged. In recent years the society as a whole has assumed a greater degree of responsibility. Consider the cases of these two retired persons.

Mr. Rolfe, age 67, is a widower whose wife *passed away* six months ago. Because his health is good, and he has many friends of his own age, he intends to live in his own house. His married daughter lives in another state; although he *misses* her and his grandchildren, he thinks he will be more comfortable in his own home.

Mrs. Taylor, age 72, has been a widow for seven years. After her husband's death she insisted on taking care of herself, so she stayed in her second-floor apartment. Her two married sons and two married daughters, who lived in the same community, *pledged* their financial support and promised to look in on her and make sure that she was all right. After she fell and broke her hip, however, her doctors said that she would not be able to get around very well. Her children, after considerable discussion, *per-*

Elderly people dining at the Aldersley Danish Retirement Home, San Rafael, California.

suaded her to live temporarily in a convalescent hospital rather than offering to have her stay with them on a rotating basis. The whole family *glossed over* the fact that the convalescent hospital might very well become her permanent home.

The decisions in both of these cases resulted from the following feelings and attitudes in the United States:

1. Parents do not like to feel dependent on their children; they *claim* that they do not want to be a burden, even if they would like very much to be with their children.
2. One generation often feels that its style of living is different from another generation's style. The feeling that each family unit should have a separate residence is characteristic. No one wants to *intrude* or be intruded upon. Both parent and child feel that the other's presence would *upset* and change the normal routine.
3. Children often do not feel an equal share of responsibility toward their parents. For example, a brother sometimes feels that his sisters are responsible for physical care of their parents, because he does not want to burden his wife with the care of his parents. One child may *resent* another's reluctance to help, *provoking* misunderstanding and bitterness. Not all of the children may be financially capable of contributing an equal share to the cost of their parents' care.

4. Children usually *rationalize* that the care in a convalescent hospital is better than what they could provide in their homes.

Once the decision is made not to take a parent into the home, children often feel guilty. In fact, they may even dread occasional visits because they *pity* and *identify with* the parent. Seeing old people forces children to realize that they and their children will someday be faced with the same situation.

Practice 1

Match the verbs on the left with the verb phrases underlined in the sentences at the right.

Examples

1. misses __b__
2. claims __a__

a. Although Helen says that she is getting along okay, I think she needs help.
b. Wayne is homesick for his hometown in the country.

1. upset _____
2. provoked _____
3. rationalized _____
4. gloss over _____
5. persuaded _____
6. passed away _____
7. resented _____

a. After John promised to pay his mother $45 a week to help her make ends meet, she felt relieved.
b. Having to make sure that some adult was always home to take care of her mother-in-law disturbed Charlotte's routine.
c. Uninvited, Mrs. Jones moved into her daughter's home. Her son-in-law felt she had forced herself into their lives.
d. Insensitive statements caused a family argument.
e. Bernard could easily imagine himself in his father's situation.
f. Mrs. Adams died two years ago. Mr. Adams tried to cover up his sadness in front of his children.
g. Bill justified putting his mother in an

8. pledge _____   h. Joyce <u>convinced</u> her father that both she and her husband would be happy if he would live with them.

9. intruded upon _____   i. Although he kept it to himself Bruce was <u>displeased and felt angry</u> at his brother's refusal to support their newly widowed mother.

10. identify with _____

Practice 2

In class, discuss the care of the aged in your countries.

An Editorial. The following passage, written in the style of a newspaper editorial, concerns the event reported in this fictitious news article. Reading the news article will help you to understand the editorial more easily.

Two Officials Indicted

BULLETIN—Late yesterday afternoon Daniel Larsen and Raymond Matheson were indicted on charges of bribery and conspiracy. Larsen, 51, 3600 Buchanan Drive, has been a member of the city Planning Commission since 1969. Matheson, 43, 4177 Victoria Avenue, has been Assistant City Manager for a year and a half. The indictments were filed after a two-month investigation of the long delay in the construction of the new city buildings.

Officials Held Accountable

Over the past several months this paper has noted with growing concern the evidence of corruption in our city government.

Yesterday, after the prosecutor had *hedged* and *stalled* for a month, the grand jury indicted two city officials. In accordance with the traditional American principle that one is innocent until proven guilty, we do not intend to *condemn* the men before their trial. However, it is our responsibility to make certain that the implications of the indictment are clear. Both men publicly *scorned* the unions for delaying construction on the new city hall, while at the same time allegedly accepting bribes to *hamper* arbitration efforts.

Naturally, responsible citizens are *outraged* by their alleged actions, but this paper particularly *resents* their attempts to *evade*, to *threaten*, and to *harass* the investigative reporters who were trying to uncover the facts.

Such irresponsible behavior can no longer be *condoned*. Officials must be held accountable for their actions. We *demand* that both Larsen and Matheson be temporarily suspended from their positions of trust for the duration of their trials.

Practice 3

To practice the verbs introduced in the previous passage, substitute a synonym from the list below for each verb cue in parentheses.

condemned	hedged
condoned	outraged
demanded	resented
evaded	scorned
hampered	threatened

A Consumer Protest

Two years ago there were reports of numerous fires caused by electric skillets which had overheated due to faulty temperature controls. A consumer rights group submitted a petition to the industry's Product Safety Board. The group (requested) _____ that the PSB require appliance manufacturers to meet higher fire safety standards. The PSB (avoided) _____ the issue for many months but finally decided to include it on the agenda.

The citizens' group (was insulted by) _____ the decision not to allow them to attend the PSB meeting. The consumers were repeatedly (held back) _____ in their efforts to send even one representative to the PSB session. The board (criticized) _____ the group for its excessive concern with a "small, insignificant problem." The citizens were (shocked) _____ when the board's decision was seven to three against changing the regulations for electric frying pans.

This year the PSB has some new members, and the citizens' group is resubmitting its petition. It hopes that the new, more consumer-oriented members will carefully consider complaints and will vote to require stricter fire safety standards for electric skillets and other small appliances.

Practice 4

Next to each blank in the following sentences, there are two words in parentheses. Choose the word which is appropriate in the context, and write it in the blank.

1. The American Indian has grounds for (resenting, accepting) _____ the "white man" for the treatment of Indian tribes in the United States for the past hundred and fifty years.
2. Congress (caught, pledged) _____ to grant the Indians land, independence, and social services.
3. In too many cases the government has ignored, exploited, and (harassed, demanded) _____ the Indians.
4. Official reports (pass away, gloss over) _____ the poor conditions in which they live.
5. Young Indians are (demanding, persuading) _____ their rights.
6. They (identify with, upset) _____ their heritage and wish to be called Native Americans, since they preceded Europeans in the New World by thousands of years.
7. United States society in general has (functioned, condoned) _____ the poor image of the Native American portrayed in movies, circuses, and amusement parks.
8. Even worse, it has (preferred, evaded) _____ its responsibility to live up to the treaties.
9. Many people give lip service to (pitying, ignoring) _____ the Indian, but do little more than that.
10. Tourists who (assume, intrude on) _____ the people in Indian communities in the Southwest should not be surprised if they are unwelcome.

11. More educational opportunities may (hedge, enable)

    _____ young Native Americans to achieve their own goals.

Practice 5

Have a class debate on this question:
   Should a minority group such as Native American Indians retain its identity or be assimilated by the mainstream society?

3.12 EVALUATIVE VOCABULARY

To develop skill in interpreting English, a student needs to know the words and phrases used to evaluate student and instructor performance and published work. This lesson will focus on three primary areas of evaluation:

1. instructors' comments on students' work;
2. students' evaluations of courses and instructors;
3. reviews of books, movies, cultural events.

Instructors' Comments

On daily homework assignments many instructors write only "OK," " √ " or a number, often from 1 to 10. On term papers and exams, however, instructors usually write comments, from one phrase to a long paragraph or more. Sometimes the comments explain why a particular letter grade was given; other times they include personal reactions or suggestions for further study. A discussion of the criteria for grading is included in the section on academic paper preparation later in this book. This lesson gives you some examples of the evaluative vocabulary commonly used at United States colleges and universities, and provides opportunities to practice evaluative vocabulary.

Practice 1

The comments below are typical of instructors' comments on students' papers and exams. Discuss them in class, and then decide which letter grade might be appropriate, according to this scale: A, B, C, D, F. Use plus (+) and minus (−) to modify the letter grades if appropriate.

Example

  __B +__   Good, careful work, somewhat lacking in creativity

  __ __   An effective, if sometimes disjointed presentation.

    _____ Clear, concise, unified—excellent work.

    _____ Sketchy, somewhat disappointing treatment.

    _____ Outstanding, both for its mature analysis and its high level of expression.

    _____ Generally well developed; your third point is shaky.

    _____ Clearly a well-thought-out argument, but Part III is unconvincing because you ignored the negative evidence.

    _____ A perceptive, coherent, and timely analysis.

    _____ This can't be your own work! See me.

    _____ Imprecise, rambling, needs revision.

    _____ Wordy, repetitious; further development is needed to explore the hypothesis.

Students' Evaluations of Courses and Instructors

Outstanding	Good	Average	Fair	Poor
5	4	3	2	1

In many United States colleges and universities, students are asked to formally evaluate their courses, including course content, course value, and instructor's teaching. Such evaluations are kept on file within an academic department; they are reviewed when the department decides to add a new course or to discontinue an existing one. They may also be considered when an instructor is up for promotion or tenure. In class, discuss the evaluation form below and determine what expectations Americans have of college instructors and how these differ from the expectations people have in your country.

Class Evaluation

Course: _____ Days, Time _____

    Please rate each of the following on the basis of the scale above. If the item does not apply to this class, put 0.

    _____ 1. Instructor's skill in eliciting relevant contributions from the students.

    _____ 2. Instructor's ability to provide a coherent, organized framework for the material covered.

_____ 3. Instructor's ability to listen and respond appropriately to student questions and contributions.
_____ 4. Instructor's availability for individual guidance and help outside of class.
_____ 5. Instructor's interest in the class.
_____ 6. Degree to which instructor provided individual help and feedback.
_____ 7. Your own interest, preparation and participation.
_____ 8. Value of the class in stimulating your interest in the subject.
_____ 9. Degree to which you felt free to raise questions of interest to you.
_____ 10. Rate the quality of the class as a whole.

How could this course be improved? Use the other side of this sheet if necessary.

Also, student groups at colleges or universities sometimes print informal course reviews to aid students in selecting courses. These booklets are not sanctioned by the university; rather, they contain tabulations of the results of questionnaires which have been filled out voluntarily by students at the end of the term. Here are two sample entries in a course review:

Computer Science 100   Introduction to Computing

R. Marshall &
G. Collier
Autumn 1977

This course was generally considered to give a good introduction to the basics of programming. There was a feeling among many of the students that the course was too time-consuming for two units of credit, that three units would be more reasonable.

Both of the instructors were praised for their articulate explanations and for their ability to analyze what the students' difficulties were. A few students in Collier's section commented that the pace at which material was covered was a little fast at times, and exam questions were either picky or ambiguous.

Art 70   Twentieth Century Architecture

M. Lloyd
Spring 1977

Several students rated the material covered as the best aspect of the course. In fact, many complained that the course was too short. "I would have attended twice as many hours if they had been offered," one student wrote enthusiastically. However, many students were less than happy with the reading material. They complained that it was too long and detailed, and most of it was dull. The exams were not unfair, drawing information from both lectures and readings. Lloyd's speaking ability and lecture organization were rated highly. The students enjoyed her mixture of traditional and innovative interpretations and her subjective comments. All of the students who responded to the questionnaire enthusiastically recommended the course.

Practice 2

In the following course evaluation, the underlined words fit in the context, but are weak, that is, too imprecise or too informal. There are other words in English which can give more explicit meaning to the paragraphs. From the words in parentheses, choose the word which fits the context in order to make a stronger, better written evaluation. Rewrite the paragraphs.

Social Sciences 230
Introduction to Graduate Study in the Social Sciences

For the past fifteen years, Soc. Sci. 230 has been the introductory course for first-year graduate students in interdisciplinary social science. There is no doubt that it was necessary (shaky, indispensable) when it was established. At that time interdisciplinary study was in its infancy: attempts to make it relevant (viable, successful) had been disconnected (disjointed, unified). This course was the first solid (general, substantive) presentation of central ideas; as such, it was quite important (influential, distracting) in shaping further graduate study.

After a generation of interdisciplinary study, however, Soc. Sci. 230 has outlived its usefulness. Today's first-year graduate has taken a fairly large (slight, considerable) number of survey courses as an undergraduate. He is eager to get beyond too basic (thorough, simplistic), sketchy (superficial, complex) survey courses to more scholarly, scientific (authoritarian, rigorous) and complete (exhaustive, fatiguing) research studies. For these students a general introductory course is not only tiresome (tedious, exciting), but also unnecessary (superfluous, extraordinary). If anything, it causes a student to question his interest in the field.

Practice 3

Write an evaluation of a course you have taken, using some of the words and phrases you have studied in this lesson.

Reviews

Reviews are a major means used to evaluate books, movies, concerts, and exhibits. Magazines and newspapers publish reviews of general interest. Many Americans read reviews to keep up to date. For a foreign student, reading reviews of general books about American society is a good means of finding out what Americans are reading and thinking.

In the United States, book reviews are recognized as an important means of evaluating scholarship and research. Reviews printed in academic journals and in magazines become an integral part of the literature. In fact, a critical review can be more important than the original book it reviewed. It is often helpful for a student to read reviews of books he is expected to evaluate. In addition, develop the habit of checking the book review section in the journals you read most often.

Libraries have several indexes which list the location of book reviews. The ones listed here are good ones to start with:

Book Review Index
Book Review Digest
Index to Book Reviews in the Humanities
The New York Times Index

When reading reviews, you will notice that certain words and phrases are used frequently. The largest group of these is adjectives, which carry a great deal of evaluative meaning. For example, certain adjectives express praise: *effective, concise, timely, intriguing, outstanding.* Other adjectives express disapproval: *repetitious, wordy, dull, outdated, disjointed, rambling.* Of course, there are many adjectives which express more subtle shades of meaning: *uneven, remarkable, substantive.*

Adverbs such as *thoroughly, extensively, heavily,* and *cheaply* have evaluative connotation. In addition to individual adjectives, adverbs, nouns, and verbs, there are many phrases which reviewers use to express praise or criticism carefully.

Practice 4

Which of the following underlined phrases are positive, and which are negative?

Examples

This book is well worth reading.   positive
I cannot recommend this book.   negative

1. He is correct in criticizing Adler, but unfortunately does not discuss the underlying reasons for his disagreement.

2. It <u>does in fact</u> cover most of the important points.
3. One <u>cannot help but question</u> the assumptions in this book.
4. I think this book <u>should be required reading</u> for anyone interested in zoology.
5. This argument <u>runs counter</u> to generally accepted fact.
6. While his <u>hypothesis is interesting, its validity is questionable.</u>
7. Chapter three <u>falls far short of my expectations</u>.
8. The editor <u>would have done well to have revised</u> the early sections.
9. Based on my familiarity with nuclear energy, <u>I found myself in disagreement</u> with his proposed solutions.
10. I disagree with Ms. Hubner's review: this book is <u>anything but</u> overrated.
11. The editorial comments in this anthology show <u>little imagination or insight</u>.
12. If this area is investigated further, <u>we may well find</u> a relationship between the two factors.
13. This biography is certainly <u>not without</u> new information about the general.

Practice 5

Cover the second part of this practice before reading the first. Read the following book review.

    Ralph Warren's book *The Primate World* (Harbor Press, 1977) is an addition to the literature on primate behavior. The first section of the book is an examination of twentieth century research in the field, though the author has a tendency to devote more space to European than to American work. In the second section he elaborates his theory of primate socialization, presenting some evidence based on experimentation to support his stand. The book has a holistic approach; unlike many others in the field, Warren does not neglect to place work with individual animal species into the whole picture of the primate world. Warren's study is reading material for any scientist with an interest in primate behavior.

Discussion: After reading the book review, answer the following questions.

1. How much do you know about the book?
2. How aware are you of the author's attitude toward Warren as a writer and as a scientist?
3. What is missing?
4. What words would you consider adding, and where?

Read the revised book review and underline the adjectives which have been added.

Ralph Warren's book *The Primitive World* (Harbor Press, 1977) is a noteworthy addition to the literature on primate behavior. The first section of the book is an exhaustive examination of twentieth century research in the field, though the author has a pronounced tendency to devote more space to European than to American work. In the second section, he elaborates his controversial theory of primate socialization, presenting some powerful evidence based on rigorous experimentation to support his stand. The book is striking for its holistic approach; unlike many others in the field, Warren does not neglect to place work with individual animal species into the whole picture of the primate world. Warren's coherent study is indispensable reading for any scientist with a serious interest in primate behavior.

Practice 6

Read this review of a (fictitious) book on solar power. Underline all of the words and phrases with particular evaluative meaning.

Lombard, Nathaniel. *The Case Against Solar Power.* New York: World Books, 1976, 237 pp.

Reviewed by Adrienne H. Andersen

Since the energy crunch of the early 1970s, the market has been flooded with books urging the development of alternative energy sources. Most of them relate the promise of nuclear, solar, and geothermal power. Although it comes as no surprise that there are several books opposing the use of nuclear power, *The Case Against Solar Power* is the first to oppose the use of solar power, and I cannot help but question what evidence in the book is convincing, even to a casual reader.

Lombard bases his objection to harnessing solar energy on the contention that it is "hopelessly impractical." A cursory examination of his four major points reveals that he has fallen into the trap of assuming that what hampers its development now will necessarily hamper it in the future.

First, he argues that solar heating systems are "worthless during most of the winter." This is simply not borne out by users who report that bright snowy days provide optimum conditions for collecting solar energy, which can then be stored for several days. Only a few rainy areas such as coastal Oregon and Washington have been found to be poor sites for the collection of solar energy. Next, he claims that because solar cannot entirely replace other forms of home heating, it is not worth developing. Clearly this is a naive and short-sighted argument. With present technology it is entirely feasible to provide 20 percent of home heating from solar power, according to environmentalist Barry Commoner. Some proponents of solar energy predict that with improved technology and improved building construction, solar can cut energy consumption in new buildings by 80 percent. The significance of that percentage cannot be questioned. Third, Lombard ignores the most obvious advantage, the virtual inexhaustibility of solar energy. Unlike petroleum or natural gas or coal or even geothermal sources, solar is not an interim source with a definite timetable. Fourth, he offers little to substantiate his statement that solar is "too costly for an average homeowner to consider." Granted, today a considerable initial investment is required to install a solar heating system in a conventional house, just as other heating systems were costly before units were mass-produced. Even with the cost for a prototype solar unit today, the owners of a solar-heated home in California calculate that their system will pay for itself within seven years. What Lombard also fails to mention is that the price of equipment for any type of heater will remain relatively stable, but the price of all fossil fuels will rise astronomically as supplies diminish. Lombard would have done well to have considered seriously the many authoritative sources which run counter to his arguments.

Although it neglects too many facts, *The Case Against Solar Power* is not without some merit; it is well written and provides both constructive criticism and thought-provoking suggestions which may well stimulate research leading to improvements in the technology for harnessing solar power.

Practice 7

Locate and read a review of a book you are interested in. After you have read it, go back through it to pick out the key evaluative vocabulary. Make sure that you understand connotations as well as basic meanings. Ask your instructor or another native English speaker to help you interpret the review.

Practice 8

Write a review of a film or television program. Use some of the phrases you have learned in this lesson.

Study Techniques

4

4.1 INTRODUCTION

Skill in study techniques is considered a prerequisite for success in American colleges and universities. It is, of course, important to become familiar with various types of examinations and exam questions. Familiarity with research vocabulary is a basic need of all college students. Good lecture notes are necessary for completing assignments and studying for exams. Making clear outlines and writing accurate summaries and paraphrases are essential organizational skills. In addition, it is important for upper division and graduate students to know how to write abstracts. Regular practice of good study techniques will enable the foreign student not only to use time more effectively, but also to adjust more readily to the American college system.

Chapter Outline

Examinations
Research Vocabulary
Taking Lecture Notes
Outlines
Summary and Paraphrase
Writing an Abstract

4.2 EXAMINATIONS

This lesson considers the kinds of examinations college instructors prepare, which in many cases differ from standardized tests such as TOEFL. While administrators of standardized tests and exams make the rules clear at the time the test is administered, instructors may assume that foreign students already know how to take several types of exams. Often there is only a minute to ask questions about procedure, and sometimes no questions are permitted. The more familiar you are with the types of exams used at American universities, the easier it will be for you to take them.

General Characteristics

Exams may be subjective (essay), objective (non-essay), or a blend of the two. Subjective questions on an exam require a student to analyze or discuss topics. Organization, completeness, and style are important. Most instructors are interested in approach as well as in factual content. Objective questions, on the other hand, generally require answers that give exact information rather than analysis or interpretation. These questions include true-false, multiple choice, matching, fill-in, and short-answer questions. Examples of various question types are included in this lesson.

Near the beginning of a course the instructor usually explains what kinds of tests will be given, and what the relative importance of each will be.

Exams may be open-book or closed-book. During an open-book exam in a classroom, students may use class notes, books, and other relevant materials announced beforehand by the instructor. Sometimes an open-book exam is a "take-home" exam; that is, students take the exam questions out of the classroom and return their answers at a specified time, which might be a few hours or even a week later. During that time each student is expected to work independently. During a closed-book exam, however, students may not use any notes, books, dictionaries, or other material.

In the American educational system, students are on their honor to do their own work, that is, *not* to cheat. To uphold a university honor code means that during an exam, students (a) will not give information to others, (b) will not receive information from others, (c) will report violations which they observe. Students can be expelled from a university for violating an honor code.

Specific Types of Tests

Generally "test" suggests shorter length than "exam." A test may cover a section of the material in a course, whereas an exam probably covers more material, for example, half of the course or all of the course.

Quizzes. An announced quiz is a short exam which usually tests specific information from a lecture or reading selection. For example, a professor may say, "There'll be a fifteen-minute quiz on chapter ten next Monday." That means students should read chapter ten and expect one or more questions based on that chapter. A "pop" or "snap" quiz is a surprise quiz for which there is no advance warning. A pop quiz often consists of a few short-answer questions and may take less than ten minutes. It is often given at the beginning of class to test students' recall of information in a reading assignment or recent lecture.

Diagnostic Test. A diagnostic test is given by an instructor to find out how much students know about a topic before it is covered in class. Usually diagnostic tests are objective so that the results can be tabulated easily. The score on a diagnostic test does not affect the student's course grade.

Midterm Examination. A midterm is given halfway through a term, covers half the course content, is usually about an hour in length, and may account for 25 percent or more of the grade for the course. Some instructors give two midterms.

Final Examination. A final is given at the end of a course, covers some or all of the content, is two or three hours in length, and may account for 40 percent of the course grade.

Types of Questions

Essays. An essay question or exam requires a student to write a well-organized, original answer. An essay question necessitates reorganization and integration of different ideas into a central theme. Often a student is expected to develop and include his own ideas in the essay. Clear development of steps is important. Length may vary from one paragraph for a short essay to ten pages or more for a take-home exam given over an extended period of time.

Short Essays (one paragraph)

Define *feedback,* give two examples, and draw figures to illustrate them.

Briefly discuss the major cause of the sharp decrease in U.S. traffic deaths in 1974.

Longer Essays

Trace the major developments in operations research from its inception to the present.

How do the principal American political parties differ from each other?

What kind of man, then, does our society need in order to function smoothly? It needs men who co-operate smoothly in large groups; who want to consume more and more, and whose tastes are standardized and can be easily influenced and anticipated. —*Erich Fromm*

Criticize or defend the above quotation. Support your argument with specific examples.

Why don't all the people who grow up speaking English speak exactly the same language?

Discuss this on the individual level, the speech community level, the regional/ethnic level, and the national level.

Problem-solving. While problem-solving questions in an exam may involve developing models or systems of equations, the intent is still to communicate information. The symbolic material should be well organized, adequately described, and complete. The method of solution is often as important as the final answer. Remember to incorporate all relevant facts included in the question.

True-False. Read a statement, decide whether it is true or false, and indicate your choice according to instructions. (Common symbols are T or F, + or 0.) Sometimes you may be asked to rewrite any statement you have marked *false;* that is, you may be asked to write a parallel sentence that is true or correct.

Circle the correct letter: T = True; F = False.

T   F   Light travels faster than sound.
T   F   CO is carbon dioxide.
T   F   Uranium is a planet.
T   F   Advertisements always influence consumers.
T   F   GNP stands for Gross National Product.

Multiple Choice. Complete a statement by selecting one of several choices. The choices are parallel in structure and must be read carefully to find the *best* answer. Circle the letter which corresponds to the best answer.

1. California is not a major producer of
    a. oranges
    b. tomatoes
    c. bananas
    d. avocados

2. Scientific writing is
    a. entertaining and formal
    b. factual and informative
    c. emotional and persuasive
    d. subjective and general

3. Freud was a
   a. physicist
   b. theologian
   c. physician
   d. all of the above
   e. none of the above

4. Satellites are not used for
   a. weather photos
   b. radio transmission
   c. television broadcasts
   d. commercial transport

Matching. Match items in one list with items in a second list. Usually one list is numbered and the other is lettered. One list may be longer than the other.

Match each capital city with the corresponding country by writing the letter of the city in the space next to the country.

1. Ecuador _____
2. Japan _____
3. Afghanistan _____
4. Austria _____
5. Nigeria _____

a. Lagos
b. Vienna
c. Bogota
d. Tokyo
e. Kabul
f. Quito

Fill-in. Read the sentence and decide which word is necessary to complete the sentence. Write the word(s) in the blank. Fill in the appropriate auxiliary verb.

Applications for admission must _____ submitted by the first of January.

Letters of recommendation _____ already been sent to the Admissions Office.

Short Answer. Answer these questions with a word or phrase. Instructions sometimes require the answer to be expressed in a complete sentence.

1. List three energy sources which are alternatives to fossil fuel.
2. When did large-scale immigration begin in the United States?
3. What is the term for a word's environment?

General Instructions for Taking Exams in Course Work

1. Before answering any question, quickly read over the entire exam to familiarize yourself with all of the instructions and to help you decide

how much time to allow for each part. Point values or recommended time limits are often indicated to help you budget your time. After distributing the exam and asking if there are any questions, the professor often leaves the room; many exams are *unproctored*.

2. Read each question *very* carefully and follow the specific instructions explicitly. Different sections may have different directions.

3. Be careful to *answer the question*. This is not as obvious as it sounds. For example, if a question asks you to define a principle, write a definition, not just some information about the principle. In addition, a question may be phrased somewhat differently than you anticipated when you were preparing for the exam. The instructor's intention may be to have you reorganize information and apply it to new situations. Do that, rather than write a "pre-planned" answer you may have developed while you were studying.

4. Before writing a long answer, organize your ideas. If permitted, use scratch paper or the back of the exam sheet to jot down an outline or ordered set of ideas. Use the outline as you write your answer.

5. When you have finished, reread the entire exam. Read each question and your answer to it. Make sure you have followed all instructions exactly and have actually *answered* each question. As you read your answers, make corrections or changes which will make your use of written English accurate and effective.

6. Be sure your name is on the exam in the indicated place at the top of the answer sheet, on the front of an exam booklet, or on all your own sheets of paper.

4.3 RESEARCH VOCABULARY

This lesson is designed to give you practice in analyzing some of the research vocabulary which is common to all academic fields; that is, the basic set of terms used repeatedly on the university level, from undergraduate survey courses to graduate research.

Precision in the use of basic research vocabulary is essential for accurate comprehension, interpretation, and writing. Much of this vocabulary may be familiar in a general sense, but it is necessary to master the specialized meanings in academic contexts. In order to develop your ability to identify, to analyze, and to use these terms, you will examine short selections from literature, such as abstracts and other scholarly papers and reports found in specialized journals. In order to make specific the basic concepts of research experimentation and reporting, this lesson begins with a description of the scientific method of experimentation and guidelines for a standard form of research reporting.

The Experimental Research Process

Statement and Hypothesis. The first step in experimentation is to formulate a problem and state it precisely. After carefully reviewing the literature on the same or closely related problems, the researcher states a testable hypothesis, including the results he expects to find.

Experimental Design. The second step is to plan an experiment that will test the hypothesis. The investigator must (1) assess resources (such as time, money, and equipment); (2) outline the procedure step by step; (3) limit and control variables; and (4) select statistical tests. While the experimental design may vary greatly depending on the field, all experiments should be designed to assure clear-cut, valid results.

Investigation and Collection of Data. The investigation or implementation of the experimental design comes next. During this stage the researcher sets up and conducts the experiment. The data gathered are often in the form of numerical values such as test scores, meter readings, temperatures, or time. Further processing of the raw data is usually required.

Compilation of Data. The fourth step is to process the data for interpretation. Handling large quantities of empirical data often requires use of a computer to organize the data and to perform statistical analyses. In some experiments the raw data must be arranged in tables or plotted on graphs.

Interpretation of Results. The researcher then examines and analyzes the results for evidence which may confirm or refute his hypothesis. The investigator compares his experimental results with the predicted results and accounts for any differences.

Evaluation. The final step in the experimental process is to decide whether the hypothesis has been supported by the evidence and to review the validity of the test.

Research Reporting

Research is reported in many forms: an address at a conference, a term paper, a short letter to the editor of a journal, a long journal article, a report for a company or a professor, or a book. The organization of research reporting is relatively standard. In journal articles, the most common form in which new findings are published, research is generally presented in the following form:

Title. The title should be short, but give as much information as possible about the content of the article.

Authors' Names. The principal author's name is printed first, followed by the names of the other authors.

Abstract. The abstract provides key words, expands the information given in the title, specifies the type of experiment, and gives the results. Based on this knowledge of the subject matter, objectives, and limitations of the paper, an individual decides if reading the paper will be worthwhile for his purpose.

Introduction. The introduction presents a theoretical framework, including a review of the literature which brings the reader up to date on the "state of the art" and current developments of the research area. Previous work is cited. A statement of the problem is included in the form of a testable hypothesis with predicted results. When a paper is published without an abstract, a summary of the results is included in the introduction.

Procedure. The procedure section includes methodology, experimental design, and collection of data. When the method used has been previously reported, the previous experiment is cited. Because readers are particularly critical of experimental procedure, it is discussed in sufficient detail so that (1) the validity of the results can be fairly judged and (2) any research worker can duplicate the experiment. Diagrams and figures are used to illustrate apparatus.

Results. In the results section the actual data obtained are presented. Both measurements, that is, raw data and derived quantities, are published. Of course, units must be carefully specified. For example, in an engineering paper, volts would not be enough information for a reader: are they international volts or absolute volts? In an economics paper, profit must be specified as net or gross profit. All symbols must be clearly identified. Tables of data are presented so that readers can easily extract specific numerical values.

Discussion. The discussion section interprets the results by presenting arguments based on the information given in the results section. Graphs, such as line and bar graphs, illustrate trends and functional relationships which cannot be seen in tables. Possible improvements on the experiment are included, as well as descriptions of any irregularities which might account for discrepancies between the predicted and the obtained results. The reader should ask himself: (1) Do I agree with the author's arguments for the results he obtained? and (2) How could the study be improved?

Conclusion. The experimental results confirming or refuting the hypothesis are summarized in the conclusion. In addition, recommendations for future research are made.

Practice 1

Examine the following abstracts for the use of research vocabulary. Compile a list of the words most frequently used to describe the research process. You will add to this list in later exercises in this class.

Size of University Classes and Student Evaluation of Teaching

For 981 undergraduate classes, many student ratings of instruction decrease with increasing class size. This relationship remains strong when other variables known or believed to influence ratings are held constant.[1]

Central Contra Costa Water Renovation Project

The Central Contra Costa (California) Sanitary and County Water districts are engaged in a joint program to renovate wastewater. The six-phase program includes a feasibility study, a sampling analysis program, plant tests and a demonstration program. A flow diagram of the pilot project is given, and design data of both current and expanded facilities are provided in a table.[2]

Practice 2

Now look at these longer abstracts. Add additional vocabulary items to your list. Which vocabulary items are used in both the short and long abstracts?

Is Scientific Achievement a Correlate of Effective Teaching Performance?

The purpose of this study was to test the hypothesis that in the context of a large health science center heavily committed to scientific activity, there would be a positive relationship between the scientific productivity of faculty members and their effectiveness as teachers. Counts of citations by others and counts of publications were used as indices of scientific productivity. The index of teaching effectiveness was derived from students' perceptions of teaching effectiveness, elicited in a questionnaire that asked students to rate teachers in terms of the presence or absence of a series of behaviors grouped under five headings called the Components of Effective Teaching.

The results of this study provide support to the notion that research and teaching are not separate and adversary phenomena each working to the disadvantage of the other, but under certain conditions are interrelated with research activity supportive of effective teaching.[3]

[1]*Journal of Higher Education*, Vol. 46, No. 4, July/August 1975.
[2]*Pollution Abstracts*, 4, no. 2, March 1973.
[3]*Research in Higher Education*, Vol. 3, 1975.

Kona Dam vs. Konatown: A Sociological Interpretation of Selected Impacts of Reservoir Development on a Community Field

The study was aimed at identifying a set of procedures useful for the delineation of environmental impacts of a public project from a sociological perspective. The research process included three major procedures: (1) analysis of Kona Dam as an action process in terms of its major phases, activities and behaviors involved during its history; (2) identification of Konatown as a community field in terms of its major constituent elements at ecological, institutional, and social levels of analysis. . . . The action project was discussed in terms of major phases, namely: (1) initiation, (2) organization of sponsorship, (3) goal setting or planning, (4) implementation of plans and (5) evaluation of the project.[4]

Conceptual Framework for Research on the Management of Interdisciplinary Research

DAVID W. CRAVENS, RAY A. MUNDY, and KENNETH W. HEATHINGTON. Interdisciplinary research in government, universities, and other institutions has become increasingly important due to the variety of disciplines contributing and interacting in large scale research projects. Yet, our understanding of effective management processes for interdisciplinary research is limited, due, in part, to the lack of research attention that has been given to this area. The existing body of knowledge concerning interdisciplinary research management is examined. Using this base of knowledge and experience, a synthesis of key concepts is developed to provide a foundation for conceptualizing interdisciplinary research management processes. A conceptual framework depicting major variables and relationships associated with interdisciplinary research management processes is presented and discussed. Promising areas of research are examined.[5]

Practice 3

In a journal, find a research study and list the headings or subtitles used in that research report. Then describe the information included under each heading.

Practice 4

Match the following words with their definitions. The first one is done for you.

---

[4]*Water Resources Abstracts*, Vol. 8, No. 14, 15 July 1975.

[5]*Operations Research Society of America (ORSA) Bulletin*, Vol. 23, Supplement 1, Spring 1975.

1. hypothesis __d__
2. empirical ____
3. research problem ____
4. table ____
5. review of the literature ____
6. pilot project ____
7. scientific method ____
8. determination of validity ____
9. "raw" data ____
10. negative relation ____

a. A discussion of the work done on a problem or problem areas up to the time of the experiment.
b. A "mini-test" done to determine what problems may appear in the larger study.
c. Whether an experiment tests what it intends to test.
d. A statement of what the experiment is intended to prove or disprove.
e. Information gathered by the researcher which has not yet been processed.
f. Subject to observations through sense perception.
g. An ordered arrangement of numerical data in rows and columns.
h. The problem to be studied; usually refers to the first step in the scientific method.
i. A procedure for carefully studying a problem, using empirical observation to find the answer to a research problem.
j. Two or more variables change in the opposite direction; as one increases the other decreases.

Practice 5

In this exercise all of the words in parentheses fit the given content, but each word has a different meaning. In class, discuss each possibility, commenting on differences in meaning and level of formality.

Example

The purpose of this study is to predict any (increase, decrease, change) in the number of foreign students in the United States between 1985 and 1995.

Discussion: increase means make greater; decrease means make smaller; change means alter, either greater or smaller.

1. (Formulating, stating, defining) a research problem is not an easy task.
2. (Planning, designing, limiting) an experiment may take longer than actually conducting it.

3. (Setting up statistical tests for, conducting) an experiment involves several steps.
4. After a researcher (obtains empirical data, makes some observations, gets some results), he tries to analyze them in terms of his hypothesis.
5. Data is often (evaluated, compiled, interpreted) with a computer.
6. Results from one experiment may or may not (refute, contribute to, support, confirm) an existing theory.
7. The discussion section of a research report (examines, interprets, graphs, accounts for) the experimental results.
8. Before beginning an experimental research project, (variables, a conceptual framework, a hypothesis) must be established after the existing (body of knowledge, literature, studies) have/has been examined.
9. The success of the (initial experiment, pilot project, public project) led the research group to believe the study would be funded.
10. The new (output, data, findings) confirmed the previous results.
11. A previous study aimed at (synthesizing, identifying, developing) two concepts.
12. The responses (taken from, gotten from, elicited from) the subjects were cited by the authors in a subsequent study.

Practice 6

The following report on research concerning dreams about earthquakes contains many terms frequently used in research reporting. For each blank, two words are listed in parentheses, but only one is appropriate. Fill in the blanks and then discuss the terms in class.

Research on Earthquake Dreams

After the 1971 earthquake in Southern California, a group of researchers decided to (conduct, buy) _____ a study of the psychological effects of the quake on children who had experienced it. In carefully (memorizing, formulating) _____ the problem to be (learned, investigated) _____ , the scientists stated their (hypothesis, hope) _____ that the children's dreams would be quake-related but decreasingly so as time passed. "Quake-related" was (defined, placed) _____ in precise psychological terms. After studying the (reasons, methodology) _____ used by researchers who had (conducted, studied) _____ fire-related dreams, they designed their (experiments, results) _____ .

Data was (gathered, picked up) _____ over a period of

two years, the time span which the researchers felt would be sufficient to (test, refute) _____ their hypothesis. Early in 1973 they began a rigid (analysis, outlook) _____ of their data, though they had (reached, existed) _____ some tentative conclusions in the course of the two years. As part of the (impact, interpretation) _____ of the data, they (elicited, calculated) _____ the values for a graph of elapsed time versus quake-related dreams.

In a preliminary report of their (findings, design) _____, given in a paper presented at a conference on child psychology held in late 1973, the researchers summarized the results they (confused, obtained) _____. Following that, they began to prepare a lengthy report for publication. In that paper, they (review, deliver) _____ the development of catastrophe-related dream research, (discuss, decrease) _____ their selection of experimental subjects, and present the evidence which (confirms, calculates) _____ their hypothesis. Finally, they (interpret, recommend) _____ future research studies which may eventually help psychologists find ways to lessen the psychological impact of natural disasters such as earthquakes on both adults and children.

Practice 7

Read the following report of a study that appeared in a journal. Make a list of general terms concerning the research process and research reporting that appear in the description. Indicate which stages they represent.

In three tests with college-aged students, Max Coltheart, Elaine Hull and Diana Slater investigated whether females and males read phonetically (by sounding words out) or visually (recognition by spelling), and if the difference is sex-related.

To study tasks that are purely visual or purely verbal, the team asked 75 British undergraduates to mentally tabulate the number of letters from A to Z containing the sound "ee" to test use of verbal aid. Writing or speaking during the test was prohibited; speed in answering was encouraged. A similar task to test visual aids in reading required the group of respondents to mentally count the number of letters containing a curve in their upper-case form. Although females were faster on the verbal test and males faster on the visual tasks, the differences, the team says, were not statistically significant (a difference of 0.9 seconds or less in both tests). But the women made fewer mistakes on the verbal test (number of "ee" sounds) while the men scored better on the visual task (letters with curves). The team says these results imply that women more often than men read words by the way they sound.[6]

Practice 8

1. Look in one of your textbooks written in English or in a magazine or a journal for a brief description of a research study. Make a list of the general research terms. In class, compare your list with those of your classmates. Discuss which terms are generally used in all fields and which are field-specific.
2. Read and analyze two articles from the literature in your field, following these steps:
    a. If they have abstracts, compile a list of the research vocabulary words and phrases found in the abstract. Add the most useful to the list you are building.
    b. Analyze the vocabulary in the main article. Add any new vocabulary to your list.

Practice 9

Using the steps of research reporting that you have learned, write a one- or two-page composition to describe research that someone in your field has conducted. Include some of the terms you have learned.

Practice 10

At the end of many research reports the author or principal investigator recommends that further study be done to test his hypothesis on a larger scale or to extend his work in a closely related area. For example,

> Having learned a great deal concerning the evolution of "competition-reducing mechanisms" from our studies of Yarrow's spiny lizards we hope to apply our data on resource division to some of the broader questions ecologists are asking.
> One question is, Does superabundance or scarcity of food result in changes in food selection, microhabitats, or activity periods? In other words, how does resources usage change under varying conditions and are these changes predictable? ... Whatever combinations of resource use may occur under different conditions, partitioning of available food is an important adaptation for coexistence within a common habitat.[7]

[6]*Science News*, Vol. 107 (15 March 1975).

[7]Carol A. Simon, "Lizard Coexistence in Four Dimensions," *Natural History*, Vol. 8, No. 4 (April 1976), p. 74.

Find a research article in your area of academic interest which recommends further study; describe the steps of the proposed study. It might be possible to describe the steps of a study to extend the research you read about for Practice 8.

Practice 11

In two or three paragraphs, describe some research you would like to do or some you have already done.

4.4 TAKING LECTURE NOTES

Taking lecture notes while studying at an American university is essential. In lectures, many American professors provide information which is *not* in the assigned text or in the outside reading for the course. Furthermore, professors who are engaged in research present lectures covering the most up-to-date information, which may be unpublished and unavailable from any other source.

The information in lecture notes is used for a variety of activities: going over the material in discussion sections or seminars; answering comprehension questions; answering open-book exam questions, and writing summaries or critiques. There is no one best way to take notes; each student must develop his own intelligible method. The guidelines below will help you take useful lecture notes.

Before the Lecture

Review the assigned readings and make a list of the key words and phrases that are new to you. Be sure to re-read the subject headings.

A looseleaf notebook is practical because pages can be inserted and removed easily.

Use ink. Pencil smears easily and often is hard to read.

For later reference, it is helpful to have the date, lecturer, and the course number at the top of the page.

During the Lecture

Avoid taking notes in full sentences. Your aim is to use short cuts which can help you write fewer words but which still enable you to reconstruct or expand the notes into full-sentence form if necessary. What you *should* have in your notes:

1. Content words—especially nouns, important adverbs and adjectives, and verbs (omit auxiliaries unless they are important, and indicate tense only at points where it changes, for example, from present to past)

2. Negative expressions or prefixes
3. Important diagrams presented by the lecturer—draw them *accurately* but *quickly*
4. Correct figures (for example, percentages, quantities)
5. Transitional expressions and subordinating conjunctions, or symbols for them
6. Anything a professor writes on the blackboard
7. Appropriate, useful abbreviations and symbols (a list appears on p. 213)
8. First initials or abbreviations of names or topics which occur very frequently—for example, if a lecture is about Newton, N may be a good symbol to use during that lecture.

What you do *not* need in your notes:

1. Articles, coordinating conjunctions between clauses (such as *and, also*), some prepositional phrases
2. Details you already know (unless they are stated in a unique way or applied in a new situation)
3. Full words written out when an abbreviation would be appropriate—for example, use *math* rather than *mathematical, tech* rather than *technical* or *technology*.

If possible, organize your notes into major groupings of ideas while the lecture is in progress.

When you have a question or idea or are unsure about something, put a symbol or note in the margin. For example, *sp?* might mean "Is the spelling correct?"; *Why?* would be a question you might like to ask during discussion.

Be alert! A lecturer uses verbal and visual cues. Listen for transitions, especially those which indicate enumeration (for example, *second, finally*) and results or conclusions (for example, *therefore, as a result*). Listen for change in emphasis in the speaker's voice. Variation in pitch, volume, or pace may be a clue to very important, or relatively unimportant, points. In addition, look at the lecturer when possible. Gestures and pauses are another indication of how important the lecturer feels certain information is.

Pay particular attention to other students' comments and questions. They may be useful and will tell you what the students think is important.

Take notes *in English*, even if you find it uncomfortable at first. If a lecturer uses an unfamiliar word or strange idiom, try to write it down as well as you can. Later you may be able to ask questions, to consult American students, or to find it in a dictionary or other source.

After the Lecture

Later the same day, read through your notes and add any other information which you remember but did not write down during the lecture. Also fill in words you have asked about or looked up. You may want to use a different color of ink for information and comments added to your original notes.

Practice 1

The following pages contain three sets of notes taken during lectures in university courses. Look at the first two sets (figures 1–3) and read and discuss the explanatory notes which accompany them. Then look at the set for course A 151 (figure 4) and discuss the student's note-taking techniques.

Lecture Notes—Sample 1–A

Notice the date and professor's name. (If one professor gave all the lectures in a course, the course number might be here instead.) Notice the title of the lecture, from the professor's course syllabus.

1. *Abbreviation*—Notice the immediate use of an abbreviation for a key word in the topic (electric).
2. *Verbal cue*—Put down 3 rather than writing out *three*. The professor may have said "There are three sources of electric power." Even if he does not say *first, second, third* when he mentions them, you know how many to expect.
3. *Question*—Notice the student's question, perhaps for discussion after the lecture, in the margin.
4. *Charts and figures*—The first table was written on the board; percentages should be copied exactly. The California table was given verbally. Write it down quickly but accurately. If you think you may have made a mistake, compare your figures with those of a friend who took notes at the same lecture.
5. *Minor point*—The student put parentheses around a minor point which relates to the discussion. It is not essential information but is useful historical information and therefore might show up on a quiz on the material.
6. *Articles*—Notice the omission of articles. The professor said, "Today in the United States the power generated by each of the three...."
7. *Essential word*—Here *main* is an essential content word. There are also three types of *fuel* sources, and without *main* you could get confused later when you read over your notes.
8. *Mathematical symbol*—Notice the use of $\sim =$ to represent "approximately equal" said by the lecturer.
9. *Vocal cue*—The word *is* is underlined to show that the professor emphasized it.
10. *Major point*—Underlining is this student's way of indicating a major area of the lecture. Another student might put it in the margin, mark it later in a different color, or give it an outline letter B if A was "3 sources of elec. power."

11. *Negative word*—The word *not* is important and must be included.
12. *Negative prefix*—*dis* is an important negative prefix.
13. *Question*—Notice the question mark by a word. The student is unfamiliar with the word and intends to look it up.
14. *Short cut*—Rather than repeating *advantage* and *disadv.* for each of the three sources, the student set up an outline level, a, b, and used it consistently under that major part of the lecture.
15. *Symbol*—The student used the chemical element symbol *U* for uranium. He was uncertain of the symbol for plutonium so wrote it out.

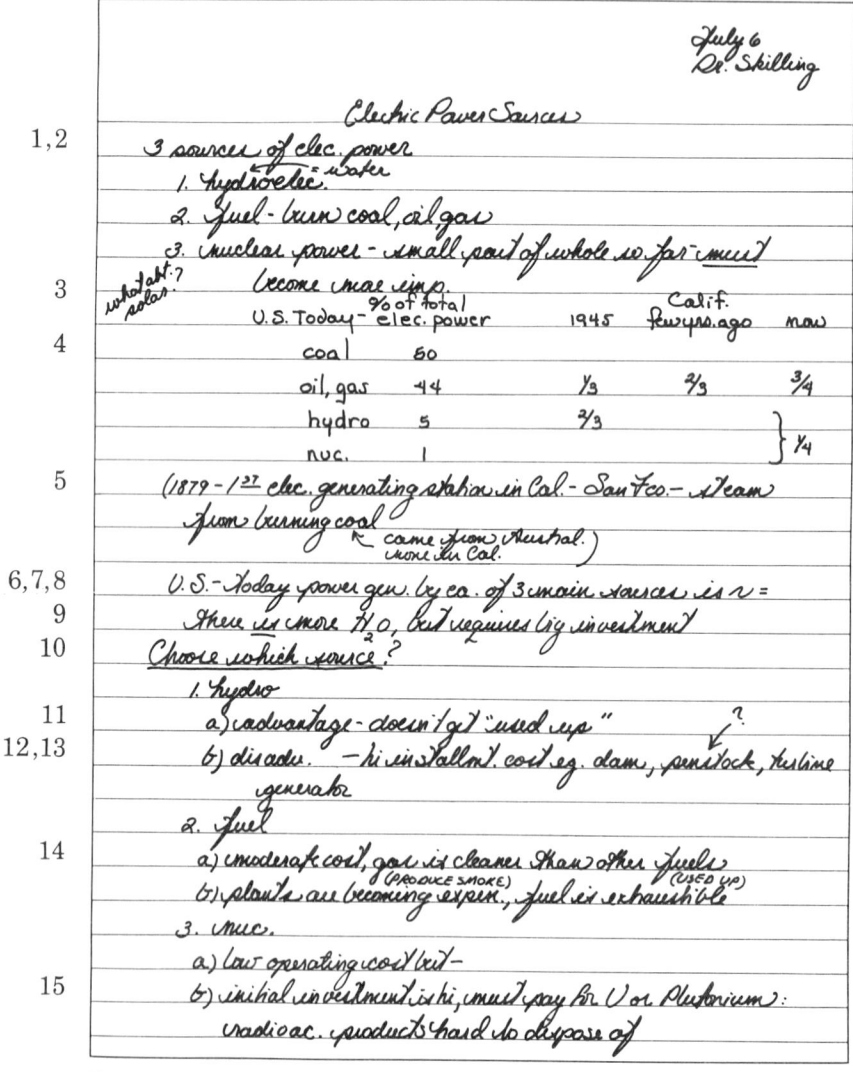

Fig. 1. Lecture notes—Sample 1–A.

Lecture Notes—Sample 1–B

16. *Emphasis*—The asterisk (*) indicates that the professor emphasized the point as critical to the decision of where to locate a power plant. Notice that the point is a complete sentence but does not contain unessential words and does not have sentence markings (capital letter and period).

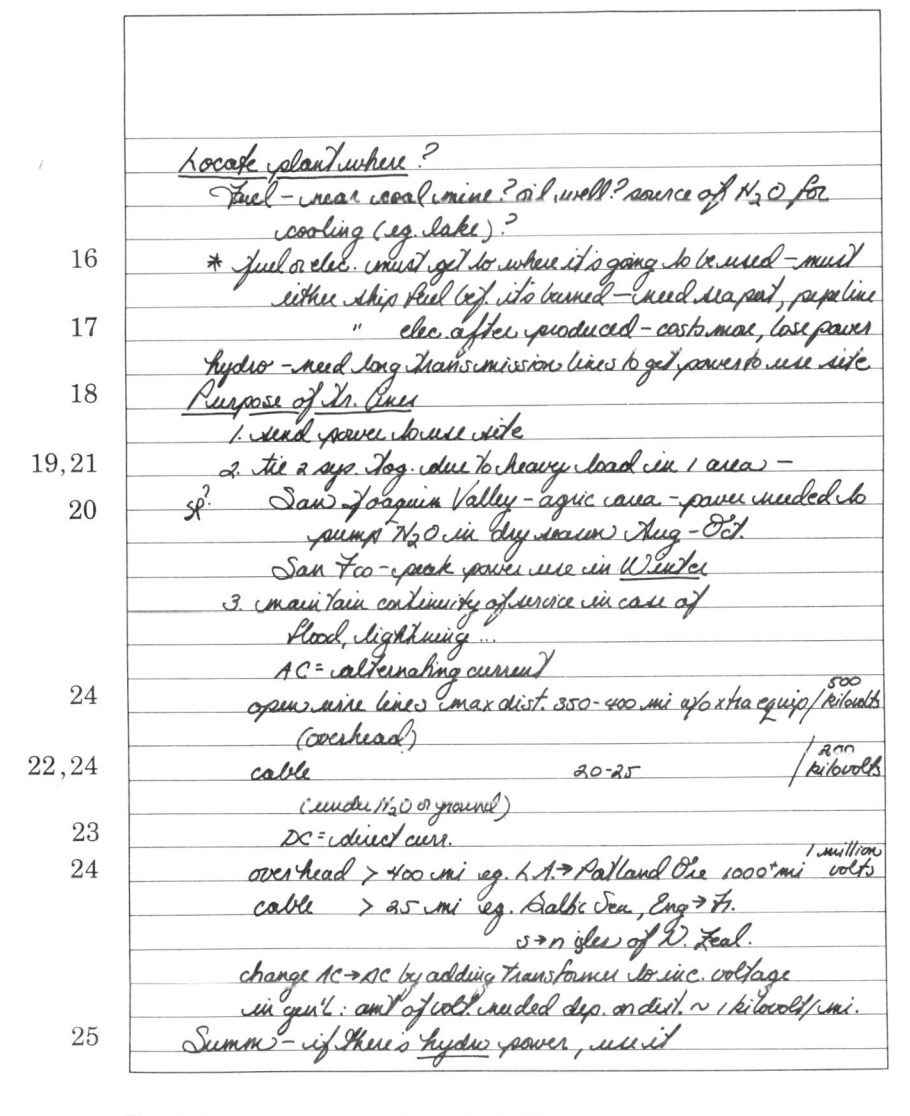

```
                Locate plant where?
                   Fuel - near coal mine? oil well? source of H₂O for
                        cooling (eg. lake)?
 16             * fuel or elec. must get to where it's going to be used - must
                        either ship fuel (ef. it's burned - need sea port, pipeline
 17                "       elec. after produced - costs more, lose power
                   hydro - need long transmission lines to get power to use site
 18             Purpose of Tr. lines
                    1. send power to use site
 19,21              2. tie 2 sys. tog. due to heavy load in 1 area -
 20             sp?    San Joaquin Valley - agric. area - power needed to
                          pump H₂O in dry season Aug - Oct.
                       San Fco - peak power use in Winter
                    3. maintain continuity of service in case of
                          flood, lightning...
                    AC = alternating current                          500
 24             open wire lines (max dist. 350-400 mi w/o xtra equip/kilovolts
                    (overhead)                                        200
 22,24          cable                      20-25                      kilovolts
                    (under H₂O or ground)
 23             DC = direct curr.                                  1 million
 24             over head > 400 mi eg. L.A. → Portland Ore 1000⁺mi   volts
                cable    > 25 mi eg. Baltic Sea, Eng → Fr.
                           s → n ples of N. Zeal.
                change AC → DC by adding transformer to inc. voltage
                   in gen'l: amt of volts needed dep. on dist. ~ 1 kilovolt/mi.
 25             Summ - if there's hydro power, use it
```

Fig. 2. Lecture notes—Sample 1–B.

17. *Short cut*—Notice the use of ditto marks to show that the same word as the above goes on that line too.
18. *Abbreviation*—*tr* may be *too short* an abbreviation. It could easily be confused with *transfer, transport,* and many other words. The only indication of what it stands for is in the note immediately above about *transmission lines*. It is important that abbreviations be clear.
19. *Important expression*—The expression *due to* (meaning *because*) is important for understanding the relationship of the two systems.
20. *Spelling*—The student put *sp?* in the margin to remind himself that he should check the spelling of San Joaquin.
21. *Important adjectives*—Several adjectives are important and should be included: *heavy* load, *agric* (agricultural) area, *peak* power use.
22. *Repetition*—It is unnecessary to repeat *max. dist.* and *mi.* (maximum distance and miles) two lines below. Notice that the student did not even put ditto marks to show the repetition of the same words, as he did near the top of the page.
23. *Abbreviation*—*curr.* is sufficient because of the parallelism between AC and DC.
24. *Student question*—A student asked the voltage carried by various means. The student included the professor's reply, even though he had to squeeze it in at the side of the page.
25. *Concluding statement*—*Summ* (summary) is an important transition indicator. This is the student's reminder to himself that the professor indicated through words or emphasis that he was giving his concluding comments.

Lecture Notes—Sample 2

Notice the course number and date.

1. *Diagram*—The student drew the diagrams clearly and quickly. Notice, for example, that he did not meticulously draw lines or arrows with a ruler.
2. *Equilibrium*—*sp?*—The student was unsure of the spelling and wrote the word down the way he heard it. He intends to look it up and make sure of the spelling.
3. *Neatness*—Notes are not meant to be "perfect." If you start to write something down and change your mind about how you want it in your notes, cross out what you started to write and keep going.
4. *Accuracy*—The student crossed out part of an equation which he began to copy incorrectly from the board. It is very important to write down mathematical formulas accurately.

EE 216
Nov 8

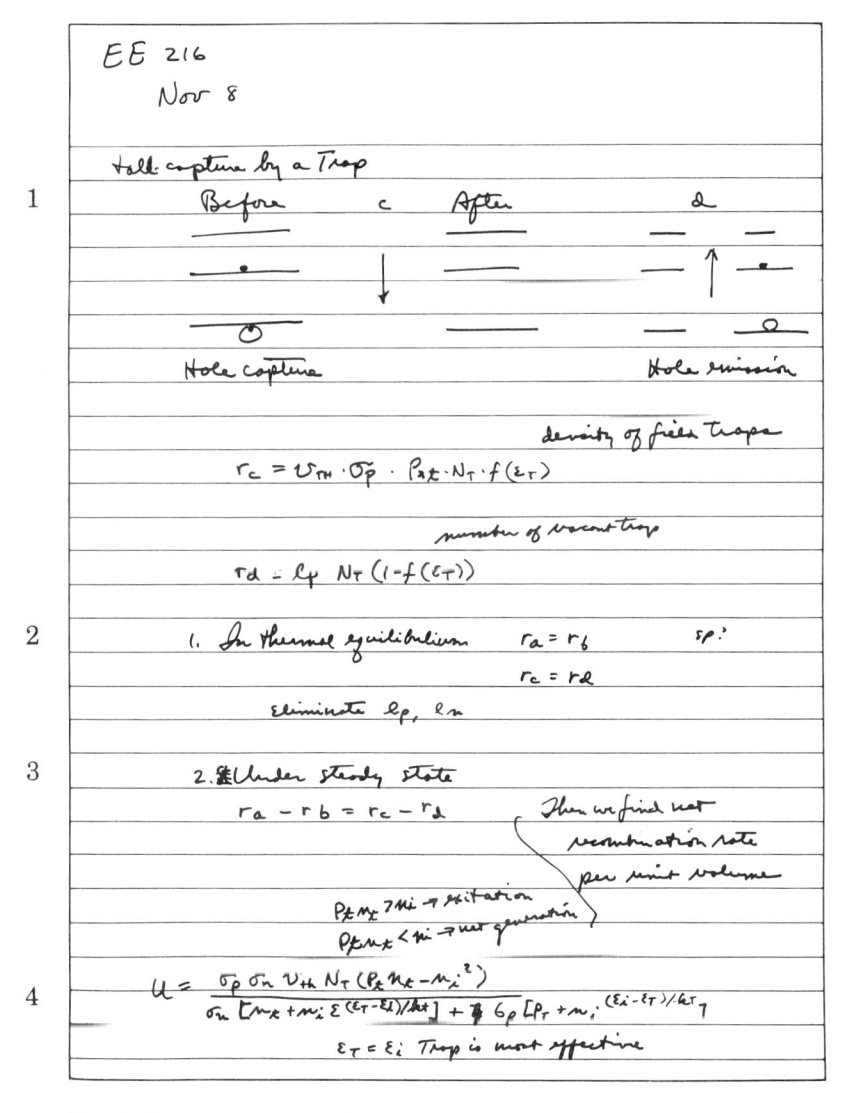

Hole capture by a Trap

1   Before   c   After   d

Hole capture   Hole emission

density of filled traps

$$r_c = v_{TH} \cdot \sigma_p \cdot P_{at} \cdot N_T \cdot f(\varepsilon_T)$$

number of vacant traps

$$r_d = e_p \, N_T (1 - f(\varepsilon_T))$$

2. 1. In thermal equilibrium $r_a = r_b$ sp:
                                  $r_c = r_d$

    Eliminate e_p, e_n

3. 2. Under steady state
    $r_a - r_b = r_c - r_d$ ⎫ Then we find net
                                recombination rate
                                per unit volume

    $p_t n_x > n_i \rightarrow$ excitation
    $p_t n_x < n_i \rightarrow$ net generation

4. $$u = \frac{\sigma_p \sigma_n v_{th} N_T (p_t n_x - n_i^2)}{\sigma_n [n_x + n_i \varepsilon^{(\varepsilon_T - \varepsilon_i)/kT}] + \sigma_p [p_T + n_i \varepsilon^{(\varepsilon_i - \varepsilon_T)/kT}]}$$

    $\varepsilon_T = \varepsilon_i$ Trap is most effective

Fig. 3. Lecture notes—Sample 2.

A 151
2/25

INTRODUCTION TO PEASANT SOCIETY

1. There are many peasants.
2. Definition.
3. Why worry about them.
4. They resist change?
5. Soc. structure.
6. World view.
7. Are they really different from other people?

1. It used to be that more people on the earth were peasants. In 1940s 57% of pop. was peasants.
Diff. People who provide the food for their own subsistence and still less than 50% of what they produce. It doesn't say to much. → anthropol. def.

1) (Wolf) (peasants):
  – Peasants are agricult. producers.
  – They have effective control on their land.
  – They are subsistence peasants rather than a profit oriented.
He distinguishes peasants from farmers.
He believes that agriculture is important to definition of peasants.

Agriculture producer (Foster and Firth) and they study patterns and fishers that are peasant – like → They are small-scale producers rather than agricultural.

Control of land: distinguish peasants from rural proletarians.
  ↳ Who don't own land but work as in a factory you do not quit – subsistence. How do they give up and go to a city?

2) Kroeber (classic definition) / Wieser
They live in relation with some kind of market town and they borrow culture from that place.
Carrican: To understand peasant you have to put yourself in the bottom of occupation and cultural values and to feel bad about yourself.
  → Two elements: subsistence and relation to towns.

The standard reason to worry about peasants is that they produce less than two times they need to survive.
Do they do not support more than a one-times family size.
→ People is trying to push them to produce more; To get them to produce more.

There are two excesses.
a) to help them produce more because they are so poor.
b) to make them participate and fully national development → part of surplus labor.
     Marxists
     Leninist
     Communist
     Maoist

Fig. 4. Lecture notes—Sample 3.

Practice 2

Read the following list of general abbreviations and symbols. Then ask three American students what abbreviations and symbols they use. Compare their abbreviations with those on the list. Present new general abbreviations in class.

Some Commonly Used General Abbreviations and Symbols

Word or Phrase	Abbreviation or Symbol
and so on, et cetera	..., etc.
approximately, roughly, close to	~
between	bet.
can be transformed into	$\Rightarrow$
change	$\triangle$
decrease	$\downarrow$
for example	e.g.
greater than, more often than	>
important	imp.
increase	$\uparrow$
less than, less often than	<
maximum	max.
minimum	min.
not the same as, different from, unequal	$\neq$
resulting in, leading to, goes to, yields	$\rightarrow$
reversible, the reverse is true	$\leftrightarrow$
such that	s.t.
the same as, equal to	=
therefore, thus	$\therefore$
with	w., w/, $\overline{w}$
without	w/out, w/o, $\overline{w}$/out
with regard to, with respect to, concerning	w.r.t.

4.5 OUTLINES

Outlining is the organizational pattern which American students are taught to use. While you are studying in American universities with American students, under American professors, it is important to fully understand how to write and use outlines, whether or not outlining coincides with the most desirable organization or style in your own language or culture. Examine the following outline.

Descriptions of Outlines

I. Definition

II. Characteristics
    A. Divisions and subdivisions
        1. Minimum of two, maximum of six
        2. Rarely only one item in any division
    B. Levels
        1. Three or four
        2. Up to six for long, complex subjects
    C. Items within any division or subdivision
        1. Equal importance
        2. Parallel structure
    D. Balance within divisions

III. Forms
    A. Types
        1. Topic
        2. Sentence
    B. Marking systems
        1. Number-letter
        2. Decimal

IV. Uses
    A. Introduction
    B. Analysis
        1. Reading
        2. Lecture notes
    C. Synthesis
        1. Forms
        2. Steps
            a. Topic selection
            b. List of ideas
            c. Division of ideas
            d. Revision
    D. Conclusion

V. Examples and practice

Definition

An outline is a skeletal framework for organizing information. The framework is a hierarchy of logically related items broken into major divisions, subdivisions, and sub-subdivisions, to as many as six levels. Each division is subordinate to the item on the level immediately above it.

Characteristics of a Formal Outline

All items within a given division are of relatively equal importance and are presented in parallel structure. Different parallelism (for example, nouns in some levels, verbs in others) may be used in different levels of the outline. See the topic outline in this section for an illustration.

There are a minimum of two but usually no more than six major divisions. There is rarely only *one* item under *any* division.

Three or four levels are customary. An outline has six levels only if the subject is extremely complex and the paper is extremely long.

Examining the outline as a whole, the *goal* of a formal outline is balance within all divisions. This goal is seldom fully realized because, for example, one idea may need more details to support it than another idea at the same level. Nevertheless, if an outline (especially on the first two levels) is *very* unbalanced, it is likely that something important has not been adequately developed or that a relatively minor item has been given too much attention.

Forms of Outlines

Types of Outlines. A *topic* outline uses single words or short phrases to present the ideas in the outline. The introduction and conclusion may also be expressed in phrases. The outline at the beginning of this section and the first sample outline, *Television Programs and Their Effect on Children*, are topic outlines.

A *sentence* outline expresses *all* items as complete sentences. Because this makes the outline quite long, the sentences should be as concise as possible. The second sample outline, *Television Programs and Their Effect on Children*, is an example of a sentence outline.

Outline Marking Systems. *Number-letter* marking is the most frequently taught system for marking outline divisions. The sequence is 1 . . . , A . . . , 1 . . . , a . . . , (1) . . . , (a) . . . .

Decimal marking, the system shown in Outline 2 in this section, is generally used for technical material such as formal reports, journal articles, and grant proposals.

Uses of Outlines

University students' outlines are used for two purposes: analysis and synthesis. Analytical skills are applied to reading material and lecture notes to find the organizational pattern in material written by others. Synthetic skills are applied in activities that involve producing organized original pieces of work, such as writing essay answers in examinations and preparing academic papers and oral presentations.

Analysis. Because much *reading* is required in college work, students often find they remember better when they take notes after they have read a chapter or an article. A very helpful means of taking notes is to write an outline of the major points and note some of the examples used by the author to illustrate those points. This, of course, assumes that the author organized his ideas well before writing the article. Headings and subheadings in an article can help locate the major divisions and subdivisions. A good introduction or abstract contains the major ideas and a suggestion of the organization of the article.

Some *lectures* lend themselves to outlining; others do not. A good lecturer prefaces his discussion with a summary of the main points he intends to cover. If he follows through on them, these points form a partial structure for an outline of the lecture. Other lecturers, even though they may not begin with a summary, present well-organized material which easily falls into an outline. Still other lecturers tend to be disorganized or go off on tangents; writing an outline for their lectures is impossible. In that case, just take notes, group them as well as possible, and later look for an organizational pattern in your notes which will best help you use the material.

Synthesis. An outline is a useful means for organizing your own material, whether it is to be presented orally or in written form.

Following the steps below will help you organize your ideas, and prepare an outline:

1. Select a topic carefully. Keep in mind specific requirements. Develop a thesis statement, that is, a statement of the central focus or idea.
2. Make a list of ideas to be included. Revise the focus if necessary.
3. Organize the ideas into major points, subdivisions of the major points, and details (such as examples) which explain or support those subdivisions. This is the basis for a tentative outline. An essay answer in an exam generally relies on a tentative outline.
4. When the end product is a paper or an oral presentation, revise the outline after further reading and thinking.

At all times an outline should be viewed as a useful *tool,* not an end in itself. Too rigid adherence to an outline, particularly in phrasing the ideas, can lead to a dull presentation or paper. Style, originality, and sentence variety are important factors in the effectiveness of the final presentation. Remember—an outline is a device to help organize ideas, but not something which specifies precisely how the final work will come out.

Practice 1

Choose one of the following topics, limit it, and write five or more points which you would include in a three- or four-page paper.

1. Movies I enjoy
2. The school system in _____ (your country)
3. The books I would take to a desert island
4. What every foreign student should know before he comes to America

Practice 2

Take the points you wrote for Practice 1 and organize them in the order you would present them in a paper. Then add details (examples, adjectives) which you would want to include in your paper.

Reading Selection and Sample Outlines

Television Programs and Their Effect on Children

Television programs regularly entertain, pacify, educate, frighten, and babysit the majority of American children from the time they are one or two years old. Most children are allowed to watch whatever program is on, with little thought on the parents' part of the effect that particular show will have on a child. Most programs can be classed as beneficial, harmful, or mediocre, according to what effect the program might have on a child.

The beneficial television programs are mainly those that educate the young. There are often nature specials on animal life that are realistic, and that teach children an appreciation for all life. There are a few regular children's programs, such as "Sesame Street" or "Electric Company," that develop the child's interest in school-type learning by stressing numbers and the alphabet, and that encourage him or her to be creative. Children's Christmas specials can offer a warm, wholesome form of entertainment, and the beneficial commercials, such as those on anti-smoking, anti-litter, and health, should be included in this category.

On the opposite side are the shows which are generally harmful to children. Many commercials, especially those sponsoring the children's programs, are deliberately written to create a desire for an unnecessary product such as sugar-coated cereals and candy. All adult programs that include violence or overdone sex scenes can at best fill a child's mind with confusing or misleading ideas, and could possibly harden the child to violence, leave him terrified, or warp his viewpoint towards human life and sexual love. Many children's cartoons should be classified as bad because of their constant ridiculing of all adults.

Many remaining programs can be classed as mediocre: not harmful to the child, but not beneficial. These would include the unrealistic situation comedies, some Saturday morning children's shows, and the "super hero" type that often contains violence. These programs are useless to the child except as a poor form of entertainment. Parents should try to interest their children in books or creative activities rather than allow them to watch and absorb useless or harmful materials.

Thoughtful parents will definitely not allow their children to view the bad programs and should discourage them from watching the mediocre ones. A child's viewing time should be limited mainly to watching educational, beneficial programs.

The following two outlines cover the reading selection you have just read. Outline 1, a topic outline, uses the number-letter system of marking divisions. Outline 2, a sentence outline, uses the decimal system.

Outline 1—*Television Programs and Their Effect on Children*

Introduction—prevalence of T.V. and parents' disregard for program selection

I. Beneficial programs
   A. Nature specials
      1. Are realistic
      2. Teach appreciation of all life
   B. "Sesame Street" and similar programs
      1. Develop interest in school
      2. Encourage creativity
   C. Christmas programs
   D. Some commercials

II. Harmful programs
   A. Many commercials
   B. Adult programs containing violence or sex
      1. Confuse the child
      2. Harden him to violence
      3. Frighten him
      4. Warp his attitudes
   C. Many cartoons

III. Mediocre programs
   A. Unrealistic situation comedies
   B. Saturday morning children's shows
   C. "Super hero" programs

Conclusion—parental control and guidance in children's selection of programs

Outline 2—*Television Programs and Their Effect on Children*

Introduction—Children watch a lot of T.V., seldom with any parental influence in choice of program. Programs can be classed in three groups which have different effects on children.

1. Some programs are beneficial, that is, they educate the young.
    1.1. Nature specials on animal life educate children.
        1.1.1. They are realistic.
        1.1.2. They teach children an appreciation for all life.
    1.2. Regular children's programs such as "Sesame Street" are beneficial.
        1.2.1. They develop interest in learning by stressing numbers and the alphabet.
        1.2.2. They encourage children to be creative.
    1.3. Children's Christmas specials offer a warm, wholesome form of entertainment.
    1.4. Some commercials, such as those on anti-smoking, are beneficial.

2. Some programs are harmful to children.
    2.1. Many commercials, especially those on children's programs, create desire for unnecessary products.
    2.2. Adult programs which contain violence or overdone sex scenes are harmful.
        2.2.1. They can confuse and mislead children.
        2.2.2. They can harden them to violence.
        2.2.3. They can terrify them.
        2.2.4. They can warp their viewpoint toward human life and sexual love.
    2.3. Many children's cartoons are harmful because they constantly ridicule all adults.

3. Most of the remaining programs are mediocre—neither harmful nor beneficial.
    3.1. Unrealistic situation comedies are mediocre.
    3.2. Some Saturday morning children's shows are useless.
    3.3. "Super hero" programs are generally mediocre, though too much violence makes them harmful.

Conclusion—Thoughtful parents should encourage their children to watch beneficial programs, discourage them from viewing mediocre ones, and not allow them to watch the harmful ones.

Practice 3

Reviewing the two outlines of *Television Programs and Their Effect on Children,* discuss in class the conventions for indentation, capitalization, and punctuation.

Practice 4

Read this passage and complete the outline that follows:

Northern California

The geography and activities of northern California are diversified. From west to east, there are three main zones: the coast, the Central Valley, and the mountains. The San Francisco Bay Area, including San Francisco, Berkeley, Oakland, San Jose, and many smaller cities, is the major urban area on the northern coast. Important coastal industries include shipping, trade, and manufacturing. Many residents and visitors find it enjoyable to take a peaceful drive on Highway 1 from Monterey along the Pacific Ocean and north through the redwood region. City visits include cultural events such as concerts, art exhibits, and museum tours; bike and walking tours; and a variety of international restaurants.

East of the coastal belt is the Central Valley. Agriculture is the area's dominant activity, from Sacramento, the state capital and regional commercial center, to Fresno, the hub of farm product processing. The California State Water Project links the two main rivers, the Sacramento and the San Joaquin, in a network of dams and canals. The massive system provides hydroelectric power and makes it possible for Central Valley farmers to irrigate their crops, thus creating one of the world's most productive regions. Much of the nation's produce (fruits and vegetables) and wine come from this area, as well as California's meat and poultry supply. On the eastern edge of the Central Valley is the Gold Country, an area of old mines and towns which flourished during the Gold Rush of the mid-1800s. Now, thousands of people visit the ghost towns.

The easternmost area of northern California lies within the Sierra Nevada Mountains. In this region, thousands of acres of evergreens and rugged terrain provide a setting for lumbering and recreation. Many of the forested areas are set aside as national forests in which logging is carefully regulated, and young trees are continually planted to renew the forest. Lake Tahoe and national parks are the major recreation spots in the area.

Waterskiing and boating in the summer and snow skiing in the winter are popular seasonal activities at Lake Tahoe. In the national parks, from Lassen in the north to Yosemite in the south, visitors go hiking and camping in the summer and skiing in the winter.

Practice 5

Analyze I, fill in the blanks under II, and construct an appropriate outline for III.

Northern California

I. Coastal areas

   A. Cities

      1. San Francisco

      2. Berkeley

      3. Oakland

      4. San Jose

      5. Smaller cities

   B. Industries

      1. Shipping

      2. Trade

      3. Manufacturing

   C. Activities

      1. Driving on Highway 1

         a. Monterey

         b. Redwoods

      2. Visiting cities

         a. Concerts

         b. Art exhibits

         c. Museum tours

         d. Bike and walking tours

         e. Restaurants

II. Central Valley

   A. Agricultural area

      1. _____

         a. Sacramento

            (1) _____

            (2) _____

         b. _____ , processing center

                2. California State Water Project

                    a. _____

                        (1) _____

                        (2) San Joaquin

                    b. _____

                        (1) Hydroelectric power

                        (2) Irrigation

                3. Products

                    a. _____

                        (1) Fruits

                        (2) _____

                    b. Wine

                    c. _____

        B. _____

            1. Old mines

            2. _____

III.

Practice 6

Using the techniques discussed in this section, write a formal outline of this composition. There are various possible outlines.

Types of Higher Education in the United States

Higher education in the United States is a complex interwoven system of colleges and technical schools with a great variety of degree programs, goals, and approaches. When a student chooses a college or university, he must examine a large number of possibilities ranging from a trade or technical school to some of the world's leading universities.

Trade and technical schools are usually private, although there are a few publicly funded institutions of this kind. They offer post–high-school programs of limited length, usually one or two years, in such fields as computer programing, electronics, and secretarial skills. A student who completes such a program usually receives a certificate rather than a degree, and is then certified by his school as competent in his field.

A large part of public higher education in many states is the system of community colleges or junior colleges. These two-year institutions, partially supported by individual communities, serve a number of functions. Many students complete their lower division courses at the low-cost community colleges, then transfer to four-year schools to earn a B.S. or B.A. Many others complete two-year A.A. degrees in programs similar to those offered in private trade schools. Still other students come to community colleges in order to take only one or two courses in a subject which they find interesting, such as photography, foreign languages, art, or music.

Most states have a system of state colleges and universities which receive funding from state tax revenues. In many cases, these schools have developed from a nineteenth-century system of teachers' colleges into the schools that educate the bulk of the college graduates in the United States. Most state colleges and universities offer undergraduate and Master's degrees and some have programs leading to doctorates. Large and often prestigious public educational institutions have many campuses which offer a wide range of programs from undergraduate education through the most advanced degrees, with specialized schools in professional fields such as business, law, and medicine. Examples of large public university systems are the University of California and the State University of New York.

In addition to the public colleges and universities, a large number of private colleges and universities offer comparable degrees. Private schools range from small liberal arts colleges, such as Reed College in Oregon, Dartmouth in New Hampshire, and Oberlin in Ohio, to universities with world-wide reputations, such as MIT, Carnegie-Mellon, the University of Chicago, and Stanford. While degrees from public and private universities are equivalent, finances are not. Because private schools do not receive tax support, their tuition is usually much higher than the tuition at a public college or university.

4.6 SUMMARY AND PARAPHRASE

The skills of summary and paraphrase are used to incorporate other people's ideas into a composition, an essay for a take-home examination, or a longer academic paper. Summarizing or paraphrasing means converting material written by others into your own words without distorting the meaning and without copying the author's exact words.

A *summary* condenses the essential information from a piece of writing into a unified group of sentences. It contains the main ideas of the original selection, stated in your own words. Usually, several sentences can be summarized in one sentence; a long paragraph can be adequately summarized in two or three sentences; and several paragraphs can be summarized in a paragraph of four or five sentences. Summaries of longer selections may be several hundred words long.

A *paraphrase* expresses a single idea and its supporting detail. In contrast to a summary, it is usually more specific and closer to the original in length.

This lesson helps you distinguish between summaries and paraphrases and helps you develop your skill in writing them. (For term paper paraphrasing, see the lessons on academic paper preparation in chapter five.)

Study and discuss the sample summaries and paraphrase of the following passage.

> The nation's newest form of public transportation is a car that runs on tracks along its own roadbed or even down the middle of a street, carrying passengers in smooth comfort and drawing its power from an electric wire strung overhead. Sound familiar? Yes, it's the trolley car, masquerading in modern dress under the new name of "light-rail vehicle" or LRV. From the brink of extinction, with only 1,068 cars serving seven American cities last year compared with 26,630 cars in service in 1940, the trolley is showing signs of making a comeback.
>
> "Clang! Clang! Clang! Trolley Coming Back,"
> The Washington Post, in Los Angeles Times,
> Vol. 94 (27 July 1975), Part 1, p. 2.

A Possible Two- to Three-Sentence Summary. The trolley, or LRV (light-rail vehicle) as it is now being called, is once again becoming a means of mass transit in the U.S. after having been used very little for over thirty years. The LRV is a car which runs on tracks and is powered by electricity from an overhead wire.

A Possible Single-Sentence Summary. The LRV (light-rail vehicle), an updated electric trolley car, is presently undergoing a revival as a method of mass transit in the U.S.

A Possible One- to Two-Sentence Paraphrase of the Final Sentence. Whereas in 1940 there were 26,630 trolley cars in use in the U.S., in 1974 there were only 1068 trolleys. There are signs this year that the trolley is coming back into use.

Basic Considerations in Summary and Paraphrase

1. Use your own words. The only exceptions are these:
   a. A word or short phrase which is the author's original term for a particular concept may be used. Occasionally a summary of a long selection includes a short quotation from the original. When you use the author's exact words, you must cite the author, making it clear that you are using his words.
   b. A word which has no synonym *(Europe, calcium)* or very few

synonyms *(research, solar energy, international relations)* may be copied.
2. Use your own writing style. Never use the author's exact word order or his individual characteristics of style.
3. Use your own organization of ideas.
4. Do not add your own ideas within the summary or paraphrase.
5. Acknowledge the source of the original information. Documentation is discussed in the chapter on academic paper preparation.

Practice 1

Write a summary of each of the following passages.

The computer is likely to have less effect on teachers than did the book, which destroyed the teacher's monopoly of knowledge by giving students the power, for the first time, to learn in private—and to learn as much as, or more than, their masters. There is reason to believe that the computer will change the teacher's role and function rather than diminish his importance.

Charles E. Silberman, *Crisis in the Classroom*
(New York: Vintage Books, 1970), p. 188.

Caliper brakes, as opposed to coaster brakes, are operated by squeezing hand levers. An experienced cyclist can moderate them faster and more easily than coaster brakes, permitting quicker, better controlled stops. But calipers have severe limitations in wet weather—our riders experienced an almost total loss of brake response in our braking tests when the wheel rims are wet. If your bike has caliper brakes, when the rims are wet, go extra slow and *walk* your vehicle down hills.

"Three-Speed Bicycles," *Consumer Reports 1975 Buying Guide*, p. 287.

Human beings have two powerful needs that are at odds with each other: to keep things the same, and to have something new happen. We like to feel secure, yet at times we like to be surprised. Too much predictability leads to monotony, but too little may lead to anxiety. To establish a balance between continuity and change is a task facing all organisms, individual and social, human and non-human.

F. Barron, M. Jarvik, and S. Bunnell, Jr., "The Hallucinogenic Drugs," *Scientific American*, Vol. 210 (April 1964), p. 11.

Few mammals actually live in the sea—whales, seals and sea otters are the only important mammalian members of the marine community. Like all mammals they possess body hair that is used for insulation. Oil pollution causes the hair to become matted, which reduces its effectiveness as a thermal insulator. The animal will therefore either freeze or succumb to diseases because of lowered resistance. Mammals are also affected by oil through the food chain. This is especially important in whales since they are plankton feeders. Reduction in the plankton population may cause whales to relocate or starve.

Bela G. Lintock, ed.,
Environmental Engineers'
Handbook, Vol. 1 (Radnor, Pa.:
Chilton Book Co., 1974), p. 1640.

Culture can be loosely defined as the body of non-genetic information which people pass from generation to generation. It is the accumulated knowledge that, in the old days, was passed on entirely by word of mouth, painting, and demonstration. Several thousand years ago the written word was added to the means of cultural transmission. Today culture is passed on in these ways, and also through television, computer tapes, motion pictures, records, blueprints, and other media. Culture is all the information man possesses except for that which is stored in the chemical language of his genes.

Paul R. Ehrlich, *The Population Bomb*
(New York: Ballantine Books, Inc., 1971), p. 13.

Music is used for many purposes today, and not all of them involve entertainment. It is used in advertising to attract attention and to promote products. Huge amounts of money are spent to create clever thirty-second "hits," which subliminally pressure consumers to make purchases. Music is also used as a pacifier; the music piped into elevators, supermarkets, airplanes, and shopping centers is designed to be ignored. It serves its purpose best when it is least obvious. This music encourages listeners to relax, slow down, and buy. Business firms provide background music for their workers, to blot out distracting noises and increase efficiency. Farmers supply the same "canned" music to their livestock to increase milk and egg production.

The unfortunate aspect of all this background music is that it has conditioned the listener to not listen. Almost in self-defense, one learns to block out such music automatically.

Robert Hickok, *Music Appreciation* (New York:
Appleton Century Crofts, 1971), pp. 365–66.

Practice 2

Write a paraphrase of each passage.

Taking lecture notes while you are studying at an American university is essential. In lectures, many American professors provide information which is *not* in the assigned text or in the outside reading for the course.

Guide to Language and Study Skills for College Students of English as a Second Language, p. 205.

Few technological developments are formidable enough to mark turning points in human history. Two such phenomena have occurred in our time: the atomic bomb and the computer.

Saturday Review, Vol. 49, No. 30 (23 July 1966), p. 15

Affluence has produced a tremendous increase in the use of credit and in the sale of all sorts of insurance policies.

Vance Packard, *The Naked Society* (New York: The David McKay Co., Inc., 1964), p. 23.

Not everyone gets the flu every time it strikes, true. But what's equally true is that not everyone who has the flu knows he has it.

Lawrence Galton, "Flu Gets Us All Eventually," *New York Times* (24 March 1974), Vol. IV, p. 6.

Few contemporary American families include grandparents, aunts, uncles, and cousins—all of whom used to be around, like the front porch, to widen the family circle. Fifty years ago, half the families in the U.S. included at least one extra adult; today, fewer than 5 percent do.

"The Parent Gap," *Newsweek,* Vol. 86, No. 12 (22 September 1975), p. 53.

The Green Revolution has contributed to widening the gap between rich and poor farmers because those able to risk more for the required fertilizer, insecticide, and water have prospered. The poor farmer, living from crop to crop, cannot afford the added costs without credit, which is expensive, if available at all.

James P. Sterba, "The Green Revolution Isn't So Bright," *This World* (20 May 1973), p. 27.

Practice 3

Read the following selection. First, write a summary of the passage. Then write a paraphrase of the following sentence from the passage: "In the next five years, it is estimated, 600 new doctors in astronomy will appear."

"Astronomy is everybody's second science." This oft-quoted phrase is used by Beverly Lynds of Kitt Peak National Observatory as an important reason for the dimensions of the current employment crisis in astronomy. The science is intellectually exciting, popular and attractive. It is relatively simple for persons trained in other branches of physical science to enter astronomy. It is relatively difficult for astronomers (their training tends to be narrow) to go into other branches. Twice as many enter as leave.

The figures are stark—a good deal worse than those for other sciences that are feeling the crunch. Four times as many astronomy Ph.D.'s are being graduated each year as there are positions to fill. In the next five years, it is estimated, 600 new doctors in astronomy will appear. Yet the same estimate gives only 50 to 100 expected openings by retirement and no more than 200 from all causes. There are now about 1,500 practicing astronomers in the United States. In 1970, 623 Ph.D.'s listed themselves as astronomers. The growth has come because of tremendous excitement in the field and because of the space program.

"Astronomy: Too Attractive Science," *Science News,* Vol. 107 (29 March 1975), p. 206.

Practice 4

From one of your textbooks or a textbook in your field, select two short passages. Photocopy the passages and document their sources. Write a summary of each selection.

Practice 5

From a magazine article or journal article of interest to you, select a short passage (a paragraph or sequence of paragraphs). Photocopy the passage and document the source. Write a summary of the passage.

Practice 6

Select one idea (one or two sentences) in *each* of the passages which you summarized in Practices 4 and 5. Write a one- or two-sentence paraphrase of each idea.

4.7 WRITING AN ABSTRACT

An abstract is a concise statement of the major points of a paper. Its purpose is to give the reader a preview of the paper. An abstract may be as short as one or two sentences or as long as 350 words. A hundred words is a reasonable length; use fewer if appropriate.

Steps to Follow in Writing an Abstract

1. Carefully read through the paper, including the outline. A well-constructed outline will help you write a thorough but brief abstract.
2. Using your outline as a guide, write a paragraph which contains the central idea and major points of the paper. When an abstract is based on original research, or on a project you designed and conducted, it should contain a brief statement of each of the following: the problem, the procedures, the results, and the conclusions.
3. Read through the paragraph and make sure you have included every major point. Determine the length and compare it to the maximum. (Do not be surprised if it is too long; this is usually the case of a tentative abstract.)
4. Revise the paragraph. Rewrite some individual sentences to make them more concise. Look for places where subordination or parallel structure can be effectively used to reduce the length. Be certain not to eliminate important content as you make your revisions. Also be certain not to include any ideas which are not in the paper. Do not include any tables or diagrams. In general, use words instead of symbols; for example, write out *NaCl* as *sodium chloride*. Make certain that the final paragraph reads smoothly

Sample Abstracts

A Survey of Selected Administrative Practices Supporting Student Evaluation of Instruction Programs

A mail survey of 333 American universities was conducted to assess the current status of Student Evaluation of Instruction. Based on a 68% return, it was concluded that there has been an increase in the popularity of student ratings as a means of evaluating faculty performance, as well as an increase in the frequency with which evaluation results are used in decisions concerning faculty status. However, at most universities, research on the rating instruments does not seem to have kept pace with the decisions that are based on the rating instruments.

Isaac I. Bejar, *Research in Higher Education*, Vol. 3, No. 1 (1975), p. 77.

The Impact of the Energy Crisis on Industrial and Consumer New Car Buyers: A Case Study

The energy crisis coupled with the recent economic recession has been creating market havoc with respect to the type and size of cars designed by consumer and industrial fleet purchasers. Based on the intentions of a random sample of 1973–75 new car buyers in Wisconsin, the paper predicts the steady state market share for full size, intermediate and compact cars. The paper also examines how the steady state market share can be expected to fluctuate with varying levels of improvement in gasoline mileage.

G. M. Naidu, Arno Kleimenhagen, and James Rothe, *Operations Research Society of America* (ORSA), Vol. 23, Supp. 2 (Fall 1975), B351.

Academic Paper Preparation

5

5.1 INTRODUCTION

Requiring students to write papers is a very common teaching device in the United States, and American students write many of them in high school. It is very important for you to have experience in writing an American-style term paper before beginning to study in an American university.

Writing a paper will help you in numerous ways:

1. It will give you practice in using a campus library system as a research tool.
2. It will acquaint you with the form, content, depth, and style required in papers written for American professors.
3. It will give you the opportunity to work on the developmental stages of a term paper with close supervision from your English instructor, and to benefit from your instructor's suggestions.
4. Most important—it will give you practice in expressing *in English* a topic of particular interest and value to you.

Chapter Outline

    Criteria for Evaluation
    Selecting and Limiting a Topic
    Library Research and Note-taking
    Preparing a Rough Draft

Documentation
Revising the Rough Draft
Typing and Proofreading

5.2 CRITERIA FOR EVALUATION

A paper is graded on its technical content and on its accurate, effective use of language. The grade is based on such aspects as depth and thoroughness of coverage, use and documentation of sources, and originality of treatment. Technical competence is usually the determining factor, but ineffective use of English may reduce the clarity of the ideas and may, therefore, result in a lower grade. For papers at the undergraduate level, professors use the letter grade system:

A excellent
B above average
C average
D barely passing
F failing

Plus (+) or minus (−) following a letter grade provides more precise evaluation, A, A−, B+, B, B−, C+, etc. In graduate schools, often only A, B, and C (with + or −) are used, with the following interpretation:

A excellent
B average
C passing

The relative value of a letter grade varies somewhat from professor to professor. A growing number of schools are using other grading systems. One of the most common of these is pass/fail, which is sometimes used as an alternative to a letter grade. A paper may be weighed as heavily as an exam. In some courses the paper grade may be the only means of course evaluation, and therefore is the course grade as well.

One criterion for a paper written for United States university professors is that it be an original piece of work. If you follow the guidelines described in these sections, you will have an original paper, a paper unlike any other paper ever written on your topic.

To write an original paper you must not plagiarize. Plagiarism is the illegal act of presenting other people's words or ideas as though they were your own. Plagiarism may be very blatant (an entire paragraph or chapter copied from elsewhere), or it may be more difficult to detect (changing words here and there without restructuring the material). Whether it is blatant or subtle, it is still theft of someone's material. It is *never permitted*.

In some universities students who are caught plagiarizing are subject to dismissal.

Correct documentation and use of paraphrasing will enable you to write without plagiarizing unintentionally.

In order to write a good paper, then, you need to paraphrase the ideas of others, fuse them with your own, and document what you have borrowed, thus creating a work of your own.

5.3 SELECTING AND LIMITING THE TOPIC

It is possible that you will change your mind many times as you decide on a particular topic. After you have chosen a general topic area, you will probably need to limit your topic to a specific topic which is appropriate to the constraints of time, length, and audience, and which is of interest and value to you.

As an illustration, let us say that four students have independently chosen the general area of noise pollution as their topic. Student A is an undergraduate interested in airplanes. Student B is an undergraduate majoring in civil engineering. Student C is an undergraduate whose hobby is playing the guitar. Student D is a graduate student in environmental engineering. Each student does some thinking about noise pollution. What does he already know about it? What would he like to learn?

Study figure 1. Notice that each of the students arrives at a different limited topic.

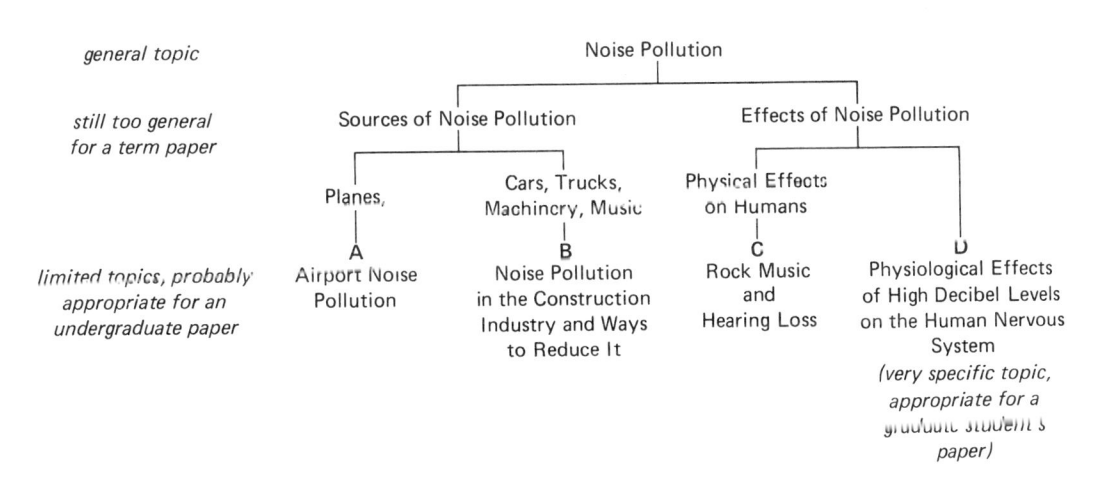

```
general topic                              Noise Pollution
                                    ┌─────────────┴─────────────┐
still too general           Sources of Noise Pollution      Effects of Noise Pollution
for a term paper            ┌───────────┴───────────┐       ┌───────────┴───────────┐
                                                Cars, Trucks,   Physical Effects
                          Planes,              Machinery, Music  on Humans
                            │                       │                │                │
                            A                       B                C                D
limited topics, probably  Airport Noise       Noise Pollution    Rock Music      Physiological Effects
appropriate for an        Pollution           in the Construction    and         of High Decibel Levels
undergraduate paper                           Industry and Ways  Hearing Loss    on the Human Nervous
                                              to Reduce It                            System
                                                                                 (very specific topic,
                                                                                  appropriate for a
                                                                                  graduate student's
                                                                                       paper)
```

Fig. 1. Narrowing a paper topic.

Practice 1

How would you limit each of the following general areas to a more specific topic? Compare your limited topics with those of your classmates.

1. The Computer
2. Education
3. Astronomy
4. Energy Sources
5. Agricultural Methods
6. Water Pollution
7. Music
8. Ocean Resources
9. Nutrition
10. Automobile Safety

Practice 2

Discuss each of the following topics. Are any too limited? Are any not limited enough? Which are sufficiently limited?

1. The Origin of Radio
2. Organ Transplants
3. Migration Patterns of Butterflies
4. The Open Classroom Concept
5. Computer Uses in Medicine
6. Movie Censorship
7. Pros and Cons of Strip Mining
8. Supersonic Transport
9. Adjusting to American Life
10. Earthquake-proof Buildings

A specific topic is not necessarily a final topic. Reevaluate the topic as you begin to find library sources. Ask yourself these questions, keeping in mind the constraints of length, time, and audience:

1. Is this a topic you will be willing to spend time on?
2. Is the topic of suitable difficulty?
   a. Is it too easy? If so, make it more specific.
   b. Is it too difficult? If so, make the topic more general or consider a new direction for limiting the original general topic.
   c. Is it suitable to your present level of education, but somewhat challenging?
3. Are there recent sources available in English about the topic? If you have not already gone to a library to find sources, that should be the next step.

5.4 LIBRARY RESEARCH AND NOTE-TAKING

Every term paper is a highly individualized piece of work. Nonetheless, there are some general rules and guidelines to follow in gathering, selecting, and recording information for the rough draft of a paper.

Using a Library

Different topics will require the use of different information sources, but there are a number of reference tools that every student should be able to use with ease. These references include the card catalog and *Reader's Guide to Periodical Literature,* as well as indexes to major newspapers and to publications in various fields. Become familiar with some of the many indexes and handbooks, such as

Reader's Guide to the Social Sciences
Business Periodicals Index
Handbook of Chemistry and Physics
Civil Engineering Handbook

A library tour and a booklet on how to use the library provide useful orientation to a campus library and its branches, but the best way to use it is to ask questions when you want more information about possible references.

Selecting References

As a starting point, you need to build a list of potentially useful sources of information about your topic. As you begin locating sources, consider these points:

1. In general it is good practice to use three or more references. A preliminary list should contain far more than three sources.
2. References should be from a variety of sources: books, periodicals (magazines, journals, newspapers), government documents, and unpublished papers.
3. It is important to use up-to-date sources. For a current topic, at least two references should be from work published within the last three years. For a historical topic, older sources may be appropriate.
4. Graduate students should rely heavily on the journal literature in their fields.
5. Sources often have bibliographies which lead to other sources. When making an initial list of possible sources, choose at least one book, chapter, or article which has an extensive bibliography or reference list. Use that list to find other sources.
6. The availability of sources may determine whether or not the topic is reasonable. It may be necessary to change or refine the topic if you cannot locate enough appropriate references.

Writing a Tentative Outline

Before scanning or reading for information, it is helpful to have a general idea of what specific areas of the topic you intend to cover, and how they might be organized. A tentative outline presents the basic organization and ideas of a topic. It may list only the major divisions. For example, a tentative outline might look like this:

1. Sources of Airport Noise Pollution
2. Present Efforts to Reduce Airport Noise Pollution
3. Future Plans for Reducing Airport Noise Pollution

A tentative outline changes and expands as you evaluate sources, select relevant information, and take notes.

Selecting Relevant Information

How do you decide what is relevant? First you need a well-defined topic, a preliminary list of references, and a tentative outline. It is better to scan or read *too many* sources and gradually eliminate some as you refine your topic than it is to read too few. You may locate sources or information you might not have found otherwise, and your paper will be improved as a result. Professors and fellow students may be able to offer potential sources of material, and it is a good idea to ask them, but before the rough draft is prepared, only *you* can decide if the information is relevant to *your* topic. As you begin examining the sources, ask yourself these questions:

1. Is the source and/or author respected in the field? This criterion applies primarily to texts, books, and journals. If you are in doubt, ask an instructor. General magazines and newspapers are acceptable for some topics.
2. Does the material relate to your tentative outline? That is, does it explain, argue against, develop, or illustrate a point in your outline?
   a. If it does, it is probably relevant and you will want to take some notes based on the material.
   b. If it does not, make a note of what it *does* contain. You may find that later you will revise your topic and outline and it will fit. Or you may find it useful for some other paper at some future date.
3. Does the material relate to your stated topic?
   a. If it relates to your outline but not to your topic, you may need to reconsider the relevance of that area of your outline to the topic, or perhaps you need to revise your topic.
   b. If it relates directly to your topic but not to the outline, you need to rethink the major developmental points of the outline.

In summary, if material in a reputable source fits into your outline in some way *and* has direct bearing on your topic, it is relevant and you should take notes on it.

Taking Notes for a Term Paper

There are as many variations of taking notes for a paper as there are students. Notes can be made mentally, or in writing on paper or cards. Some students retain tremendous amounts of detailed information and citations in their minds and recall them when necessary. They write rough drafts on the basis of mental notes and then go back to the source to make sure they have not distorted the ideas or facts presented. This method is *not* recommended for foreign students beginning their work in American universities.

Written notes are preferable because they are easier to retrieve. Notes for a paper may be taken on sheets of paper, small slips of paper, or index cards. Because of the need to *sort* information after gathering it, large sheets of paper may be inconvenient. To sort the material, you have to cut the paper or keep mental track of each bit of information on it. Slips of paper lend themselves to sorting, but they are easily damaged or lost and are hard to keep together. Index cards (three-by-five- or four-by-six-inch size) are durable, easy to sort, and easy to carry around. For these reasons it is recommended that you try using index cards at least once. You will need to write down two kinds of information: the source itself and relevant facts or ideas from the source. The guidelines below refer specifically to note cards but should be followed regardless of the method you decide to use.

Source Cards (Bibliography Cards). A source card for a book should record author (last name, first name, middle initial), title, place, publisher, and date of publication. A source card for a journal should record author, title of article, journal title, volume and issue number, and range of pages of the article (for example, pp. 37–43).

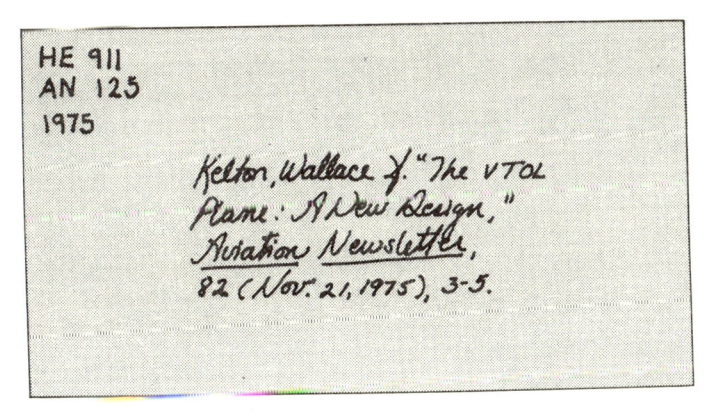

Fig. 2. Source card.

Try to follow these guidelines when writing your own source cards:

1. Be consistent in the way you put down the source information; it will save time later. For one possible form, see the sample card in figure 2.
2. Write each source on a separate card.
3. Write general notes about the content on the back of the card, if you feel they will be useful.
4. Put the library call number on the cards for sources you wish to locate again; this saves time.
5. Use a different color of card for source cards to distinguish them from information cards.

Information Cards (Notecards). An information card should contain the exact source, a topic heading, and notes.

1. Code the source by writing the author's last name or the title of the work. You need just enough information about the source to identify it precisely.
2. Write the *exact* page number which contains the information, whether the material is paraphrased or quoted.
3. Put a topic heading (based on your outline) on the card to make future sorting easier.

Notes on an Information Card. Put only *one* idea or bit of information on a card. Though it may sound wasteful, it facilitates sorting and integrating material from different sources when it is time to write the rough draft. Figure 3 shows a sample information card.

When you select information you can write it down in an exact quote or a *paraphrase;* most of your note-taking should be paraphrasing, a skill that

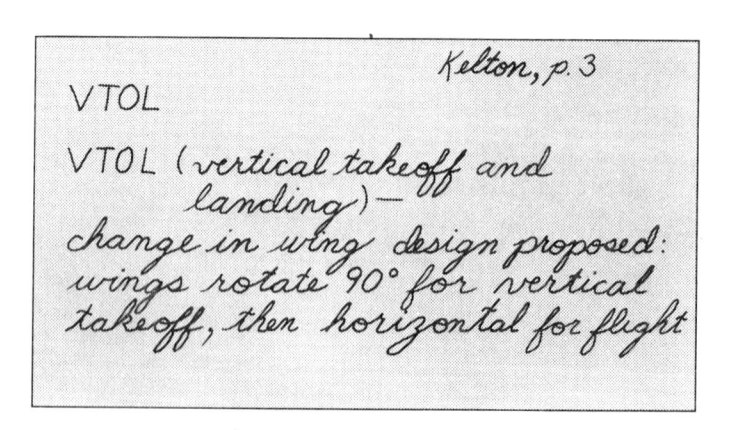

Fig. 3. Information card.

combines what you practiced in the lessons on summary and paraphrase and lecture note-taking. Your goal is to make your paraphrased notes full enough to enable you to write complete sentences in your rough draft, but not so full that they are too time-consuming or nearly identical to the original source in expression or organization. Accordingly, write your notes in phrases, using these conventions from lecture note-taking:

1. Include content words; negatives; accurate statistics; and possibly some transitions, subordinating conjunctions, articles, and prepositional phrases.
2. Use abbreviations and symbols. Develop abbreviations for words which are central concepts or which will be used frequently in your paper.
3. Write down your reactions to the material as you read and paraphrase it, and record also any related ideas that occur to you at that time. Put your ideas on the card at the bottom or on the back. Using a different color of ink, putting your own comments in brackets [ ], or marking comments with your initials will distinguish them from the source material. Later, as you organize your cards according to outline sections and start to interrelate material from various references, you will already have some of your own ideas jotted down.
4. Document all figures, diagrams, and graphs used in your paper. A card helps to keep track of what a specific figure contains and exactly where it is located. Later you can look at the card, decide if the figure should be included, and if so, go back to the source to copy it exactly.

As you take notes for your paper, keep in mind your topic and outline, your intended reader, and constraints of time and length. Do not hesitate to modify your outline as you proceed, but do not completely change topics unless there is still sufficient time to do a thorough job on the revised topic. Use notetaking both as a tool for gathering information to integrate with your own ideas *and* as a means for broadening your understanding of an area of your field.

Practice 1

Read the following excerpt from a newspaper article and examine the source and information cards based on the selection (figures 4, 5, and 6). Then write two more cards based on other information in the article.

   Nearly a fifth of all Americans move in any given year. A total of 36.1 million changed addresses in a recent 12-month period surveyed by the Census Bureau....
   Among the migrants are students seeking college educations away from home, newly marrieds setting up their first households, corporate "gypsies" following their careers, academics seeking better positions, and elderly people looking forward to a sunny retirement. Others are not so much lured to greener pastures as they are driven from their homes.

These include migratory blacks seeking work in Northern cities, and farm families who can no longer compete with corporate agriculture. The farm population, which reached its peak of 32.5 million in 1916, fell from 15.6 million in 1960 to 9.7 million in 1970, and is still falling.

While the exodus from rural to urban America continues, the most explosive population movement in recent years has been from the central cities to the suburbs. This trend had been accelerating for 50 years before it became a tidal wave in the Sixties. Today, seven of every ten Americans live in metropolitan areas and of that seven, four live in the suburbs.[1]

> Deans, Ralph C. "Millions on the Move," *Palo Alto Times* (May 3, 1973), 31

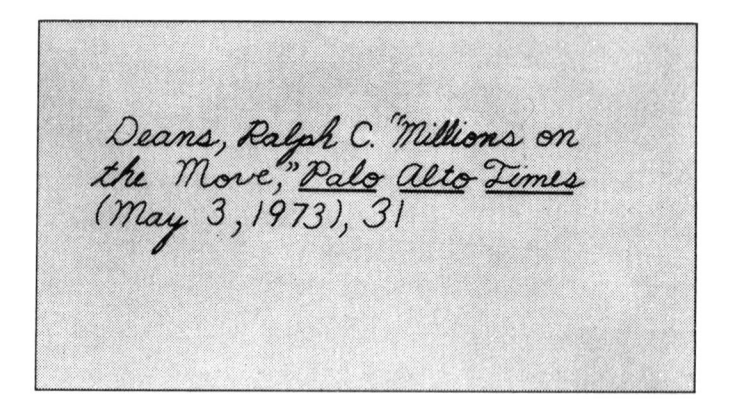

Fig. 4. Source card.

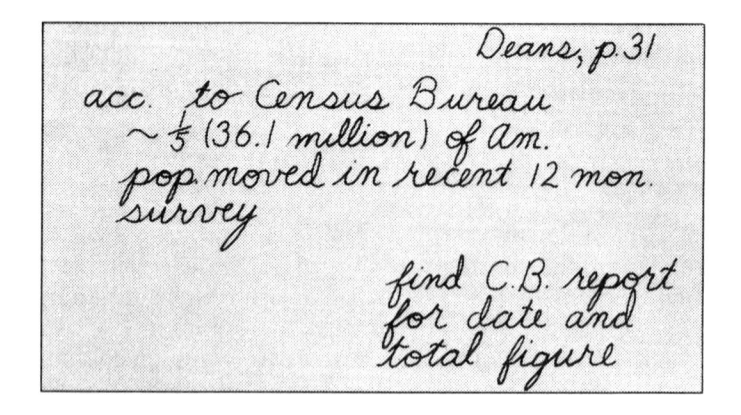

> Deans, p. 31
> acc. to Census Bureau
> ~ ⅕ (36.1 million) of Am. pop. moved in recent 12 mon. survey
>
> find C.B. report for date and total figure

Fig. 5. Information card A.

[1]Reprinted by permission from Ralph C. Deans, "Millions on the Move," *Palo Alto Times*, No. 106 (3 May 1973), p. 31.

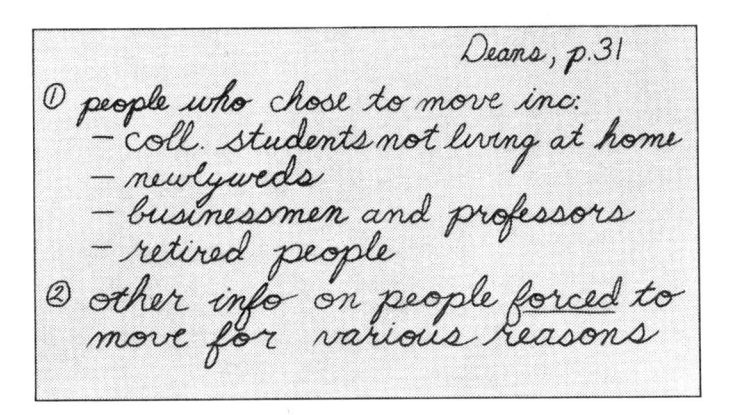

> Deans, p. 31
>
> ① people who chose to move inc:
>   – coll. students not living at home
>   – newlyweds
>   – businessmen and professors
>   – retired people
> ② other info on people _forced_ to move for various reasons

Fig. 6. Information card B.

Practice 2

Read the following selection from a journal article. Write a source card and two or more information cards based on the passage.

   The vast rural-to-urban migration that was the common pattern of U.S. population movement since World War II has halted and, on balance, even reversed. In the eyes of many Americans, the appeal of major urban areas has diminished in recent years and the attractiveness of rural and small town communities has increased. The result is a new trend that is already having an impact and that modifies much that we have taken for granted about population distribution. . . . Since 1970, changes in rural and urban population flows have occurred so rapidly that nonmetropolitan areas are not only retaining people but are receiving an actual net immigration.[2]

Practice 3

Select two magazine or journal articles on a topic of interest to you. From each article select a passage that contains information on which you can base several notecards. The passages should be related to the same major idea. For each passage do the following:

1. Write a source card.
2. Write three or more information cards. Paraphrase rather than quote the material on at least two of the cards.
3. Provide your instructor with a copy of the page(s) from which you took the information, so that the accuracy of your cards can be verified.

   [2]Calvin L. Beale, "Renewed Growth in Rural Communities," *The Futurist*, Vol. 9, No. 4 (August 1975), p. 196.

5.5 PREPARING A ROUGH DRAFT

The next step in writing an academic paper is the preparation of a first version of the paper, called a *rough draft*. In this first version, you integrate the information in your notes with your own ideas, producing an unpolished but complete version of the paper, which contains the revised outline, the text of the paper, rough diagrams, charts and other illustrations, footnotes, and bibliography. Before beginning to write, revise and expand your tentative outline. For practice in writing outlines, see the section on outlines.

Arrange your notecards according to the divisions in your outline and begin to write, keeping these guidelines in mind:

1. Use your own organization of ideas. Do not copy the sequence of ideas in any of your sources. Introduce and conclude the topic effectively.
2. Use formal English and your own writing style, within the accepted conventions for an American academic paper (discussed below).
3. Document any information which comes from other sources, whether it is summarized, paraphrased, or quoted.
4. Develop the topic clearly for your reader. Support your major points effectively with examples, definitions, statistics, and diagrams.

Stylistic Conventions

There are three main elements of the language style used in American academic writing: levels of formality, person, and voice. An academic paper is a formal piece of writing which requires the use of formal wording. It is inappropriate, for example, to begin a paper with "Last year a couple of guys figured out." An appropriate beginning would be "Recent investigations have shown." Also, formal writing does not contain contractions, such as "doesn't," "he's," and "there'll." The level of formality should be maintained throughout the paper.

Person and voice must also be considered. Academic papers are usually written in the third person (he, she, it, they). *You, we,* and *I* are avoided. On occasion, *I* is used in the conclusion of a paper when an author states personal views. In addition, passive constructions are used when the identity of the author of a source of information is not as important as what was discovered or discussed. Passive constructions are used to provide a means for a writer to explain what he did without using *I*. For example, "Next, I added 5 cc of H_2O to the solution" is better stated: "Next, 5 cc of H_2O were added to the solution." Balanced use of active and passive voice is important. See the lesson on passives in the first chapter.

For more information on stylistic conventions, consult leading journals in your academic major.

Practice 1

Each of the following three pairs of passages contains academic information presented in two styles. In class, compare each pair in terms of formality, person, and voice.

Anyway, if we look in Wilson's book, we can easily see that the majority of voting age citizens who don't vote are the rural poor, the urban slum people, the old, and the people who don't have any kind of a job.	According to Wilson, the majority of nonvoters of voting age are the rural poor, the urban poor in slums, the elderly, and the unemployed.
I've already told you that a pump is any gadget that can increase the pressure of a liquid. The kind that is different because of the way it increases the pressure is the one people call a centrifugal pump.	A pump has been defined previously as any device that can increase the pressure of a liquid. A centrifugal pump can be distinguished from other pumps by the principle it uses to increase the pressure.
In this paper I'm going to take a look at this new area of decision analysis and show you how relevant it is in my field, communication management. What I'm trying to do here is write an introduction to what's going on in the field.	The emerging field of decision analysis is defined, and its relevance to communication management is examined.

5.6 DOCUMENTATION

You *must* document *all* sources used in your paper, whether they are concepts or interpretations. All writers are expected to give credit to material in the paper which is not their own. Check your rough draft page by page to make certain that you have documented the following information with a footnote or citation:

1. Direct quotations of any length
2. Tables, graphs, figures, or diagrams from other sources
3. Key ideas, conclusions, or opinions of other people, even though you have summarized or paraphrased them in your own words
4. Factual information which is not common knowledge to the reader

In addition, footnotes are occasionally used to refer the reader to other sources which give more detail on a specific point and to provide information which does not fit smoothly into the paper, but which an interested reader would find worthwhile to know.

Two commonly used methods of citing sources used in a paper are discussed below. Some journals, departments, and fields of study use footnotes (or endnotes) and a bibliography. Others list all references at the end of the paper, either numbering the references consecutively as they occur in the text or alphabetizing them according to author.

Method One: Footnotes and Bibliography

Basics of Footnoting. A footnote should contain the following information:

1. Author, first name before last name
2. Title of work
3. Publishing information
4. Page(s) used for that specific material.

There are many forms for presenting footnote information. You are advised to use the form accepted by your department, or by a major journal in your field if your department has no specific requirements. One accepted form is used in the examples below.

Commas are used to separate author from title, and publishing information from page numbers. For example:

[4]William R. Brown, *The Future Role of Computers* (New York: J. Smithton Co., 1976), p. 235.
[5]Eric T. Garrett, "New Computer Applications in Medicine," *Computer Science Journal,* 13 (October 1975), 23.

In the form illustrated above, footnote 4 refers to a book and shows publishing information in parentheses (notice there is no comma before the parenthesis). The publishing information is the city, the state if the city is unfamiliar, the publisher, and the date.

Footnote 5 refers to a journal article and shows the author, article title in quotation marks, the journal title italicized, volume number of the journal (again no comma before the parenthesis), then the journal issue, and the page number (in this form a journal page number is not preceded by *p.* for page).

When the same work is referred to again, a shortened form of footnote may be used. For example:

[6]Brown, p. 239.
[7]Ibid., p. 240.

Footnote 6 refers to the book previously noted, and uses the author's last name only, plus the page. If there is more than one Brown in the list of sources, you repeat the first initials. For example, if the bibliography includes a book by William R. Brown and an article by Thomas L. Brown, footnote 6 would be:

[6]W. R. Brown, p. 239.

If there is more than one work by the same Brown, you would mention the title again.

Footnote 7 refers to the same book, immediately after it has been mentioned, and uses the Latin abbreviation *Ibid.* to refer to the work in the immediately preceding note. The new page number is indicated.

Footnote Placement and Typing. As the word suggests, these are notes placed at the foot (bottom) of the page and are numbered consecutively throughout the paper. The number is typed a half-space above the typed line at the end of the borrowed material (for example, . . . as stated by Brown[4]). The same number is typed at the bottom of the page, in raised position, before the corresponding footnote.

Footnotes are separated from the text on each page by a line about one and a half inches (15 spaces) long, beginning at the left margin and using the underline key. This line should be a single-space below the text and a double-space above the first footnote on the page.

Each footnote is indented five spaces for its first line. It is single-spaced and separated from the next footnote by double-spacing.

Footnoting more complicated references:

[8]John B. Shaw, "Looking Ahead," in *Advances in Technology,* ed. by Allen L. Price (Boston: Slauson Press, 1972), p. 287.

Footnote 8 is an example of an article in a book which contains articles by many different authors.

[9]Walter R. Downey, *A Study of the Radio* (London: Brownstone Press, 1958), p. 42, cited in Bernard M. Rosen, *The New Media* (New York: Cohen Co., 1975), p. 328.

Footnote 9 is an example of a source (called the primary source) cited in another source (called the secondary source). The reader has consulted the secondary source but has not read the primary source.

Some professors or departments will accept footnotes listed all on one page immediately after the body of the paper. The form is exactly the same. These footnotes are sometimes referred to as *endnotes.*

Bibliography. The bibliography is an alphabetical list of sources used in the paper. Its order is based on author's *last* name or, if there is no author, on the first word in the title which is not *a, an,* or *the.*

If several works by the same author are used, they are arranged according to the alphabetical order of the titles. In the bibliographic entries following the first one by that author, do not repeat the author's name, but indicate it is the same as the one above by using a seven-space solid line. See the example below.

Each entry should begin at the left-hand margin with following lines indented five spaces. Each entry should be single-spaced, with double-spacing between entries.

Sample Bibliography

Brown, William R. *The Future Role of Computers.* New York: J. Smithton Company, 1976.

———. *Man's Helping Hand—The Computer.* Menlo Park, California: K. T. Wilson Press, 1959.

Downey, Walter R. *A Study of the Radio.* London: Brownstone Press, 1958. Cited in Bernard M. Rosen. *The New Media.* New York: Cohen Company, 1975.

Garrett, Eric T. "New Computer Applications in Medicine," *Computer Medicine Journal,* 13 (October 1975), 21–32.

Shaw, John B. "Looking Ahead," *Advances in Technology.* Edited by Allen L. Price. Boston: Slauson Press, 1973.

For an article the pages of the article are indicated. As in footnotes, there is no comma immediately before a parenthesis. Every entry ends in a period.

The bibliography is typed on a separate page and is usually the last page of a paper. The page should be titled *Bibliography.*

Method Two: Reference List and Numbered Citations

This method presents a coded list at the end of the paper of all sources used in the paper, and the same code is placed after each piece of information in the text which is being documented. There are three ways in which this may be done.

Variation A. As each source is cited for the first time, it is numbered. That number is repeated in the text whenever the same source is referred to again. Generally the number immediately follows mention of an author's name, or a specific experiment, method, or result. A list of citations titled *References* appears at the end of the paper. References are numbered consecutively, with each source preceded by its number. The specific page of the reference used is usually included in the text of the paper; or it can be placed at the end of the citation. The sources are only listed once, and it is, of course, important that each reference be complete.

An example of text and an excerpt from the corresponding reference list follow:

> Hansen (6, p. 173) has demonstrated that outdoor illumination in Chicago is increasing dramatically, as shown in figure 3. His results agree with the findings of the Illinois Power Company (7, p. 3) which show that Chicago illumination has increased at an annual rate of between 7 and 10% since 1965. The Illinois Power Company predicts that by 1980. . . .

> *References*
>
> 6. Hansen, Roger K. "The Threat of High Illumination to Astrophysical Observation," (Unpublished Ph.D. Dissertation, No. P3218R, Department of Physics, University of Chicago, 1973).
> 7. Illinois Power Company, "A Report on City Illumination," *Bulletin of the Illinois Power Company,* 17 (March 1972).

Variation B. With this form all sources in the reference list are alphabetized and numbered. Then those numbers are used in the paper as described under variation *A*.

Variation C. In another similar form, all sources are alphabetized in a single list, but no numbers are assigned. Instead, the year of publication of the source is inserted in the text. Using the example given in variation *A*, the text would read: "Hansen (1973) has demonstrated." The citation is even more useful if the page number is also included, for example, "Hansen (1973, p. 173) has demonstrated." When the method of year plus page number is used, the entry in the references list for an article shows the range of pages of the article, as the reader already knows precisely which page has been cited.

Documentation within the Text

> The following sentences are from a journal article. Read the excerpts and notice these three conventions of incorporating paraphrases and quotations into the text of a paper:
>
> 1. Introductory expressions
> 2. Deletions, shown with three dots
> 3. Additions, put in brackets
>
> Another reason that policy makers have not done more about employment policy is that they assume more jobs will come as a by-

product of economic growth (17). Rosenstein-Rodan argues that Latin America must "aim at absorbing unemployment at a high level of productivity through large-scale, capital intensive but highly productive industrialization. This implies high savings and investment, and a high rate of economic growth—5.5 to 6.5 percent for the economy as a whole, and around 9 to 10 percent per annum in the industrial sector. It will take at least 5 to 10 years to reach full employment that way—but it is the way of defeating poverty . . ." (18).

Examining the history of most developed countries, one finds that the ratio of manufacturing jobs to urban employment remained essentially constant over long periods of time—and at much higher levels (27).

The inability to absorb labor is not confined to manufacturing. One recent report claims: "Even construction, while much less capital-intensive than manufacturing, has apparently become more capital-intensive, with cranes and bulldozers and other labor-saving machinery being substituted for labor" (28).

Even today, U.S. agriculture harbors a surprisingly large amount of surplus labor. In our country, redundant labor resources have not only funded their own sustenance, they have been called upon to supply a large proportion of the overhead capital necessary for such social benefits as public schools. Owen has called this phenomenon, which is usually unnoticed, "farm-financed social welfare" (35).

It seems as though our policy makers—and the American public—do not realize that, in the words of Robert Heilbroner, ". . . development [in Latin America] is much more than a matter of encouraging economic growth within a given social structure. It is rather the modernization of that structure, a process . . . that requires the remaking of society in its more intimate as well as its most public attributes" (43).[3]

Introductory Expressions

Often a paraphrase is incorporated into the text of a paper without an introductory phrase which cites the author of the idea. A quotation is always introduced. Many times, however, paraphrases as well as quotations are introduced. The preceding excerpts illustrate some of the ways to introduce them. Some other commonly used introductory expressions are: *according to x, as x states, as x observes, as x has shown.*

Remember that a footnote is needed, even when an introductory expression is used.

[3]William C. Thiesenhusen, "Latin America's Employment Problem," *Science*, Vol. 171 (5 March 1971), 868–74.

Deletions

Sometimes parts of a quote are relevant, but other phrases or even sentences are not. In that case the writer of the paper uses three dots (called ellipses) to indicate that material in the original has been deleted. It is important that the text read smoothly, despite the deletion.

Additions

Occasionally when phrases or sentences are deleted, it becomes necessary to add an essential word so that the context is smooth. Paragraphs preceding the last example had mentioned Latin America, but the *specific* sentence which was quoted did not. The author of the article inserted the specific reference and put it in brackets which indicate that the words were added.

Practice 1

As a class, develop a list of as many introductory phrases as you can.

Practice 2

Using the note cards based on Deans and Beale in section 5.4 of this chapter, write a paragraph on population shifts in the United States. Use information from both sources and document the information.

Practice 3

Using the note cards you wrote based on sources you selected in Practice 3 under Note-taking (section 5.4), write a paragraph or short composition on the subject. Use information from both sources and document the information sources.

Practice 4

Select a limited topic appropriate for a two- or three-page paper and find three recent sources on the topic. Take notes and integrate the information into a short, documented paper. You may want to consider one of the following areas for your topic:

1. A famous living person
2. A recent news event discussed in magazines and newspapers
3. A very limited current issue which pertains to your country and the United States

5.7 REVISING THE ROUGH DRAFT

It is very important to reread a rough draft and to examine it critically before putting the paper in final form. When rereading the paper, be particularly aware of organization, development, and coherence of ideas. Add transitions if needed, and rewrite sentences to make them more effective. Also, look for and correct structural errors and check to see that punctuation is used appropriately. Refer to the *Guide to Proofreading Your Paper* at the end of the academic paper section for a list of specific things to look for in the paper. In addition, be certain that all borrowed information has been documented adequately, and that the method of documentation is consistent throughout the paper.

Finally, prepare a final outline, appendixes, if any, and an abstract if one is required. The paper is then ready to be put in its final form.

Final Outline

Reexamine your expanded outline. Revise it, if necessary, to match the revised organization and content of the paper. The final outline forms the basis for the table of contents of the paper and would also be useful for organizing an oral presentation on the same topic.

In the section on library research (5.4), a tentative outline for the topic "Airport Noise Pollution" is given. A final outline for the same topic might look like this:

Airport Noise Pollution in Populated Areas

Introduction—extent of the problem

I. Sources of airport noise pollution
    A. Quantity of air traffic
    B. Low approaches of planes

II. Present efforts to reduce airport noise pollution
    A. Changes in planes
        1. Use of engine mufflers
        2. Greater use of jumbo planes
    B. Changes in traffic patterns
        1. Angles of descent and takeoff
        2. Directions of descent and takeoff

III. Projected ways of reducing airport noise pollution
    A. Relocation of airports
    B. Use of vertical takeoff and landing (VTOL) planes
    C. Use of alternate means of transportation

Conclusion

Appendix

Use of an appendix is optional. A writer uses appendixes for diagrams, tables, field notes, or photographs which are not essential to the text of the paper, but which he feels an interested reader would appreciate examining as a supplement to the paper. Reference to items contained in the appendix is made in the text of the paper.

Abstract

An abstract is often required in a graduate paper; an undergraduate paper seldom has an abstract. Sample abstracts and guidelines for writing an abstract are given in section 4.7.

Order of Presentation of the Parts of the Paper

1. Title page
2. Abstract, if required
3. Table of contents
4. Body of the paper, including footnotes
5. Appendixes, if any
6. Bibliography (or a reference list instead of footnotes and bibliography)

5.8 TYPING AND PROOFREADING

The final version of an academic paper must be legible and neat. For this reason, many instructors in American universities require that papers be typed. Others will accept papers either typed or handwritten, as long as they are readable and neat. If no requirement or preference is stated by the instructor, it is the student's responsibility to find out which form is acceptable for that course.

This section presents general and specific instructions for an acceptable, widely used format for a typed paper.

General Instructions

1. The paper should be typed on standard size, 8½-by-11-inch, unlined white paper, on one side only.
2. Standard margins for a paper are 1½ inches on the left, 1 inch on the right, and 1 inch to 1¼ inches at the top and at the bottom.
3. The paper should be double-spaced. Exceptions are mentioned below.
4. It is a good idea to protect the paper in a folder which binds the pages together on the left side. Some instructors require that a paper be submitted in a folder. If you do not use a folder, be sure to staple your pages together.

Specific Typing Instructions

Title Page. Type the title of the paper entirely in capital letters, about halfway down the page. Do not underline the title. Two inches below the title, center the word *by,* double-space, then type your name. Several inches from the bottom of the page, type the course name, the instructor's name, and the date. These items should be on separate lines, single-spaced. There should be a 1- to 1¼-inch margin below the final item. See p. 258 for a sample title page.

Abstract. Title the page *Abstract* and double-space the abstract. Indent the first line five spaces.

Table of Contents. Type the table of contents after typing the rest of the paper and numbering the pages. Type *Table of Contents* or just *Contents* near the top of the page. List the main divisions of the paper and give the number of the page on which each division begins. After listing the major divisions, some writers list the figures contained in the paper. The appendix and the bibliography are the final items in the table of contents.

A sample table of contents for "Airport Noise Pollution," for which a final outline is given in the preceding section, might be:

Table of Contents

Introduction	1
Sources of Airport Noise Pollution	2
Present Efforts to Reduce Airport Noise Pollution	4
Projected Ways of Reducing Airport Noise Pollution	7
Conclusion	9
Appendix	10
Bibliography	11

Body of the Paper

Spacing. Double-space the body of the paper. Exceptions are some elements of documentation (see section 5.6) and long quotations (see *Quotations* below).

Margins and Page Numbers. Observe the standard margins mentioned in the general typing instructions. On the first page of the body, leave a 3-inch top margin, type the title as before, triple-space, and then begin the text, or the heading before the text.

The number *1* should be centered at the bottom of the first page of the body. On following pages, type consecutive arabic numbers in the upper right-hand corner. (*Note:* In some departments the customary procedure may be to center the page number at the top of the page, other than the first page.) Pages, except the title page, that precede the body may be numbered with lowercase roman numerals centered at the bottom of each page.

Headings. The introduction and conclusion may be integrated into the body of the paper without headings, or they may be separate. If they are separate divisions, each should be preceded by a heading.

Headings are often used in long papers which have many major sections, but generally do not need to be used in a short paper. There are many formats for headings. The general rule is that the more major the division is in your outline, the more dominant it should appear on the typed page. Relative importance may be shown by using all capital letters, underlining, or position on the page.

Hyphenation. In general, try to avoid breaking words at the right-hand margin. If you do need to break a word, hyphenate the word at a syllable break. Consult a dictionary for correct word division. Refer to the section on punctuation for examples.

Quotations. If a quotation is short (less than three typed lines), it generally is included in the text in quotation marks. The section on documentation contains some examples.

If a quotation is longer than five lines, it should be introduced by a colon, single-spaced, and indented. The first line is indented eight spaces; successive lines are indented five spaces. Double-space above and below the indented quotation to separate it from the main text. An indented quotation is not put in quotation marks.

Footnotes. Detailed instructions for typing footnotes are given in the documentation section.

Appendixes. Type *Appendix* on the top of the page. If there is more than one appendix, each appendix should begin on a separate page. Appendixes are numbered with roman numerals or capital letters (I, II; or A, B).

Bibliography or Reference List. Specific instructions are given in the documentation section.

The format described above is one of many acceptable methods for presenting a paper. An individual instructor or department may recommend or require a slightly different system. In addition to finding out the recommendation of your instructors or department and looking at style sheets accepted by journals in your field, you may wish to consult one or more of the following books for a more thorough treatment of acceptable forms used in academic papers:

A Manual of Style, 12th ed. Chicago: The University of Chicago Press, 1969.

Turabian, Kate L. *A Manual for Writers of Term Papers, Theses, and Dissertations,* Fourth edition, revised. Chicago: The University of Chicago Press, 1973.

Proofreading—the Final Step. There is one more step after the paper has been put in final form—proofreading. Take the time to read through the paper one last time before submitting it to an instructor. This is the final chance to find mistakes, particularly typing errors ("typos"), and to correct them. Make corrections as neatly as possible. Erase carefully, and make additions with a black pen. If many corrections need to be made on a single page, it is best to type the page again.

The "Guide to Proofreading Your Paper" which follows is a series of key questions to ask yourself as you reread your paper.

Guide to Proofreading Your Paper

Organization and Development

1. Is there a clear statement of purpose?
2. Have you effectively introduced and concluded your topic?
3. Are the ideas developed systematically?
4. Have you adequately supported your main points? (This may include examples, graphs, figures, and other devices.)

Coherence

1. Are there transitions where they are needed—within sentences, between sentences, between paragraphs?
2. Are the ideas stated clearly and concisely?
3. Are pronoun references clear?
4. Have you rewritten or eliminated awkward or repetitious sentences?

Sentence Structure and Punctuation

1. Are there any fragments or run-on sentences?
2. Does every subject agree with its verb?
3. Are various verb tenses constructed and used correctly?
4. Have you used passive when it is appropriate, and have you constructed it correctly?
5. Have you used acceptable word order in every sentence?
6. Are there articles where needed, and not where they are *not* needed?
7. Are words spelled correctly?

8. Have you looked up or asked about two-word verbs and phrases with prepositions that you were uncertain about?
9. Have you used only those abbreviations which are acceptable in your field?
10. Have you used punctuation where it is needed, and *not* where it is unnecessary?
11. If you have divided any words on two lines, are they divided correctly?
12. Have you written numbers correctly?

Format

1. Have you left adequate margins?
2. Are long quotations indented and single-spaced?
3. Have you documented information wherever it is necessary?
4. Does every reference number in the text correspond to a footnote or to a source in a references list?
5. Have you been consistent in your use of a documentation system?
6. If you have used headings, have you been consistent in indicating the relative importance of various divisions and subdivisions of the paper?
7. Has proper spacing been used for quotations, footnotes, bibliography, and other special cases?
8. Are the parts of the paper in the correct order?
9. Are all pages in order?
10. Are the pages numbered correctly?
11. Have erasures and corrections been made neatly?
12. Have you corrected all errors indicated in your rough draft?

Finally

Have you done your best to check both technical content and English?

Appendix

STUDENT PAPERS

Two student papers, one written by an undergraduate and one written by a graduate, are included here as samples.

The undergraduate wrote his paper for his English class; he had not chosen his field yet, although he was considering medicine. The graduate student wrote his paper for an advanced course in his field; he assumed that his readers were professionals. Clearly, the papers differ in complexity of information, degree of usage of technical terms, and use of data.

There are two differences in paper form. The undergraduate used a table of contents; the graduate used an abstract. There are two styles of documentation: one used endnotes and bibliography, and the other, references.

Cordoba, Juan. *Physical Effects of Marijuana Use.* Unpublished paper, 22 May 1976.

Niku, Salar. *Adsorption: Granular Activated Carbon, Practice and Economics.* Unpublished paper, 11 March 1975.

PHYSICAL EFFECTS OF MARIJUANA USE

by
Juan Cordoba

English IA
Howard Rapp
May 22, 1975

Table of Contents

Introduction 260
Short-Term Effects 260
Long-Term Effects 262
Conclusion 263

Introduction

Marijuana (Cannabis sativa) is one of man's oldest and most widely used drugs. It has been consumed in various ways as long as medical history has been recorded and is currently used throughout the world by hundreds of millions of people. A fairly consistent picture of its short-term effects on users is presented in many publications. There are, however, strongly contradictory opinions about whether the ultimate effects are harmful, harmless, or beneficial to human functioning. Many of the old reports suffered from multiple problems such as biased sampling, lack of control groups, and use of substances of unknown potency.[1] However, recent scientific literature presents a clear, well-documented case.

Several factors have to be taken into consideration in order to evaluate some of the research. The first aspect is the amount of the dose of Δ^9-tetrahydrocannabinol (THC), the major ingredient in marijuana.[2] Another factor is the kind of person using marijuana. Also, the non-drug factor of setting must be considered in evaluating the results of experimental studies.[3] These points are not going to be detailed or discussed although they have a very strong influence on an individual who smokes "pot."

Our study may be divided into two categories: (a) at the beginning of use, and (b) when a user is into the situation. It could also be divided with reference to the level of the physical effects in man. In order to study physical effects rather than how they are produced, this paper proposes a third classification based on the duration and intensity of marijuana's effects. Therefore, short-term and long-term or chronic effects are chosen as divisions.

Short-Term Effects

The most consistent physiological sign is an increase of pulse rate. For example, doses of 14 mg. Δ^9-THC have resulted in higher than average pulse rates immediately after smoking.[4] Another symptom found by Berke and Hernton is reddening of the eyes.[5] Other researchers support these findings but find no evidence for claims that pupils dilate.[6] Little or no effect on respiratory rates, lung vital capacity, or basal metabolic rate is noted.

Other symptoms frequently reported are dryness of the mouth and throat and increasing frequency of urination.

Short-term biochemical effects are also an important consideration. Reports of increased hunger especially for sweets during Cannabis intoxication have focused attention on possible changes in blood sugar level.[7] Many of Berke's subjects experienced appetite stimulation and general hunger.

Neurological experiments have not revealed major abnormalities during marijuana intoxication. Muscle strength and performance of simple motor tasks do appear to be affected.[8] Cannabis users often report increased auditory sensibility, visual acuity, and aesthetic appreciation of music.[9]

Berke divides short-term physical effects reported by subjects into two groups: the major symptoms are nausea, vomiting, and dizziness; less enduring ones are headaches, exhaustion, feeling faint, cold, and sweating.[10] In his interviews he found that in general these effects last from fifteen minutes to an hour. One of his interviewees said:

> I have been ill physically about four times, when I attributed it to hash or pot smoking. I became very dizzy, hot flushes, sweating, and vomiting in 3 of the occasions. It lasted once 10 minutes, once about 2 hours or so, and the other time about half an hour. When the illness left, I was perfectly fit and was left very stoned indeed. On one occasion, it occurred after the first smoke of the day, and on the other after three or four smokes, so I deduce no connection with quantity.[11]

To summarize what Berke tries to explain with this example, the physical effects of Cannabis depend upon the experience which an individual has with it, and that is the point which people have to consider when they talk about physical effects. He makes this point strongly in an explanatory list of physical symptoms versus frequency in 257 people:[12]

From 257 People

Nausea	95	Vomiting	62
Sick, sickness	92	Dizziness, giddiness	59

Headache	25	Sleepiness, sleep	5
Exhaustion	20	Buzz in head	2
Feel faint, faint	18	Discoordination	9
Heaviness	15	Gastric distress	2
Feel Cold	14	Head feel bad	2
Sweating	11	Other	14

Long-Term Effects

After having dealt with short-term effects we must discuss long-term effects. Long-term effects are not classified according to their frequency but according to their duration and intensity. It is difficult to find a chronic symptom caused by marijuana.

Silverstein and Lessin stated that smoking marijuana does not produce any impairment of cellular immunity.[13] Nothing was found in the application of standard skin tests of an antigen to 22 chronic marijuana users. In contrast, Nahas concluded from a study of 51 subjects that cellular immunity of an individual can be diminished or weakened by the chronic use of marijuana.[14]

More recent experiments performed by Nahas[15] on long-term "pot" smokers, show that THC interferes with the body's production of DNA, which is the genetic material that causes cell division and hereditary characteristics. Nahas uses the slowing down of the DNA process in order to explain that the weakness caused by marijuana stimulates the production of virus-fighting white blood cells.

Dr. Morton A. Stenchever and his associates discovered that a high percentage of marijuana users develop a significant increase in chromosome breaks, compared to nonusers.[16]

At the Reproductive Biology Research Foundation in St. Louis, Dr. Robert C. Kolodny[17] has found that men smoking at least ten marijuana cigarettes a week had a lower level of testosterone (principal male sex hormone) than non-smokers. In thirty percent of the users (6 of 20), sperm counts were relatively low.

Experiments carried out by Dr. Forest S. Tenant, Jr., in the U.S. Army's drug program in Europe, found in teenage smokers up to their 20's (a) a type of acute bronchitis, and (b) tissue changes in lung biopsies, abnormalities which were the same as those associated with lung cancer.[18]

There are other suspected or reported effects which are produced when the smoker is unstable physiologically or psychologically. Nutrition, sanitation and climate, potency, drug dose level and frequency of use, and use of other drugs are conditions which influence the body. Consequently, it would be easier for marijuana to cause disorders which are not really attributed to it.

Conclusion

While much has already been learned about the acute physiological effects of Cannabis, much remains to be learned. It is also important to understand the possible influence of other constituents of Cannabis which may not in themselves be psycho- or physical-active but may nevertheless influence the action of those constituents which are.

In spite of the increase of marijuana research papers in the last 10 years, some actions of marijuana are incompletely understood and their possible significance for health cannot at present be evaluated. These areas are discussed under the classical organ systems approach commonly used in medicine. Cardiovascular systems, gastrointestinal function, liver function, neuroendocrine effects of marijuana, and lung function are, from my point of view, the main areas to be investigated.

Endnotes

[1] Joseph Berke and Calvin Hernton, *The Cannabis Experience* (London: Peter Owen, 1974), pp. 14-15.

[2] Stanley D. Glick and Svetlana Milloy, "Tolerance, State-Dependency and Long-Term Behavioral Effects of Δ^9-THC," in Mark L. Lewis, ed., *Current Research in Marijuana* (New York: Academic Press, 1972), p. 1.

[3] Berke, p. 13.

[4] Rhea L. Dornbush et al., "21-Day Administration of Marijuana in Male Volunteers," in Mark F. Lewis, ed., *Current Research in Marijuana* (New York: Academic Press, 1972), p. 122.

[5] Berke, p. 113.

[6] *Ibid*.

[7] Berke, pp. 108-9.

[8] Berke, pp. 117-32.

[9] Berke, pp. 150-63.

[10] Berke, p. 233.

[11] Berke, p. 234.

[12] Berke, p. 279.

[13] Melvin J. Silverstein and Phyllis J. Lessin, "Normal Skin Test Responses in Chronic Marijuana Users," *Science*, 186 (November 22, 1974), pp. 740-41.

[14] Nahas et al., *Science*, 183 (1974), p. 419, cited in Silverstein.

[15] "The Alarming New Evidence about Marijuana's Effects," *Good Housekeeping*, 180 (February 1975), p. 162.

[16] Edward M. Brecher, "Marijuana: The Health Question," *Consumer Reports*, 40 (March 1975), p. 144.

[17] Brecher, p. 145.

[18] "The Alarming New Evidence," p. 162.

BEGIN NEW PAGE

Bibliography

"The Alarming New Evidence About Marijuana's Effects," *Good Housekeeping*, 180 (February 1975), pp. 161-62.

Berke, Joseph and Hernton, Calvin. *The Cannabis Experience*. London: Peter Owen Limited, 1974.

Brecher, Edward M. "Marijuana: The Health Question," *Consumer Reports*, 40 (March 1975), pp. 143-49.

Lewis, Mark F., ed. *Current Research in Marijuana*. New York: Academic Press, 1972.

Silverstein, Melvin J. and Lessin, Phyllis J. "Normal Skin Test Responses in Chronic Marijuana Users," *Science*, 186 (November 22, 1974), pp. 740-41.

ADSORPTION: GRANULAR ACTIVATED CARBON
Practice and Economics

by
Salar Niku

Civil Engineering 271A
Professor James Leckie

March 11, 1975

Abstract

Activated carbon is the most promising means of efficiently treating water and wastewater by adsorption. This paper covers two approaches to the use of granular activated carbon as a tertiary step.

Major applications are listed, economic factors are considered, and a table of estimated capital and operating costs at one treatment plant is presented.

Practice Processes

At the present time, activated carbon holds the most promise for efficient treatment of water and wastewater by adsorption. In the last ten years, granular activated carbon has been utilized for municipal and industrial treatment of wastewater. The process has become much more attractive for widespread use due to the development of economical regeneration methods and equipment.

Almost 17 percent of solids present in raw wastewater are refractory organics which cannot be removed by the biodegradable aspects of conventional treatment processes. Activated carbon adsorbs a great variety of dissolved organic materials at its large surface areas. This is attributable to its highly porous structure. Granular activated carbon typically has surface areas of 500-1400 m^2/gram (6). Much of the surface area available for adsorption in granular carbon is found in its pores, created during the activation process.

The most commonly used types of granular activated carbons suitable for purifying municipal and industrial wastewaters are made from bituminous coal and lignite (4). Bituminous coal carbons generally have more surface area in very small pores, while lignite carbons have more total pore volume.

Numerous types of carbon contactor systems have been developed (6): (a) Upflow packed beds; (b) Upflow expanded beds; (c) Downflow packed beds in gravity and pressure units in series or parallel; (d) Various combinations of the above. Upflow beds have an advantage over downflow beds in the efficiency of carbon use because they can more closely approach continuous countercurrent contact operation, which results in the minimum use of carbon, or the lowest carbon dosage rate. The principal reason for using a downflow contactor is to use the carbon for two purposes: Adsorption of organics, and filtration of suspended materials. Downflow beds may be operated in parallel or in series. Valves and piping are provided in series installations to permit each bed to be operated in any position in the series sequence. Expanded bed columns can work for several months without undergoing any head-loss or necessitating any backwash, so they operate with less trouble than packed beds.

There are two approaches for the use of granular activated carbon in wastewater treatment (4) (6).

One approach is the use of activated carbon in a "tertiary" treatment sequence following conventional primary and biological secondary treatment. Figure 1 shows a typical treatment flow diagram utilizing carbon adsorption as a tertiary step. There are several benefits if biological treatment and filtration precede carbon treatment: (1) The BOD, COD and other organic applied loads on carbon will be reduced; (2) The headloss through the bed of carbon, which is applied by suspended and colloidal solids will be reduced and may aid in solving problems of physical plugging, ash buildup and progressive loss of adsorptive capacity of carbon particles; and (3) the problems of biological growth and hydrogen sulfide protection may be decreased.

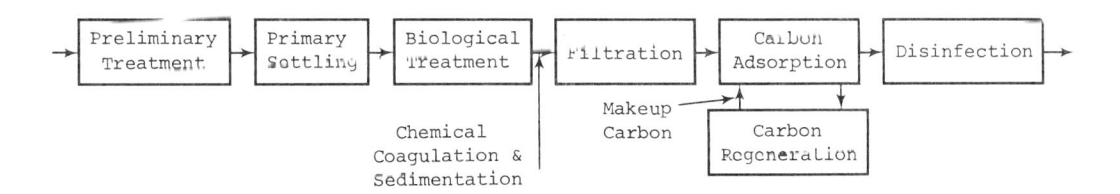

Fig. 1 Typical treatment scheme utilizing carbon adsorption as a tertiary step (4).

Another approach is to use activated carbon in a "physical-chemical" treatment (PCT) process (Fig. 2). In this process raw wastewater is treated in a primary clarifier with chemicals prior to carbon adsorption. Filtration and disinfection may also be included but biological processes are not used. PCT is also applicable in cases where the presence of biological toxic materials or space limitations prevent the use of biological processes. It has been shown in several cases that when biological oxidation, chemical coagulation, filtration, and adsorption are operated in series as separate processes, the quality of effluent will be optimized. PCT will result in capital cost savings when compared with biological treatment followed by tertiary treatment.

Examples of Major Applications in the Wastewater Field

There have been many examples of experiments that successfully use activated carbon in the treatment of domestic and industrial wastewater in recent years. Tofflemire et al. (5) used carbon adsorption to polish a strong combined domestic and paper mill waste. Brunotts et al. (1) removed 94 percent of TOC by activated carbon adsorption columns. There are four full-scale tertiary treatment plants in operation (4) which utilize granular activated carbon in the treatment process: (1) South Lake Tahoe, California, with a capacity of 7.5 mgd., which treats activated sludge effluent; (2) Windhoek, South Africa, with a capacity of 1.3 mgd. in which wastewater is treated for subsequent use in the city's municipal water system; (3) Colorado Springs, Colorado, with a capacity of 3 mgd.; and (4) Piscataway, Maryland, with a capacity of 5 mgd.

There are many full-scale physical-chemical treatment plants under design or construction (4): Zurn Environmental Engineers did Labora-

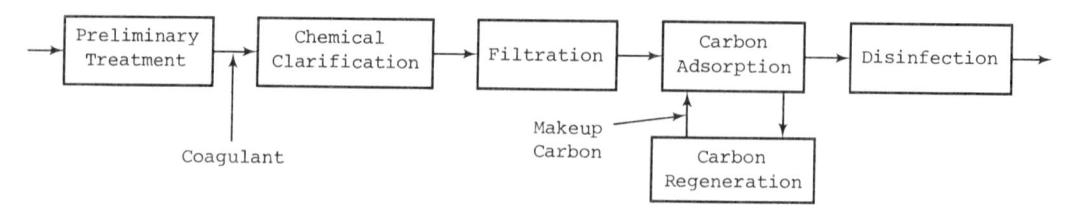

Fig. 2 Typical physical-chemical treatment (PCT) scheme (4).

tory investigations on raw sewage at the Westerly Plant in Cleveland, Ohio. In a process of coagulation, settling, filtration, and granular carbon adsorption, 86.5 percent BOD and 92.4 percent COD removals have been accomplished. By physical-chemical treatment of raw wastewater at Blues Plains, 95 percent BOD, 95 percent COD, and 99 percent total phosphorus were removed over a 10-month period. The carbon columns in Waterford (5) afforded 75 to 85 percent organic nitrogen removal.

Some problems with the generation of hydrogen sulfide in the carbon columns also occur under certain conditions. In plant design, proper considerations should be taken to provide flexibility for dealing with problems of hydrogen sulfide production.

Economics and Estimated Costs

For an economical design various factors should be considered. Capital, operation, and maintenance costs for the various components of activated carbon treatment system are the most important.

1. *Capital Cost*. Capital cost depends on the type of contactors. There is little cost difference between upflow packed and expanded beds. Downflow parallel operated packed beds are about the same cost as upflow contactors, while downflow series packed beds are more expensive. An economy scale analysis shows that (6) the two-stage series downflow units having a volume of v/2 would cost approximately 28 percent more than single stage contactors of volume v.

Materials of construction will also influence contactor system costs. Shop-fabricated steel vessels are more economical for small contactors (up to 12-feet diameter) whereas with diameters greater than 12 feet, field fabrication is necessary and concrete construction is competitive in cost. To obtain total capital costs, the construction costs must be adjusted to account for engineering, legal, administrative, land, and interest expenses.

Carbon performance, which determines the carbon usage rate or dosage, is the major economic variable. The carbon usage rate is the rate at which carbon must be removed from the adsorption system and replaced with fresh carbon to maintain the purification levels required. Carbon usage rate will vary directly with the amount of impurities which must be removed. A very rough rule-of-thumb for biologically active municipal wastewater systems is (4): For every 10 ppm COD which must be removed, a dosage of about 250 lb. carbon per million gallons will be required.

2. <u>Regeneration Systems</u>. Economical application of carbon depends on an efficient means of regenerating the carbon for reuse after its adsorptive capacity has been reached. Granular carbon can easily be regenerated by oxidizing the organic matter in a furnace. Almost 10 percent of the carbon will be destroyed in this process and must be replaced (6). Complete regeneration system costs add about 50 percent to the basic installed furnace costs.

Economic research studies (6) show that, for plants with carbon usage less than 200 lb/day or for tertiary treatment plants having a carbon usage of about 250 lbs/mg and smaller than 800,000 gpd capacity, and for PCT plants having a carbon usage of about 1200 lbs/mg and smaller than 170,000 gpd capacity, carbon regeneration facilities should not be provided. In this case the cost of regenerated carbon equals the cost for granular carbon used on a throw-away basis, and it would be more economical to operate regeneration on a regional basis, to serve several plants with one regeneration furnace. When average carbon regeneration requirements exceed 1500 lbs/day, construction of on-site carbon regeneration facilities is economical. This includes tertiary plants with capacities greater than 6 mgd and PCT plants with 800,000 gpd capacity or more. For carbon usage between 200 and 1,500 lbs/day, the cost of on-site regeneration must be compared to the costs of central regeneration and to the costs of alternate treatment methods for removing refractory organics.

Note also that a pump station will be required to force effluent through the contactor system. In this case the costs of pump stations, which vary with location and total dynamic head requirements, should be considered.

3. <u>Operation and Maintenance Costs</u>. In a typical municipal and industrial wastewater granular carbon system, operating at a reasonably steady state in a stable economic climate, 85-95 percent of the total operating cost is contributed by constant factors; e.g.: depreciation, overhead, labor, and maintenance (3). Only 5-15 percent is related to variable factors, e.g.: carbon performance, carbon makeup, carbon cost, and utilities. Estimated capital and operating costs at the South Lake Tahoe treatment plant, based on a flow 7.5 mgd is shown in Table 1 (6). All capital costs were adjusted to EPA, STP Index 127.0, during 1969-1970, amortized a percent for 25 years.

Table 1

Item	Carbon adsorption $/mill gal.	Carbon regeneration $/mill gal.	Unit costs
Operating Costs:			
Electricity	6.31	0.30	$0.012/kwh
Natural gas	–	0.82	
Makeup carbon	–	9.39	$0.305/lb
Operating labor	3.27	12.25	$6.11/hour
Maintenance labor	0.44	2.16	$5.05/hour
Repair material	0.15	0.16	
Instrument maintenance	0.57	0.25	
Total operating cost	10.74	25.33	
Total capital cost	16.30	5.20	
Total cost	27.09	30.53	

Conclusion

The use of activated carbon for removal of dissolved organics from water and wastewater has been demonstrated to be feasible and promising. Two prominent methods utilizing activated carbon are tertiary treatment and physical-chemical treatment. By these processes, a high quality effluent can be obtained. A high percent removal of BOD, COD and NOD (on the order of 95 percent) has been provided in some treatment plants.

For a granular activated carbon to be economical in most treatment systems, carbon must be regenerated for reuse. Makeup carbon cost is an important item and is quite predominant in large systems. The exact value for the cost items will differ according to the design features of the system, treatment processes, labor rates, utility costs, and other considerations. Since the relative magnitudes of the cost items will be similar in all cases, data presented here can be used as a general guide.

References:

1. Brunotts, V. A., et al. "Granular Carbon Handles Concentrated Waste," *Chem. Eng. Program*, 69 (1973).

2. Hutchins, R. A. "Economic Factors in Granular Carbon Thermal Regeneration," *Chem. Eng. Programs*, 69 (1973).

3. Metcalf & Eddy, Inc. *Wastewater Engineering*. McGraw-Hill, New York (1972).

4. Suhr, L. G., and Culp, G. L. "State of the Art--Activated Carbon Treatment of Wastewater," *Water and Sewage Works* (Oct. 1974).

5. Tofflemire, T. J., et al. "Activated Carbon Adsorption and Polishing of Strong Wastewater," *Jour. Water Poll. Cont. Fed.*, 45 (1973).

6. U.S. Environmental Protection Agency, Technology Transfer Office. *Process Design Manual For Carbon Adsorption*. Oct. 1973.

Index

a, 11–12
a-, as negative prefix, 95
abbreviations
   in lecture notes, 213
   of names of organizations, 161
   in newspapers, 83
abstract nouns, 2–3
abstracts
   examples, 229–30, 266
   typing, 252
   writing, 229
academic paper, 231–72
   documentation, 243–49
   grading, 232
   library research for, 234–36
   note-taking for, 237–41
   order of parts, 251
   outline for, 235–36, 242, 250
   proofreading, 254–55
   rough draft, 242–43, 250
   samples, 257–72
   style of language in, 242–43
   topic selection, 233–34
   typing, 251–55
   use of passive and active in, 66–67
active vocabulary, 88
active vs. passive voice, 58–67
adjectives, 124–43
   for objects, 125–32
   for people, 132–43

adverbs
   adverb clause punctuation, 78
   word order (place, manner, etc.), 26–37
ago, 39
agreement of subject and verb, 1–7
an, 11–12
Anglo-Saxon vocabulary origin, 88
-ant, as noun suffix, 108
anti-, as negative prefix, 98
apostrophe, 81
appendix
   typing, 253
   use in academic paper, 251
articles, 1, 7–20
-ate, as verb suffix, 111

bibliography
   examples, 246, 254
   explanation, 246
   typing, 246
bibliography cards, 237–38, 240. *See also* Source cards
bilingual dictionary, 90
brackets, to show addition, 249

capitalization, 82
cardinal numbers, and use of *the,* 15
checklist of errors, 1

cities, and use of *the,* 15
collective nouns, 2–3
colon, 77
comma, 77–80
conjunctive adverbs, with semicolon, 76
connotation, 89
context, 88
contra-, as negative prefix, 98
coordinative conjunction, with comma, 77
count nouns, 2–3
counter-, as negative prefix, 98
countries, and use of *the,* 16

dash, 81
data, plural, 75
de-, as negative prefix, 75
definite article, 8–12
degree adverbs, 26–37
denotation, 89
description
    of objects, 125–32
    of people, 132–43
determiners, 7–20
dis-, as negative prefix, 98
do and *make,* 118–24
documentation, 243–49
    bibliography, 246
    footnotes, 244–45
    reference list and citations, 246–47
    within the text, 247–49
doubling consonants in spelling, 68–70

ei, spelling, 74
ellipses, 249
endnotes
    definition, 245
    sample, 264
English-English dictionary, 90
-ent, as noun suffix, 108
-er, as noun suffix, 108
examinations, 192–96
    instructions for taking, 195–96
    questions in, 193–95
    types of, 192–93
exclamation mark, 76
expanding vocabulary, 87–94

footnotes, 244–45
formality
    of level of writing, 242–43
    of vocabulary, 88

frequency adverbs, 26–37
frequently used word groups, 117–90

gerund, 43–58
get, 59
government and politics, 162–70
grading of papers, 183–84, 232

have + participle, 37
headings, use of in academic papers, 253
headlines in newspapers, 155
health, 143–51
height adjectives, 133
how clauses, 33–37
human characteristics, 134–43
hyphen, 80

-ian, as noun suffix, 108
ie, spelling, 74
-ify, as verb suffix, 111
il-, as negative prefix, 95
im-, as negative prefix, 95
in-, as negative prefix, 95
indefinite articles, 11–12
infinitive vs. gerund, 43–58
information cards, 238–39
    samples, 238, 240, 241
insurance vocabulary, 151–55
ir-, as negative prefix, 95
islands, use of *the* with, 17
-ist, as noun suffix, 108
its, 81
-ize, as verb suffix, 111

journal, 92

Latin vocabulary origin, 88
lecture notes, 205–13
    abbreviations and symbols in, 213
    guidelines for taking, 205–7
    sample notes and explanation of, 207–12
legal vocabulary, 170–77
letters, sample, 36, 153
library research for academic paper, 234–36
likelihood adverbs, 26–37
locations
    capitalization of, 82
    use of *the,* 17

make and *do,* 118–24
mal-, as negative prefix, 100

manner adverbs, 26–37
margins in academic paper, 251–53
mass nouns, 2–3
means adverbs, 26–37
mis-, as negative prefix, 100
mountains, and use of *the*, 17

names, and use of *the*, 14
negative prefixes, 94–107
negative second verbs, 55
negatives to emphasize positive, 106
newspaper language, 155–61
no longer, 106
non-, as negative prefix, 95
non-count nouns, 2–3
non-essential agent, 59–63
nonrestrictive clauses, 79–80
not at all, 106
notecards, 238–39. *See also* Information cards
notes
   for an academic paper, 237–41
   of lectures, 205–13
noun agent suffixes, 108–11
numbers, and use of *the*, 15

object receiver, 58–61
oceans, and use of *the*, 17
-or, as noun suffix, 108
ordinal numbers, and use of *the*, 15
outlines, 213–23. *See also* Academic paper
   examples, 218–19, 250
   types, 215
   uses, 216–17
over-, as negative prefix, 100

paraphrase, 223–29
participle
   passive voice, present perfect, 37–43
   punctuation, 78
parts of a group, 1, 20–26
passive vocabulary, 88
passive voice, 1, 58–67
   balanced use of active and passive, 66–67
   present perfect passive, 38
   use in academic paper, 242
past vs. present perfect, 38–43
people, 2
period, 76
place adverbs, 26–37
plagiarism, 232–33

plural
   count nouns, 8–12
   unusual, 75
politics and government, 162–70
position of adverbs, 1, 26–37
possessive
   use of *the*, 8
   with verb *-ing*, 53–54
prepositions
   punctuation, 78
   with verb *-ing*, 50–53
present perfect, 37–43
proofreading, 254–55
punctuation, 1, 75–85
purpose adverbs, 26–37

question mark, 76
question word clauses, 32–37
quizzes, 193
quotations
   in academic paper, 247–49
   typing of, 253
   use of colon with, 77

recording new vocabulary, 90
reference list
   examples, 247, 272
   explanation, 246–47
remember, 48
research vocabulary, 196–205
   process, 197
   reporting, 197–98
restrictive clause, 79–80
reviews of books, movies, etc., 187
rivers, and use of *the*, 17
rough draft
   preparation, 242–49
   revision, 250

say, synonyms of, 159–60
seas, and use of *the*, 17
semicolon, 76
sentence outline, 215, 219
since, 39
singular count noun, 3, 8–12
so far, 39
some, 11–12
source cards, 237–38, 240
spacing, in academic paper, 251–52
spelling, 1, 67–75
stop, 48
streets, and use of *the*, 15
structural errors, 1
style, in academic paper, 242–43

subject-verb agreement, 1–7
subject-verb word order, 33–37
summary, 223–29

technical nouns, 3
tense of verb
    past vs. present perfect, 37–43
tentative outline, 235–36
term paper, 231–72. *See also* Academic paper
tests, 192–96. *See also* Examinations
the, use of, 8–12, 15–17, 20–25
third person verb ending, 1–7
time expressions
    adverbs, 26–37
    present perfect vs. past, 39–40
    use of *the,* 17
titles, and use of *the,* 14
to, 43–58
to + verb (infinitive) vs. gerund, 43–58
    punctuation, 79
topic outline, 215, 218–19, 250
transitional phrases, with semicolon, 76
two-word verbs, 89
typing

of academic paper, 251–55
of bibliography, 246
of footnotes, 245

un-, as negative prefix, 92
under-, as negative prefix, 100

verb-forming suffixes, 111–15
verb-*ing* (gerund) vs. infinitive, 43–58
verb tense, past vs. present perfect, 37–43
verbs expressing attitudes, 177–90
vocabulary cards, 90
vocabulary development, 87–115
vocabulary notebook, 92

weight adjectives, 133
wh- clauses, 32–37
whose, 81
word order
    adverbs, 26–32
    question word clauses, 32–37
writing, use of passive and active in, 58–67

yet, 40

germ, circ MONTGOMERY COLLEGE LIBRARIES PE 1128.G8
Guide to lang

0 0000 00171711 5